Introduction To Music Fundamentals And Lead-Sheet Terminology

David Nivans

California State University Dominguez Hills

World Bet Books

Copyright © 2012 by David Nivans

All rights reserved. No part of this publication may be reproduced, transmitted, stored in a retrieval system or a database in any form or by any means, be it graphic, electronic, or mechanical, including but not limited to photocopying, recording, scanning, digitizing, or otherwise, without prior written permission of the publisher.

World Bet Books
www.worldbetbooks.com
worldbetbooks@gmail.com

ISBN 978-1-937214-03-6

Library of Congress Control Number: 2011934472

This book is printed on acid-free paper.

To the Memory of

Wally Bower

1929–2008

About the Author

David Nivans holds a Ph.D. in historical musicology from University of California Los Angeles. He has taught courses in music fundamentals, harmony, counterpoint, musicianship, world music, music appreciation, music and art appreciation, music history, and surveys of popular music, jazz, rock, and film music. Dr. Nivans is also the author of *Finding The Right Pitch: A Guide To The Study Of Music Fundamentals* and *Finding The Right Pitch II: A Guide To The Study Of Basic Harmony*.

TABLE OF CONTENTS

Preface ix

Chapter 1 Time and Performance 1
    Ties and Dots 3
    Meter and Beat 4
    Divisions of Beats 5
    Time Signatures 5
    Counting Note Values 7
    Rhythm 9
    Syncopation 9
    Displacement 10
    Hemiola 11
    Repeat Signs 12
    First and Second Endings 13
    Da Capo al Fine, Dal Segno al Fine, Da Capo al Coda, and *Dal Segno al Coda* 14
    Performance Marks 16
    Tempo 16
    Dynamics 17
    Simple and Compound Meter Exchange 17
    Triplets 18
    Duplets 22
    Asymmetrical Meter 23

Chapter 2 Pitch 25
    Accidentals and Enharmonic Equivalency 26
    Chromatic and Diatonic Half Steps 28
    The Great Staff and Clefs 29
    Octave Registers 31
    Octave Signs 33

Chapter 3 The Major Scale 35
    Moving the Major Scale to Octaves Other Than C with the Addition of Sharps 37
    Moving the Major Scale to Octaves Other Than C with the Addition of Flats 40

Chapter 4 Major Key Signatures 43
    The Circle of 5ths 45
    Identifying Major Key Signatures 47
    Diatonicism, Chromaticism, Tonality, and Atonality 47

Chapter 5 Intervals 49
    The Essential Diatonic Intervals of Major 50
    Two Principles for Recognizing and Constructing the Qualities of Intervals 51
    When the Bottom Pitch of the Interval Is Not Scale Degree 1 of C Major 54
    When the Bottom Pitch Does Not Correspond to One of the Fourteen
        Transpositions of C Major 57
    The Principle of Like Inflection 58
    Compound Intervals 59
    Interval Inversion 60
    Consonance and Dissonance 61
    The Suspension 63

Chapter 6 The Minor Mode 65
    The Natural Minor Mode 65
    The Relative Minor 66
    The Parallel Minor and the Parallel Major 67
    The Relative Major 68
    The Circle of 5ths for Minor 69
    The Harmonic Minor Mode 71
    The Melodic Minor Mode 72
    The Ascending Form of the Melodic Minor 72
    The Descending Form of the Melodic Minor 73
    Finding the Variable Scale Degrees in the Melodic Minor 74
    Comparing the Three Forms of Minor 74

Chapter 7 Triads 77
- Triad Quality 79
- Triad Qualities in Major 81
- Inverting the Major Triad 82
- Inverting the Minor Triad 83
- Inverting the Diminished Triad 84
- Inverting the Augmented Triad 84
- Triad Qualities in Minor 85
- Roman Numeral Chord Symbols 87
- Tonality and the Names of the Scale Degrees 90
- The Harmonic Series 92

Chapter 8 The Church Modes 95
- Major and Minor Prototypes 97
- Relating the Church Modes to the Major Mode 99
- Mode Transposition 99
- Given the Key and Mode, Find the Right Key Signature 103

Chapter 9 Seventh Chords 109
- Adding the Seventh to the Triad 109
- The Origin of the Seventh Chord 110
- The Real Seventh Chord 111
- The Four Principal Types of "White-Key" Seventh Chords 111
- The Formation of Seventh Chords in the Church Mode System 112
- The Formation of Seventh Chords in the Major Mode 116
- Inversions of the Seventh Chord 116
- The Treatment of the Dissonant Seventh 118
- The Seventh Chord of the Leading Tone 119
- The Formation of Seventh Chords in the Minor Mode 120
- The Added 6th 121

Chapter 10 Lead-Sheet Terminology 123

Triads 123
The Major Seventh, Dominant Seventh, Minor Seventh, and
   Half-Diminished Seventh 125
Inversions of the Major Seventh, Dominant Seventh, Minor Seventh, and
   Half-Diminished Seventh 126
The Added 6th and Added 9th 127
Chords of the Ninth 128
The Fully Diminished Seventh, Minor-Major Seventh, and Augmented-Major Seventh 129
Inversions of the Minor-Major Seventh and Augmented-Major Seventh 130
The Suspension 130
The Altered Fifth and Altered Ninth 131
The Altered Fifth and Altered Ninth Together 133
Chords of the Eleventh and Thirteenth 134
Altered Eleventh and Thirteenth Chords 135
Simplifying the Notation 139
Other Abbreviations and Symbols 140

Glossary 143

Index 153

Preface

Introduction To Music Fundamentals And Lead-Sheet Terminology is intended for the beginning commercial musician. This book assumes no technical knowledge of music and starts from the premise that the reader is either currently (or soon to be) involved in private music study with someone who teaches an instrument (or voice) or plans to become proficient through self instruction and practical experience. The concise format presented here offers an accelerated program that gets the beginning musician up and running within a relatively short span of time.

Chapters 1 through 9 provide a technical foundation for the survey of chord descriptions in Chapter 10. The opening chapter introduces notes and rests, concepts in rhythm and meter, repeat signs, and performance directions. Chapters 2, 3, and 4 present the subjects of pitch, scale, and key signature. Intervals, the minor mode, triads, and seventh chords follow in Chapters 5, 6, 7, and 9. Since a significant portion of commercial music and jazz involves scales and modes that are neither major nor minor, the topic of church modes is explored in Chapter 8. Chapter 10 outlines and analyzes the chord symbols typically represented in lead sheets.

Access To Worksheets

Worksheets are not included with this text; however, they are integral components of *Finding The Right Pitch: A Guide To The Study Of Music Fundamentals* and *Finding The Right Pitch II: A Guide To The Study Of Basic Harmony*. Most of the worksheets for both volumes can be used with *Introduction To Music Fundamentals And Lead-Sheet Terminology*. At this writing, they are available as free downloads at www.worldbetbooks.com.

Three Additional Resources

The preeminent reference for the study of lead-sheet terminology remains Carl Brandt and Clinton Roemer's *Standardized Chord Symbol Notation: A Uniform System for the Music Profession* (Sherman Oaks: Roerick Music Company, 1976). Chapter 10 of *Introduction To Music Fundamentals And Lead-Sheet Terminology* supports Brandt and Roemer's system, but also acknowledges a few of the alternative chord symbols informing the common practice of commercial music and jazz literature.

For a comprehensive excursion into the world of music fundamentals, see *Finding The Right Pitch: A Guide To The Study Of Music Fundamentals*. Designed primarily (though not exclusively) for college students, this book prepares music majors for the study of harmony and meets the needs of non-music majors who would complete a course in music fundamentals as an elective. Depending on the priorities of the student and/or instructor, certain items will serve as reference, whereas other topics will merit immediate consideration. *Finding The Right Pitch* includes

(1) discussions of pitch, scale, major and minor modes, and key signatures;
(2) a rigorous exploration of both elementary and advanced concepts in rhythm and meter;
(3) drills and step-by-step guides for the construction of intervals;
(4) drills and step-by-step guides for the construction of triads within the major-minor tonal system;
(5) four-part texture and principles for doubling the chord tones of triads;
(6) singing triads in all positions from a common bass pitch;
(7) the church modes, the cadential six-four chord, the dominant seventh, cadences, and nonharmonic tones;
(8) singing the dominant seventh in all positions from a common bass pitch;
(9) practical exercises in rhythm and meter, including several patterns for two hands that promote bilateral hand-to-hand coordination—a skill usually reserved for drummers.

Ninety worksheets follow the index of *Finding The Right Pitch*. As suggested above, many of these worksheets can be used with my *Introduction To Music Fundamentals*, particularly Chapters 1–7. Worldbetbooks.com provides a free download of worksheets for the chord symbols discussed in Chapter 10 of this text.

Finding The Right Pitch II: A Guide To The Study Of Basic Harmony, also for college students, focuses on voice leading, a process that controls the linear succession of tones in each voice (i.e., melodic line), optimizing how each voice moves through time in relation to the rest of the musical texture. *Finding The Right Pitch II* covers

(1) the formation and construction of triads within the church mode system;
(2) singing, transposing, and identifying the church modes;
(3) the principles of voice leading;
(4) the different types of six-four chords;
(5) cadence formation;
(6) harmonic and contrapuntal progressions;
(7) the properties of seventh chords;
(8) the formation of seventh chords within the church modes and the major-minor tonal system;
(9) using the interval of the 7th to improve voice leading;
(10) real and apparent seventh chords;
(11) interlocking seventh chords;
(12) harmonic and contrapuntal sequences;
(13) the two-progression framework;
(14) singing seventh chords in all positions from a common bass pitch;
(15) the utility of nonharmonic tones for correcting faulty motion between chords;
(16) the application of voice-leading principles and chord progression to the piano keyboard.

Ninety worksheets follow the index of *Finding The Right Pitch II*. Additionally, they are available as free downloads at www.worldbetbooks.com. Most of the worksheets for Chapters 2, 5, and 8 of *Finding The Right Pitch II* may be used with Chapters 8 and 9 of *Introduction To Music Fundamentals*.

Acknowledgments

I extend my lasting gratitude to the following people for giving generously of their time to review portions of the manuscript: Marius Sapkus; Tommy Harrison, Jacksonville University; Alyson McLamore, Cal Poly San Luis Obispo; Tom Owens, El Camino College; Ted Stern, Glendale College; and David Bradfield, California State University Dominguez Hills.

Wally Bower

Introduction To Music Fundamentals And Lead-Sheet Terminology is a tribute to my teacher, the late Wallace Henry Bower, Jr., professor of music theory at El Camino College in Torrance, California. Sometime in the mid-1970s, Wally began teaching lead-sheet terminology in his harmony classes. The survey of chord symbols presented in Chapter 10 underscores the extent to which he valued the study of lead sheets in music education.

David Nivans

Chapter 1 Time and Performance

The creation of music involves the organization of two complementary elements: sound and silence. An aural art that depends on the unfolding of time for its performance and appreciation, music is produced from fixed units of duration called notes and rests. Notes represent musical sound while rests represent musical silence. Musical sound and silence are signified in written form by the shapes of the notes and rests that exist on a set of five parallel lines and four spaces called a **staff**.

Example 1–1 illustrates the differences in the shapes of the various musical sounds on the staff. Both whole notes and half notes appear as oval hollowed-out structures. This structure is called the **note head**. Quarter notes, eighth notes, sixteenth notes, thirty-second notes, and sixty-fourth notes all have filled-in note heads.

All notes smaller than the whole note contain a **stem** (1–1). Eighth notes, sixteenth notes, thirty-second notes, and sixty-fourth notes also carry a **flag**, an additional component that is always attached to the right side of the stem. Eighth notes have one flag, sixteenth notes two, thirty-second notes three, and sixty-fourth notes four. As we shall soon see, any two notes with flags may be joined together with a thick horizontal line called a **beam**. Since half notes and quarter notes do not have flags, neither can they have beams.

Example 1–1: note values on the staff

Another significant aspect of a note's musical shape involves its location on the staff and the position of its stem (1–1). If a stemmed note in a single vocal or instrumental part occurs above the center line, then the stem proceeds downwards from the left side of the note head. If a stemmed note in a single vocal or instrumental part occurs below the center line, then the stem proceeds upwards from the right of the note head. If a stemmed note is located on the center line, then the stem may point in either direction according to the musical context. In most cases, however, the stem of a note on the center line points down.

The staff is also the means by which **pitches** (see Chapter 2) can be distinguished from one another in written form. The relative highness or lowness of any pitch corresponds to the highness or lowness of the line or space of the staff on which the pitch is located. In 1–1 above, the notes with downward stems are higher in pitch than those with upward stems. (Although the highness or lowness of a pitch is best represented with a staff, musical durations can be indicated without a staff.)

Example 1–2 displays the shapes of the corresponding rests for each of the notes discussed above. Both the whole rest and half rest resemble a black rectangular box. Counting the lines from the bottom of the staff, the whole rest hangs on the fourth line, while the half rest stands on the center line. Unlike the notes on the staff, which can appear on any space or line, the rests are always located in the same position.

Example 1–2: rest values on the staff

1

The design for the quarter rest, consisting of diagonal and curved lines, is dissimilar to all the other rests, resembling a bird flying sideways at a 90-degree angle to the earth. The remaining eighth, sixteenth, thirty-second, and sixty-fourth rests have one, two, three, and four hooks respectively, with each hook pointing towards the left. The eighth-note rest, with its single hook, resembles the number 7; while the sixteenth, thirty-second, and sixty-fourth rests add to this number one hook for each shorter rest value.

As indicated in example 1–3, half notes, quarter notes, eighth notes, sixteenth notes, thirty-second notes, and sixty-fourth notes have a mathematical relationship to each other and to the whole note. Assuming that the duration of the whole note carries a relative value of "one," two halves, four quarters, eight eighths, sixteen sixteenths, thirty-two thirty-seconds, and sixty-four sixty-fourths will all fill the span of a single whole note.

Further, two quarters fill the duration of a single half note, two eighths equal a single quarter, two sixteenths equal a single eighth, two thirty-seconds equal a single sixteenth, and two sixty-fourths equal a single thirty-second. Thus, smaller note divisions in relation to the whole note exhibit the following equivalent durations:

Example 1–3: mathematical relationships between note values

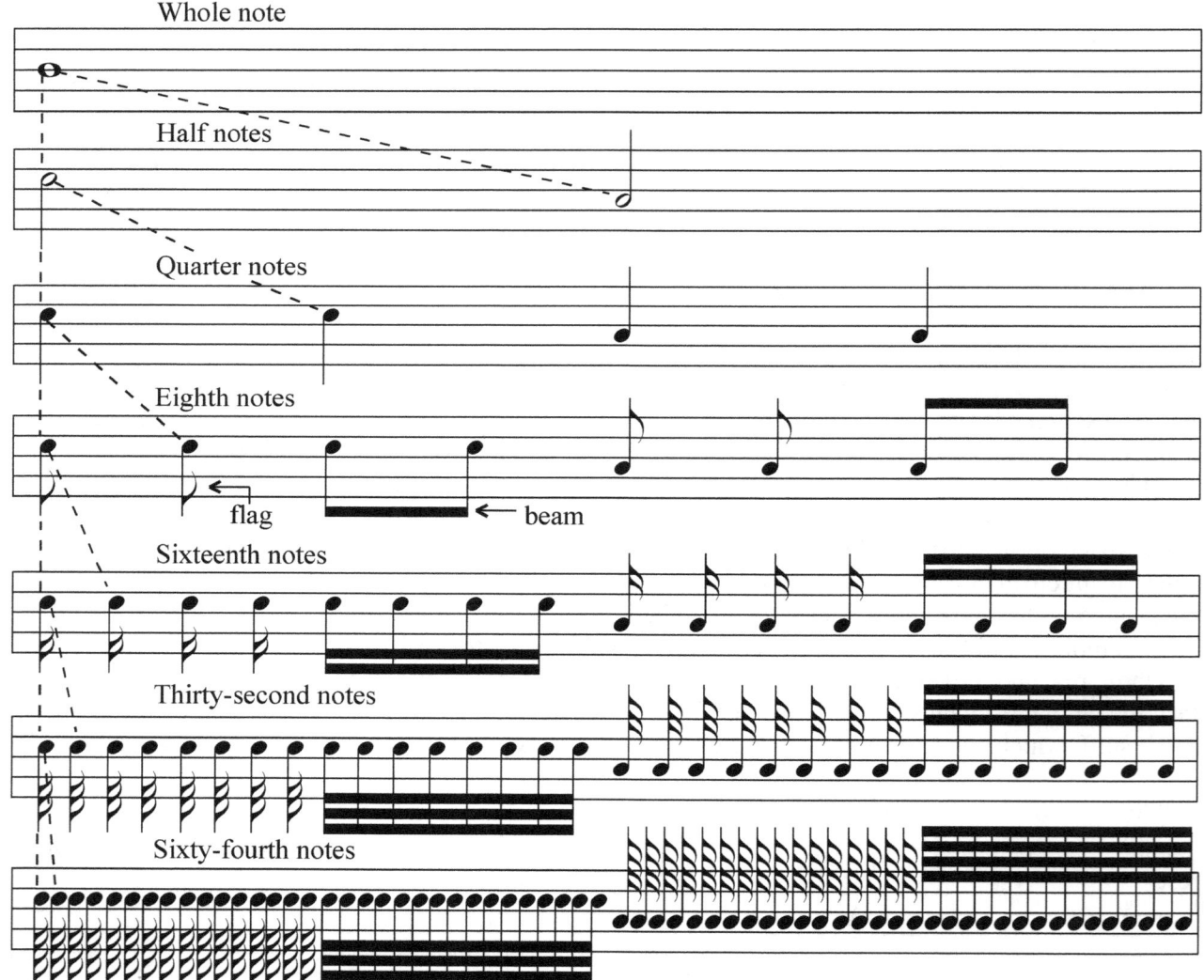

Example 1–3 above demonstrates how two or more notes with flags may be joined together with a corresponding number of beams. Eighth notes may have one beam, sixteenth notes two, thirty-second notes three, and sixty-fourth notes four. The common practice in music today is to use beams rather than flags whenever both options are available, as beamed notes are easier to read than flagged notes. In vocal music, however, the former practice was to assign one or more flags to any duration smaller than a quarter note that carried a single syllable of text.

It is also possible to group different note values together with beams. Moreover, in certain cases, the use of beams may appear to contradict the principle of stem position. For example, if most of the notes of a group take upward stems, then all of the notes will be stemmed up and beamed above the notes. Conversely, if most of the notes of a group take downward stems, then all of the notes will be stemmed down and beamed below the notes (see the dotted lines and circled notes in example 1–4).

Example 1–4: stem direction

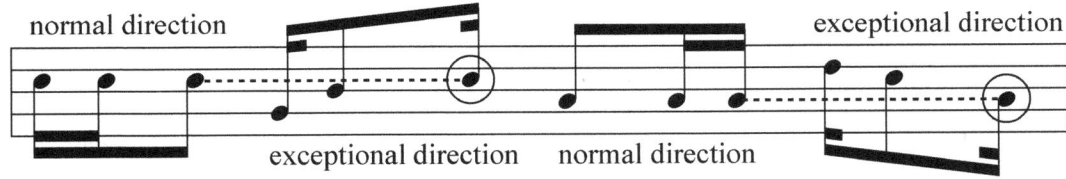

Ties and Dots

There are two different ways to extend the duration of any note: with a **tie** or a **dot**. A tie, as shown in example 1–5, is a curved line that connects two or more notes together; however, only the first note of any tied pair or group of notes is articulated. The second note of the tied pair (or group of notes) is sustained for the duration of the note values presented. Tied notes are particularly useful for extending the duration of a note across the **bar line** (we shall discuss the bar line in the next section).

The second way to extend the duration of a note is to add a dot to it, as shown in example 1–6. The addition of a dot extends the duration of a note (or rest) by *one half its original value*. The tied notes in 1–5 correspond to the dotted note and rest values in 1–6. Thus, the whole note tied to the half note on the center line of 1–5 corresponds to the dotted whole note on the center line of 1–6. The same holds true for the other tied and dotted values on each of the lines and spaces in both examples.

Adding a second dot extends the duration of a note (or rest) by *one half the value of the first dot*. Therefore, if a single dot extends the duration of a quarter note by one eighth, then a second dot extends the duration by one sixteenth. If a single dot extends the duration of a half note by one quarter note, then a second dot extends the duration by one eighth.

4 Chapter 1 Time and Performance

Meter and Beat

In music, notes and rests are organized into a series of pulses, or beats. Some of these beats are theoretically stronger and receive more emphasis than others. The stronger beats, or stressed beats, are called **primary accents**. Indicated in example 1–7 with the uppercase letter P, they are the first accents we perceive when hearing a stream of accents unfold in time as a piece of music is being performed. The weaker beats, or unstressed beats, are called **secondary accents**, indicated in 1–7 with the letter s.

Usually, the notes and rests that signify both the primary and secondary accents of a musical composition are arranged in various configurations that produce a larger temporal framework called **meter**. As demonstrated in 1–7, it is the distance between primary accents that determines the meter (see the brackets in the example), a distance measured by the number of intervening secondary accents that both precede and follow the primary accents.

At least two basic types of meter, namely, duple and triple, arise from the distances that span any two primary accents. Duple meter (1–7a) has one intervening secondary accent between primary accents: P s P s. Quadruple meter (1–7b), a subcategory of duple meter, has three intervening secondary accents: P s S s P s S s, the second of which receives more stress than the first or third (notice the uppercase S). The other main type of meter, triple meter (1–7c), has two intervening secondary accents: P s s P s s. Duple, quadruple, and triple meters are all considered to be **symmetrical meters** because they can be divided evenly by either 2 or 3.

The distance between two primary accents, in addition to producing meter, constitutes a unit of measured musical space. And each unit so measured is marked off by vertical lines called bar lines, or measure lines. The spaces these lines enclose are called **measures**, or **bars**.

The value of the beat for the measures of duple, quadruple, and triple meters displayed in 1–7 is the quarter note. To count primary and secondary accents within duple, quadruple, and triple meters, we use the numbers: 1-2, 1-2-3-4, and 1-2-3 respectively.

Example 1–7: the distance between primary accents in duple, quadruple, and triple meters

a. duple meter (two beats per measure, one secondary accent between primary accents)

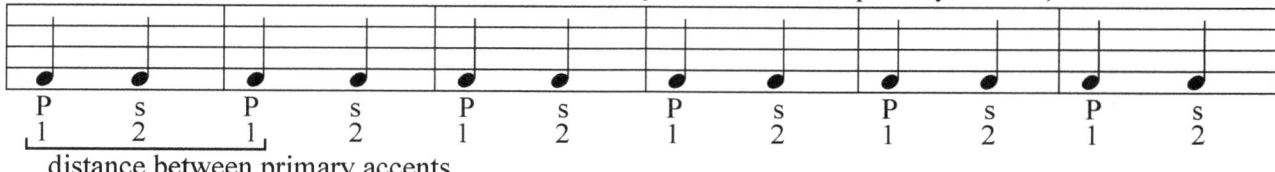

b. quadruple meter (four beats per measure, three secondary accents between primary accents)

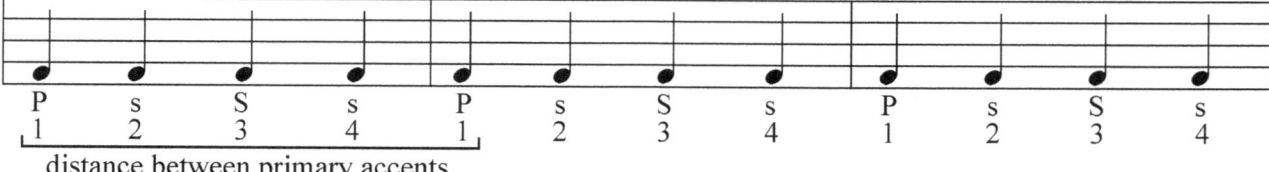

c. triple meter (three beats per measure, two secondary accents between primary accents)

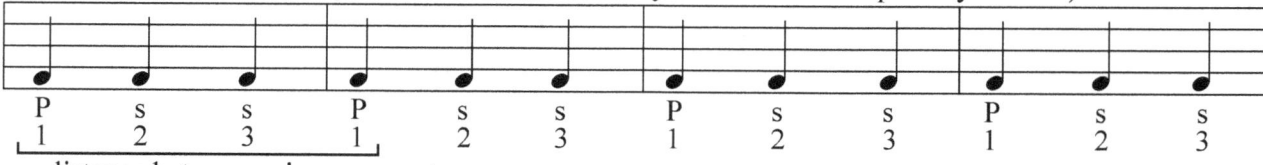

Divisions of Beats

There are two basic ways to divide the beat of any meter. If each of the beats is divided into two equal parts (or multiples of two), then the meter is classified as **simple**. If, however, each of the beats is divided into three equal parts (or multiples of three), then the meter is classified as **compound**. Therefore, any duple, quadruple, or triple meter may have either a simple division or compound division of the beat.

As shown in example 1–8, the first simple division of the quarter-note beat is the eighth note while the second division is the sixteenth note (on beat 2 of the first measure, a quarter rest is used instead of a quarter note). A plus sign indicates the location of where the second half of each quarter-note beat falls.

Example 1–8: simple duple meter

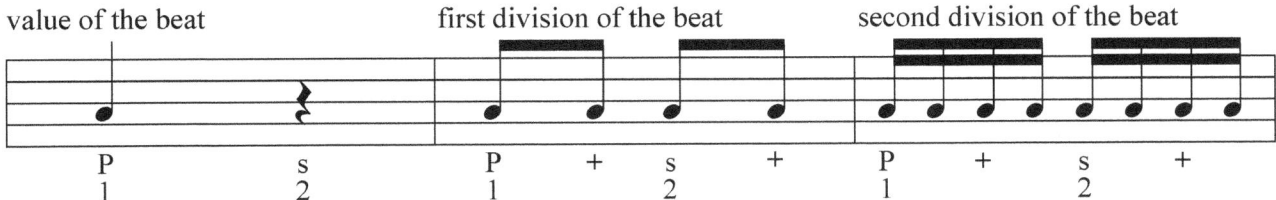

The next example illustrates the difference between a duple meter with a *simple* division of the beat and a duple meter with a *compound* division of the beat. In the latter (example 1–9b), the value of the beat is a dotted quarter note (on beat 2 of the first measure, a dotted quarter rest is used instead of a dotted quarter note). As we have said, the beat of a compound meter is divided into three equal parts or multiples of three. A dotted quarter can be divided into either three eighth notes (the first compound division) or six sixteenth notes (the second division).

Example 1–9: simple and compound duple meter

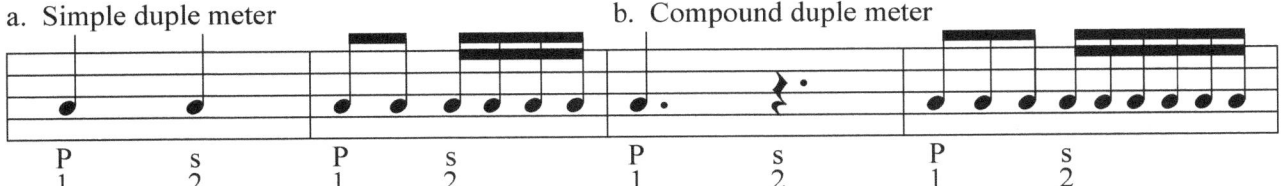

Time Signatures

Examples 1–8 and 9 demonstrate how some of the most basic configurations of notes and rests may occur within simple and compound meters. It is not difficult to see where these configurations of notes and rests coincide with the primary and secondary accents because they are clearly marked. Since the primary and secondary accents are not so identified in actual music, it would be helpful to have a sign or symbol that could tell us the value of the beat and how many beats are distributed across each measure.

The **time signature**, or **meter signature**, provides this valuable information. Consisting of two components, the time signature appears as a pair of Arabic numbers, one located directly above the other. If the meter is simple, then the top number designates the number of beats per measure and the bottom number reveals the value of each beat. All simple meters are read in this way.

If, therefore, the bottom number is 4 in a simple meter, then the value of the beat is the quarter note. There are two quarter-note beats per measure in example 1–10a, four quarter-note beats per measure in 1–10b, and three quarter-note beats per measure in 1–10c. Had the bottom number in examples 1–10a, 10b, and 10c been 16, the value of the beat would have been a sixteenth note. Had the bottom number been 32, the value of the beat would have been a thirty-second note.

Example 1–10: simple meters

The reading of compound time signatures is somewhat more complicated. If we attempt to read the meters represented in example 1–11 according to the method for reading simple meters described above, then 1–11a would have six eighth-note beats per measure, 1–11b would have twelve eighth-note beats per measure, and 1–11c would have nine eighth-note beats per measure. But as we shall see presently, this is usually not the way to interpret compound signatures, unless the meter is performed very slowly (see below, p. 8).

In order to identify, read, and classify compound meters accurately, it is necessary to perform a basic arithmetic operation. If dividing the number 3 into the top number of the time signature results in a quotient is 2, 3, or 4, then the number of beats per measure is 2, 3, or 4 (for an example of a time signature with a quotient greater than 4, see the last section of this chapter). To determine the value of the beat, take the note value that the bottom number represents, proceed to the note value that is one denomination higher, and add a dot to that note value.

If the bottom number is 8, which signifies an eighth note, then proceed to the quarter note and add a dot; therefore, the value of the beat is a dotted quarter. In examples 1–11a, 11b, and 11c, the value of the beat is the dotted quarter note with two, four, and three beats distributed across each respective measure. Had the bottom number in examples 1–11a, 11b, and 11c been 16, the value of the beat would have been a dotted eighth. Had the bottom number been 32, the value of the beat would have been a dotted sixteenth.

Example 1–11: compound meters

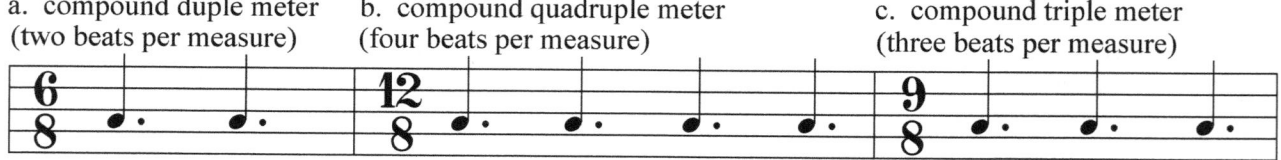

Nearly all time signatures resemble those shown above: pairs of Arabic numbers with one number located directly above the other. There are, however, two principal exceptions to this practice, each of which involves a symbol that looks somewhat like the letter C. The first symbol (example 1–12a), often referred to as "common time," is the equivalent of $\frac{4}{4}$ time. The second symbol (1–12b), often referred to as either "cut time" or *alla breve*, is the same as $\frac{2}{2}$ time. Here, the value of the beat is the half note while the first division of that beat is the quarter note.

At this point, we will dispense with marking primary and secondary accents with P and s and instead use numbers to represent each beat. The first division of the beat is indicated with a plus sign on the second half of each beat. Counting beats and half beats will be explained in more detail in the following section.

Example 1–12: common time and cut time

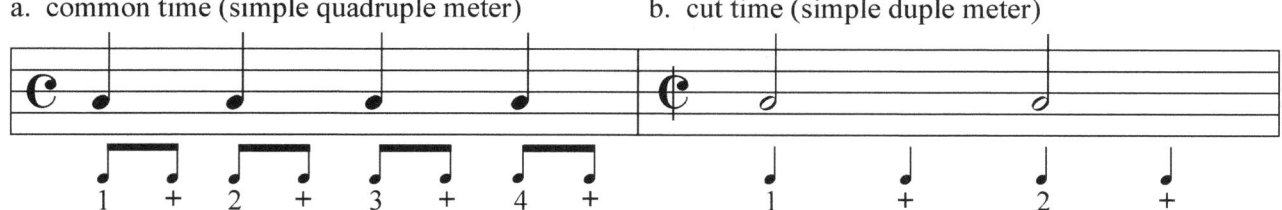

Counting Note Values

When performing or reading note values such as those put forward in examples 1–8 and 12b, musicians vocalize or internalize the numbers and plus signs. Usually, musicians counting aloud replace the plus sign with the word "and." Accordingly, both the beat and the first division of the beat in, say, 1–12b would be expressed as: "one and two and." If we include the second and third divisions of the beat, as in example 1–13, then additional syllables may be used.

With the quarter note as the value of the beat, the second division brings us to the level of the sixteenth note—four sixteenth notes fill the duration of one quarter. For each group of four sixteenths, the syllables "e" (pronounced ee) and "a" (pronounced uh or ah) are applied to the second and fourth sixteenth notes respectively. Counting at the level of the third division requires no other syllables beyond those already employed for the second division.

We avoid adding syllables below the second division of the beat in simple meter because vocalizing or internalizing syllables and words becomes unwieldy if the note values are performed at a very quick pace. In any event, it can be seen that the note values in 1–13 all have a mathematical relationship to each other: a single quarter note can be divided into two eighths, four sixteenths, or eight thirty-seconds (the "in 2" designation in the example means that there are two beats to each measure).

Example 1–13: counting the first, second, and third divisions of the beat in simple duple meter (in 2)

Earlier, we said that the reading of time signatures for compound meter is more complicated than reading those for simple meter. Two different methods for counting aid the performance and reading of note values in compound meter. Example 1–14 illustrates the first method. The value of the beat is the dotted quarter note. The first division of the beat would be counted as: 1 + a 2 + a ("one and uh two and uh").

Notice that for the second division of the beat, every other sixteenth note does not receive a syllable. For the third division of the beat, only six of twenty-four thirty-second notes are counted. As in example 1–13, the note values in 1–14 all have a mathematical relationship to each other: a dotted quarter note can be divided into three eighths, six sixteenths, or twelve thirty-seconds.

Example 1–14: counting the first, second, and third divisions of the beat in compound duple meter (in 2)

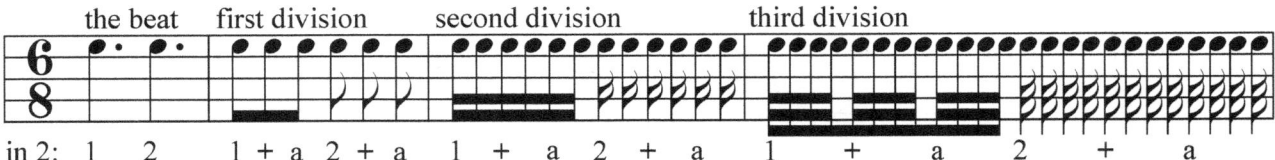

The second method for performing and reading compound meter appears to contradict the process of classifying time signatures by dividing three into the top number and by adding a dot to the note value that is one denomination higher than the bottom number (see above, p. 6). That compound meters are sometimes performed very slowly accounts for the apparent contradiction. When a compound meter such as $\frac{6}{8}$ is performed slowly, we hear the first division rather than the dotted quarter note as the value of the beat. Thus, the meter in 1–14 above would be interpreted as having not *two* beats per measure but *six* and the value of the beat would be the eighth note, not the dotted quarter.

Example 1–15 demonstrates how the preceding example would be counted if the notes were played slowly. When interpreting the first division of a compound meter as the value of the beat, the note values are counted with the syllables used in simple meter. According to this method, the second division of compound meter is counted as if it were in simple meter with every note receiving a syllable (1 + 2 + 3 + 4 + 5 + 6 +).

Example 1–15: counting compound duple meter with six beats to the measure

Showing the two methods of counting together, the numbers and syllables for both the beats and first divisions of beats in $\frac{6}{8}$ meter should coincide according to the pattern indicated in example 1–16.

Example 1–16: counting compound duple meter (in 2 and in 6)

Example 1–17 illustrates the coincidence of numbers and syllables for both the second and third divisions of the beat in ⁶⁄₈ meter.

Example 1–17: counting compound duple meter (in 2 and in 6)

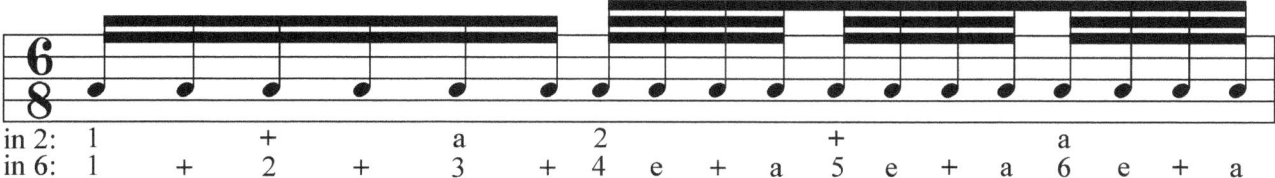

Rhythm

If meter is the distance between two primary accents, then **rhythm** is the measurement of both the primary and secondary accents within that meter. Rhythm involves how the accents are organized, or configured. In the preceding exercises and examples, we have seen various types of rhythmic configurations. Some of the rhythms presented in this chapter are quite simple to read, count, and interpret, while others are more challenging for the beginning music student.

It would be instructive to tap out the rhythm to the song "Jingle Bells" to see if your friends can identify the music without actually hearing the words or the tune. Not surprisingly, most listeners recognize the music from hearing only the rhythm. To be sure, the song has a very distinctive rhythmic profile. But in any case, we can take from this exercise the following lesson: *rhythm is that particular arrangement of notes and rests within each measure that ultimately helps to inform the individuality of a musical composition.*

Syncopation

Under normal musical conditions, we expect notes of longer duration to fall on primary accents and those of shorter duration to occur on secondary accents. When divisions of beats are emphasized and/or when the strongest part of the primary accent is left either unarticulated or weakened in some way, it disrupts the regular distribution of note values and creates an effect known as **syncopation**. *Syncopation makes strong that which is otherwise weak.*

Musicians produce syncopations by using ties, rests, or shorter notes followed by longer ones. The syncopated figure in example 1–18a shifts the focus to the first division of the quarter-note beat by introducing an eighth note on the strongest part of the primary accent and following it with a quarter, a note value that is twice as long as the preceding eighth.

Example 1–18: four types of syncopation

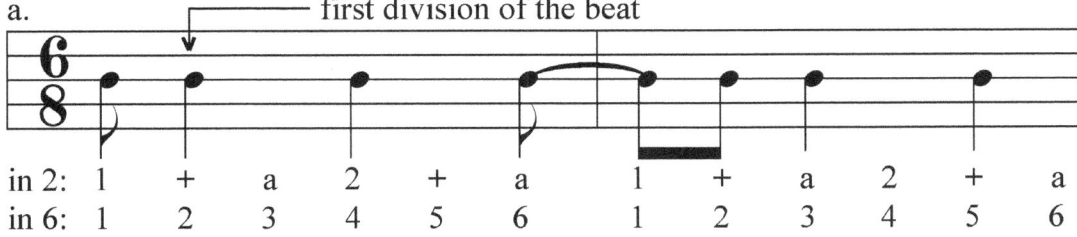

10   Chapter 1   Time and Performance

Example 1–18b shows syncopation within the second division of the beat at the level of the sixteenth note. The rhythmic syllables in parentheses indicate that their inclusion here adds nothing to the basic count and that their absence would not obscure the recognition of any of the beats or first divisions of beats.

An eighth rest produces the syncopation in the first measure of 1–18c. The second measure of 1–18c weakens the first part of the primary accent with the placement of two sixteenth notes followed by an eighth tied to a sixteenth.

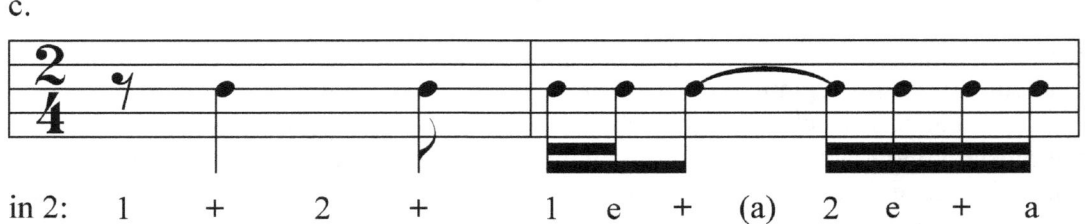

The first measure of 1–18d exhibits the same kind of syncopation as the first measure of 1–18a and even uses identical notes values. Notice, however, that the meter and therefore the counting in both examples is completely different, which underscores the importance of knowing the value of the beat and whether the meter is simple or compound.

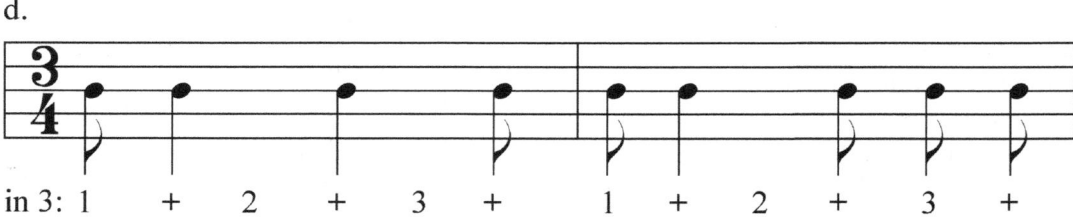

Displacement

If the normal rhythmic flow has been disrupted at the level of the beat rather than the division of the beat, this procedure is distinguished from syncopation and is usually referred to as either a **cross accent** or a **displaced accent**. In example 1–19, the secondary accent carries the longer note value, which is then tied into the primary accent of the next measure. Although the primary accent appears to be weakened, it has been shifted, or displaced, to another part of the measure (see brackets).

Example 1–19: the displaced accent (cross accent)

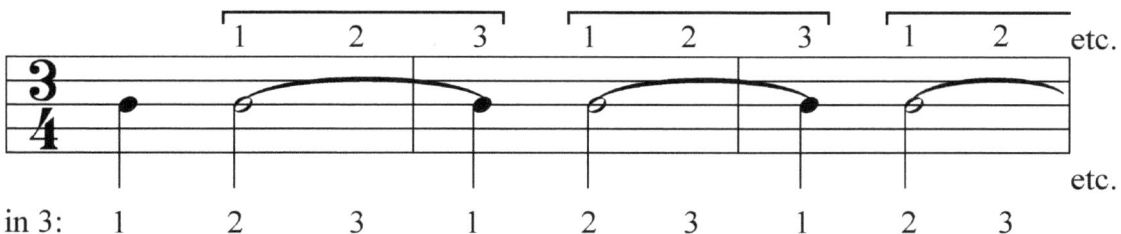

Hemiola

Hemiola is a process by which a composer may displace the accents in such a way that it transforms either a duple meter into what sounds like a triple meter or a triple meter into what sounds like a duple meter. It may occur within the measure, as in examples 1–20a and 20b, or across measures, as in 1–20c and 20d (see brackets).

In 1–20a, a measure of $\frac{3}{4}$ is placed within the metric context of $\frac{6}{8}$. Example 1–20b shows the opposite process: the transformation of $\frac{3}{4}$ into $\frac{6}{8}$. Three measures of $\frac{2}{4}$ span two measures of $\frac{3}{4}$ in 1–20c. Grouping three quarter notes of duration together by dots and ties transforms three measures of quadruple meter (a subcategory of duple) into four measures of triple meter in 1–20d.

Example 1–20: types of hemiola

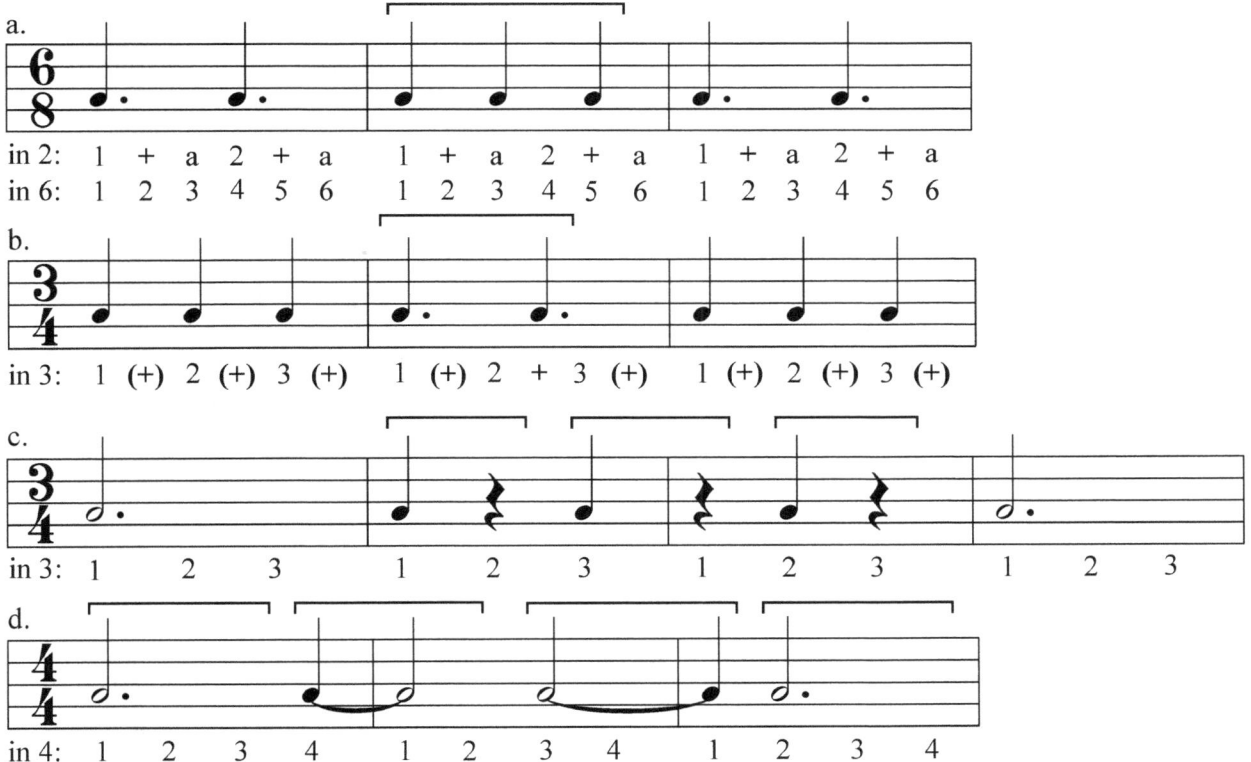

12 Chapter 1 Time and Performance

Repeat Signs

It is possible to repeat sections or passages of music without actually writing the notes out twice. Composers use various signs to indicate where such repetitions should occur. A **repeat sign** consisting of two dots on the second and third spaces of the staff followed by a **double bar** tells the performer that everything before the sign should be played again from the beginning.

The double bar itself has one narrow bar line and one thicker bar line. Upon reaching the double bar, as shown in step 2 of example 1–21a, the performer starts over from the beginning (step 3) and then continues with the rest of the music, passing through the first double bar until a second double bar, one without dots, indicates the conclusion of the composition. As we shall see in example 1–23, another common type of double bar, consisting of two narrow bar lines of the same thickness, is used to close off a section of music *before the end*.

Example 1–21: types of repeat signs

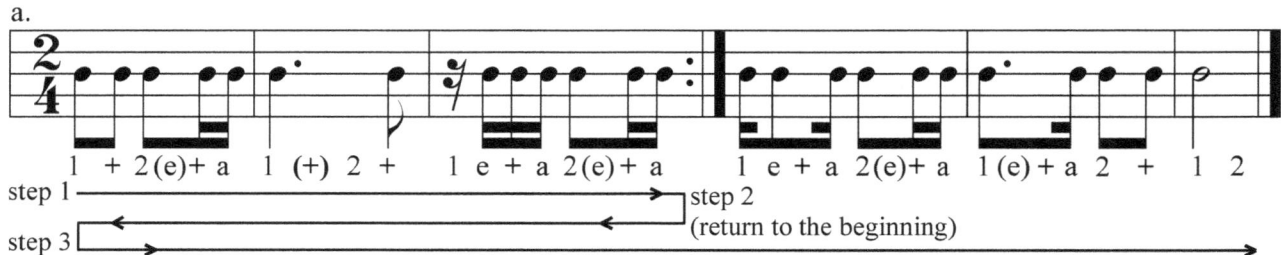

An additional double bar with dots placed after the beginning of the composition, but before the double bar shown in the foregoing example, may be used to limit the amount of repetition; here, the performer is directed to execute a single repetition of the music within the two double bars before continuing with the rest of composition (1–21b).

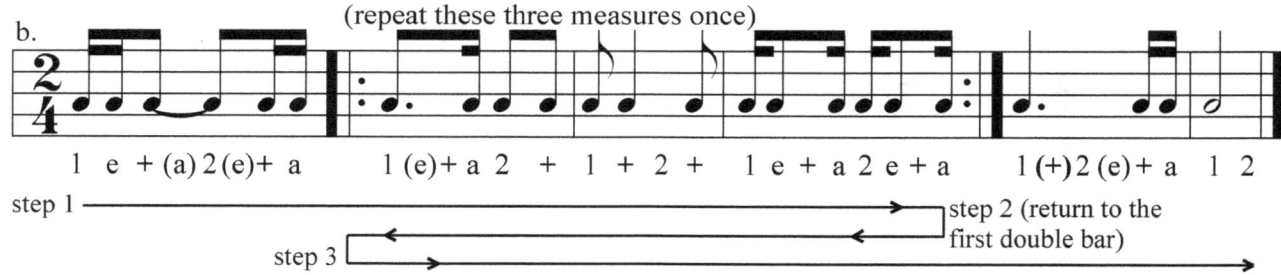

If the repeat involves just a single measure, then the sign consists of a diagonal slash and two dots (1–21c).

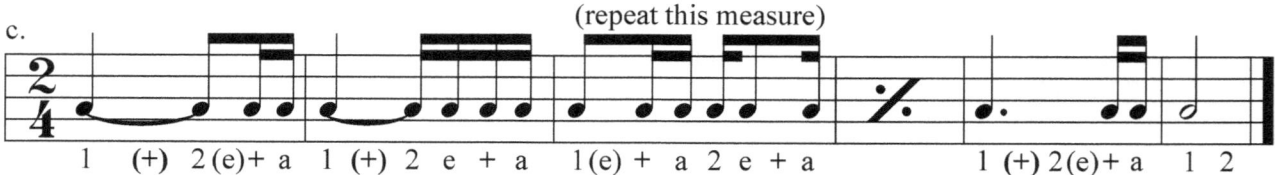

A sign resembling the single-measure repeat but crossing over the bar line instructs the performer to repeat the previous two measures, rather than just one. Sometimes the sign includes the number 2 above the bar line to clarify that the repetition should include only two measures (1–21d).

The Latin word *bis* (which means twice) may also be used to show a two-measure repeat (1–21e). According to this practice, *bis* is enclosed in a bracket and appears directly over the bar line.

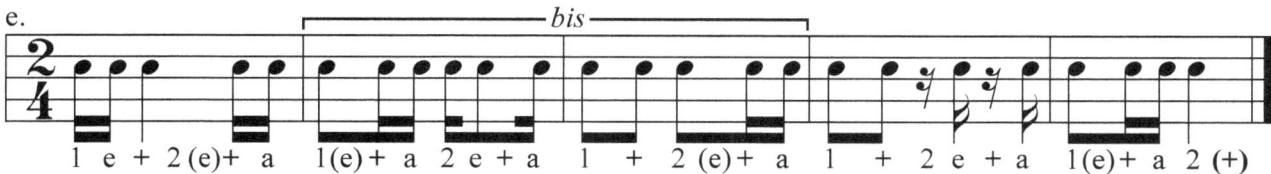

First and Second Endings

Alternate endings for compositions or musical passages are indicated with first and second endings (numbered 1 and 2 respectively in example 1–22). The **first ending** directs the performer to return either to the beginning of the composition (1–22a) or to an earlier repeat sign (1–22b). After the music has been repeated, the performer takes the **second ending** rather than the first.

Example 1–22: first and second endings

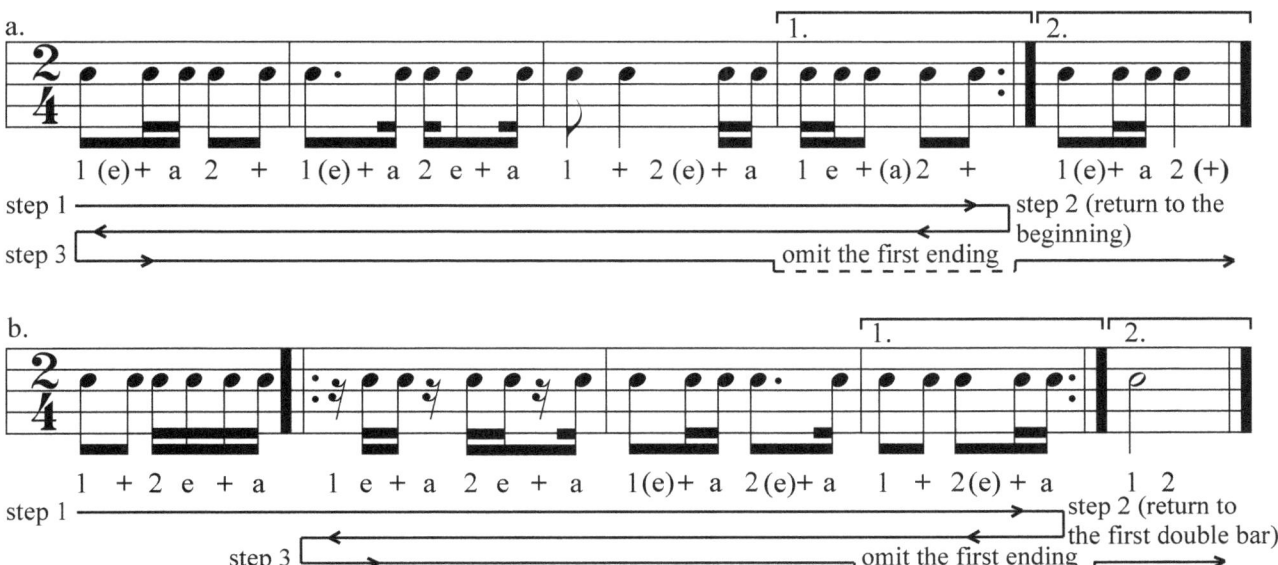

14   Chapter 1 Time and Performance

Da Capo al Fine, Dal Segno al Fine, Da Capo al Coda, **and** ***Dal Segno al Coda***

Other repeat signs include the following Italian expressions: *Da Capo al Fine, Dal Segno al Fine, Da Capo al Coda,* and *Dal Segno al Coda*. The abbreviation *D.C.*, shown in example 1–23a, stands for *Da Capo*, which means "from the head," or in this context "from the beginning." The English word for *Fine* is end; therefore, the expression *D.C. al Fine* directs the performer to repeat the music "from the beginning to the end." Notice that the final double bar coincides with the single word *Fine* rather than with the last measure of the example.

Example 1–23: *Da Capo al Fine, Dal Segno al Fine, Da Capo al Coda,* and *Dal Segno al Coda*

The words *Dal Segno*, abbreviated as *D.S.* in 1–23b, means "from the sign." The expression *Dal Segno al Fine*, which translates as "from the sign to the end," indicates that the music repeats back to the point where the sign (𝄋) first appears and then stops at the word *Fine*. In the second measure of the example, the note values include two thirty-seconds; representing the third division of the beat, the second of the two thirty-second notes does not receive a syllable (*).

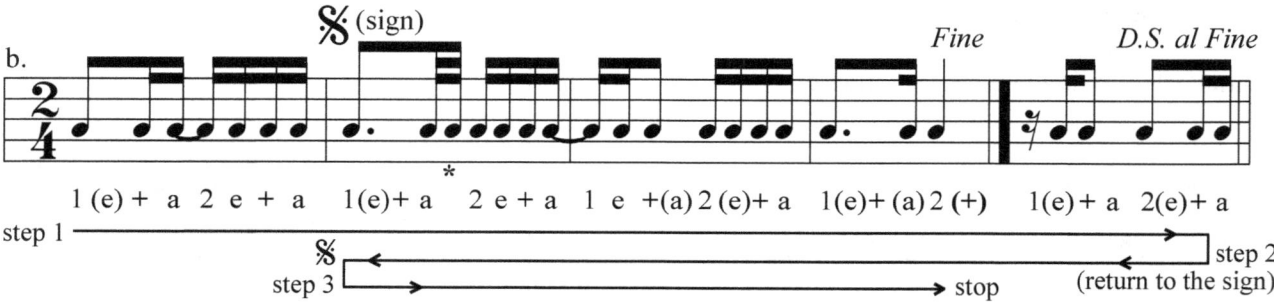

Da Capo al Coda, shown in 1–23c, denotes a return to the beginning and a continuation up to the coda sign (⊕). Upon reaching the coda sign, the performer skips ahead to the next appearance of the coda sign and then proceeds to the end.

At the conclusion of the example over the last note of the final bar, there is a sign called a **fermata** (𝄐). The fermata suspends the counting of the beat and extends the length of the note or rest beyond its original value. There is no precise duration for the extension of the note or rest that carries the fermata, but usually, the suspension of time will be longer in a slow **tempo** than in a fast tempo (see below, p. 16).

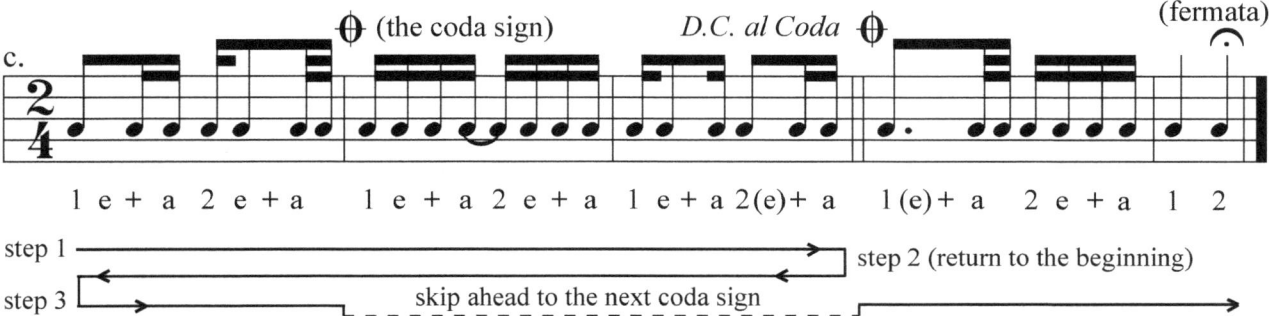

As demonstrated in 1–23d, the expression *Dal Segno al Coda* directs the performer to repeat the music from where the sign first appears (𝄋) until reaching the first coda sign (⊕); after arriving at the first coda sign, the performer skips ahead to the appearance of the second coda sign. From the second coda sign forward, the performer proceeds to the end of the composition.

The example below begins with a measure that does not contain all of the note values required to constitute a complete measure according to the given time signature. Indeed, not all compositions begin with the primary accent of the first measure. In such cases, the first measure is incomplete; the traditional practice is to complete the measure at the end of the composition, that is, to include the missing note values in the final measure of the work.

The incomplete measure at the beginning is known variously as the anacrusis, the upbeat, or the pickup; it is considered to be the upbeat for the following downbeat of the first complete measure. The downbeat is always the first primary accent of the composition.

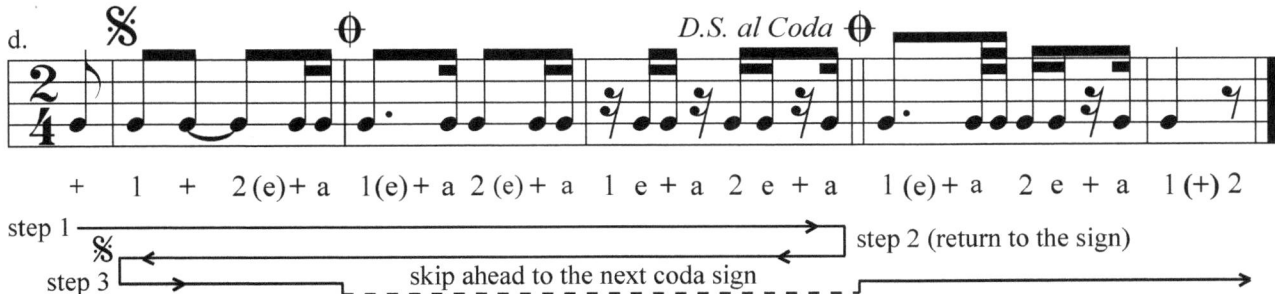

Performance Marks

If the performance of a musical score consisted only of written durations and pitches without any other elements of expression, the result would be little more than a mechanical rendering that could just as easily be produced by a machine or a computer. A musical score, however, contains a variety of words and symbols to help supplement, shape, and refine the performance of a composition. These words and symbols help the performer to understand the composer's intentions so that a more faithful interpretation of those intentions can be presented.

Two of the most important indications for shaping the expression of a composition involve both the speed and the volume of the performance. These indications are known as tempo and **dynamics**.

Tempo

Tempo is the rate of speed at which the beat in a music composition is performed. Earlier in this chapter, we referred to fast and slow performances of note values. The traditional language of choice for words such as fast and slow is Italian; however, one might encounter descriptions of tempo in other languages as well, most notably, German and French.

Words signifying tempo are usually placed above the staff. Below is a list of some of the Italian words used to indicate the relative speed of the music, progressing from slower to faster tempos:

largo	very slow	*moderato*	moderate (faster than *andante*)
grave	slow, serious	*allegretto*	moderately fast
lento	slow	*allegro*	fast
larghetto	slow (not as slow as *largo*)	*vivace*	fast
adagio	slow	*presto*	very fast
adagietto	slow (faster than *adagio*)	*prestissimo*	as fast as possible
andante	moderately slow		

The tempo signs shown above are general and imprecise. Any two musicians will probably have a slightly different feeling for what is very slow, slow, moderately slow, moderate, moderately fast, fast, very fast, and so on. Since the early nineteenth century, composers have been using a device called a **metronome** to provide more precise tempo indications. The metronome produces a steady and repeated click that helps the musician to know exactly how fast or slow to play a composition. Usually, a metronome marking appears at the beginning of a composition in one of two ways: M.M. ♩ = 60 or ♩ = 60.

The M.M. abbreviation stands for Maelzel's metronome, after Johann Maelzel (1772–1838), the first person to mass produce and popularize the device. The note value preceding the equal sign designates the value of the beat, or pulse. The number of clicks the metronome generates ranges from 40 to about 208 beats per minute. In the present instance, the number 60 indicates 60 clicks per minute. Although a quarter note was given here, any note value may be used as part of the metronome marking.

Sometimes, the musical score may contain an instruction directing the performer to change the prevailing tempo. The two most common instructions for changing the tempo are represented by the Italian words *ritardando* and *accelerando*. *Ritardando* directs the performer to gradually slow down while *accelerando* means to gradually increase the speed of a musical passage.

Dynamics

The term dynamics refers to marks in the musical score that instruct the performer to play within a wide range of volume levels, from a barely audible whisper to an excruciating roar. Relative degrees of loudness and softness are expressed most commonly with Italian words, although one might encounter dynamics in other languages as well, particularly German and French.

The following list of Italian words presents the most prevalent dynamics, progressing from softer to louder volume levels. The abbreviation for each word is also indicated, as dynamic marks are usually abbreviated in musical scores and placed below the staff.

Italian	Abbreviation	English
pianissimo	*pp*	very soft
piano	*p*	soft
mezzo piano	*mp*	moderately soft
mezzo forte	*mf*	moderately loud
forte	*f*	loud
fortissimo	*ff*	very loud

Another dynamic instruction to the performer may involve playing certain notes louder than others; this type of mark is called a **dynamic accent**. The most common symbol for a dynamic accent is $>$ and it usually appears either above or below the note head.

Directions for gradual increases or decreases in volume are represented by the Italian words *crescendo* and *decrescendo*; both terms are signified by elongated wedges (also called "hairpins"), as shown below. (The sign for the *decrescendo* symbol should not be confused with the symbol for the dynamic accent. The *decrescendo* is more elongated in appearance than the latter and may be used in conjunction with a large number of notes, whereas each dynamic accent mark occurs with a single note, is placed directly adjacent to the note head, and is much smaller in appearance.)

Italian	Abbreviation	English	Sign
crescendo	*cresc.*	getting louder	$<$
decrescendo	*decresc.*	getting softer	$>$

Simple and Compound Meter Exchange

In music, it is possible and often desirable to place either a simple division of the beat into a compound meter or a compound division of the beat into a simple meter. A simple (two-part) division of the beat occurring in a compound meter is referred to as the **duplet**. A compound (three-part) division of the beat used in a simple meter is called the **triplet**.

Triplets

To understand the triplet, let us compare two duple meters: $\frac{2}{4}$ and $\frac{6}{8}$. In $\frac{2}{4}$ time (example 1–24a), the value of the beat occurs at the level of the quarter note; in $\frac{6}{8}$ time (1–24b), however, the value of the beat is the dotted quarter note. The first division of the beat for both meters is the eighth note. Because both $\frac{2}{4}$ and $\frac{6}{8}$ are duple meters and have beat values of the same note denomination (i.e., the quarter note and the dotted quarter note), we refer to these meters as "parallel duple meters."

Example 1–24: parallel duple meters

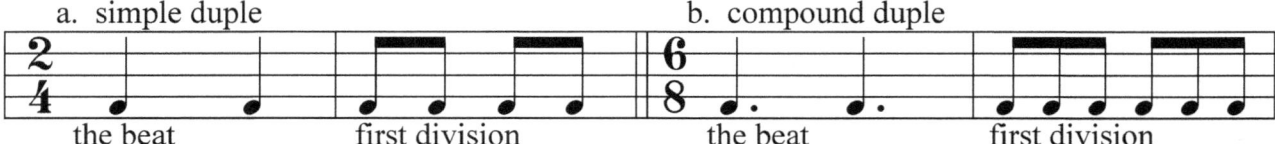

When a simple meter borrows the first division of the beat from a compound meter, the first division carries the number 3 above the note group and is referred to generally as the triplet; in this text, the triplet of the first division is termed "the small triplet." Examples 1–25a and 25b show how the triplet appears in $\frac{2}{4}$, first with all three notes beamed together (1–25a) and then expressed as a quarter note and eighth (1–25b). The method for counting the triplet is taken from compound meter (1 + a 2 + a).

If the triplet is not beamed (1–25b), then the figure adds a bracket to the number 3 in order to show the correct grouping of the notes. In example 1–25b, the first two eighth notes of the triplet are replaced by a quarter note, thereby modifying the triplet's basic three-note framework. In example 1–27 below, we shall discover that *smaller* note denominations can also replace any of the first-division note values of the triplet.

Example 1–25: the small triplet

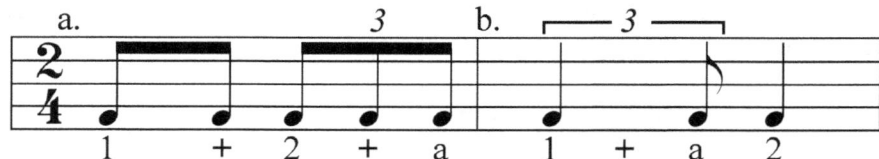

The triplet on beat 2 of 1–25a above occurs within the same span of time as the two eighth notes that normally constitute the first division of the beat. In simple meter, the triplet forms an irregular grouping of notes that conflicts with the two-part division of the beat. Example 1–26 shows the placement of the triplet in relation to the two eighth notes of the first division. Here, the triplet is notated with stems down and combined with another rhythmic line with stems up; the latter shows the first simple division of the beat. The second half of beat 2 (measure 1) falls between the second and third notes of the triplet.

Example 1–26: placement of the small triplet

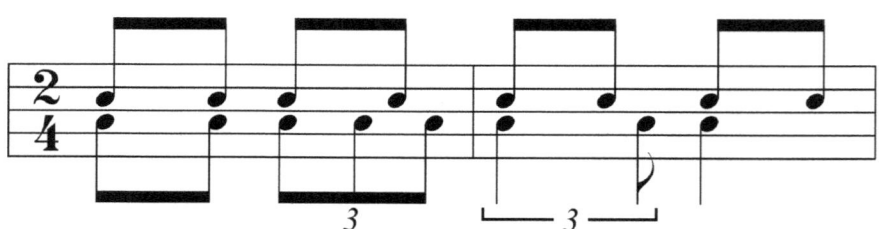

As we have said, any triplet with note values that are equivalent to the note values of the meter's first division (such as the triplets in examples 1–25 and 26 above) will be referred to as the small triplet. Other varieties of triplets discussed in this chapter include "the micro triplet" and "the large triplet." These other triplets use note values that either correspond to the second division of the beat or span two beats within the measure.

Earlier, we noted that smaller note denominations, such as those of the second division, could replace any of the first-division values of the triplet. Example 1–27 presents some of the ways in which these substitutions within the small triplet take place. In each instance, the basic three-note framework of the triplet figure has been changed: either two sixteenths replace one eighth (examples 1–27a and 27b) or four sixteenths replace two eighths (1–27c). Notice that the second sixteenth note of each pair of sixteenths does not receive a count (or syllable).

Example 1–27: using second-division note values with the small triplet

Example 1–28 illustrates another type of triplet, one that occurs at the level of the second division, the sixteenth note in $\frac{2}{4}$ time. We refer to this triplet as the micro triplet. The micro triplet is notated with stems down in the example and is combined with another rhythmic line with stems up; the line with stems up shows both the first division of the beat in eighths (1–28a) and the second division of the beat in sixteenths (1–28b, the second half of beat 2). Each micro triplet carries the number 3.

Example 1–28: the micro triplet

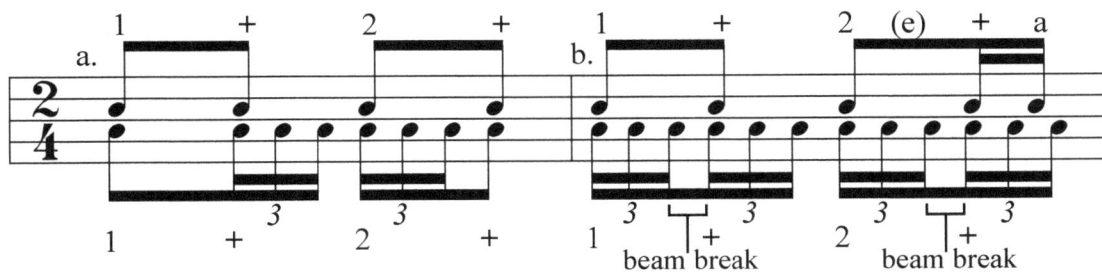

As indicated in example 1–28 above, the micro triplet may appear on the first part of the beat, the second part, or both. In 1–28a, the micro triplet falls alternately on each half of the beat, whereas in 1–28b, it is placed on both halves. When the micro triplet appears on both parts of the beat, there is usually a *break in the beam* to make the second half of the beat easier to read.

Example 1–29a shows where the small triplet falls in relation to both the first and second simple divisions of the beat. Example 1–29b presents a decidedly different operation at the level of the second division; for here, we have two micro triplets beamed into a single group of six notes on each beat. The six notes carry the number 6 instead of the number 3.

The notation for the group of six notes changes because the accompanying rhythmic line (i.e., the line with stems up) does not emphasize the second half of the beat. On beat 1 of 1–29b, the second half of the beat has been subsumed within the eighth note that falls on the syllable "e" (see the circled "e"). On beat 2, the second half of the beat occurs within the larger context of four equally-spaced sixteenth notes. Thus, in the line that has the six notes, there is no need to clarify the second half of the beat with a beam break. In effect, each pair of micro triplets has become a single group of six notes called the sextuplet.

Example 1–29: the small triplet, sextuplet, and second division of the beat

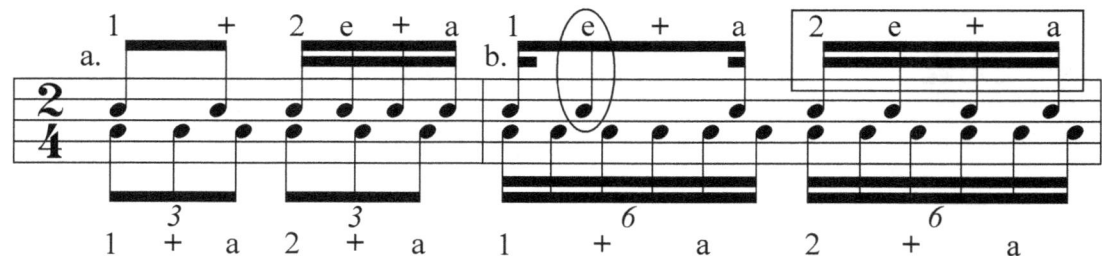

In the foregoing paragraphs, we saw how the small triplet substitutes three notes for two notes of the first simple division. The micro triplet can replace either one half of the beat or it can occur on both halves of the beat, resulting in a single group of six notes. Although the small triplet and the micro triplet are each confined to the duration of one beat, they can be repeated in a series of successive beats in a variety of combinations and configurations.

The large triplet, however, extends its note values across two beats. Example 1–30 demonstrates how the large triplet is created and placed over two beats: the six eighth notes of two small triplets in $\frac{4}{4}$ time are tied together in pairs, which ultimately produces the equivalent of three quarter-note durations that in turn fill the space of two quarter-note beats. (Remember that only the first note of any tied pair of notes is articulated; the second note of the tied pair is sustained for the full value of the second note's duration.)

Since both the value of the beat and the note value for the large triplet in $\frac{4}{4}$ time are exactly the same (i.e., the quarter note), it follows that *the note value of any large triplet corresponds to the value of the beat for the meter in which the large triplet occurs.*

Example 1–30: converting two small triplets in $\frac{4}{4}$ time into one large triplet

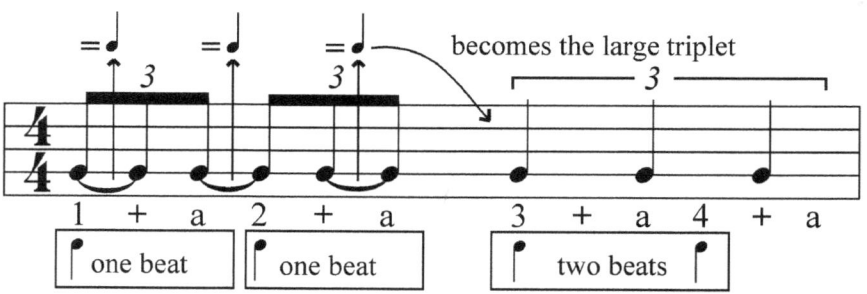

In example 1–31, the large triplet exists in $\frac{4}{2}$ time at the level of the half note and extends across two half-note beats. Since the first division of the beat occurs at the level of the quarter note, the small triplet also uses the quarter note.

Example 1–31: converting two small triplets in $\frac{4}{2}$ time into one large triplet

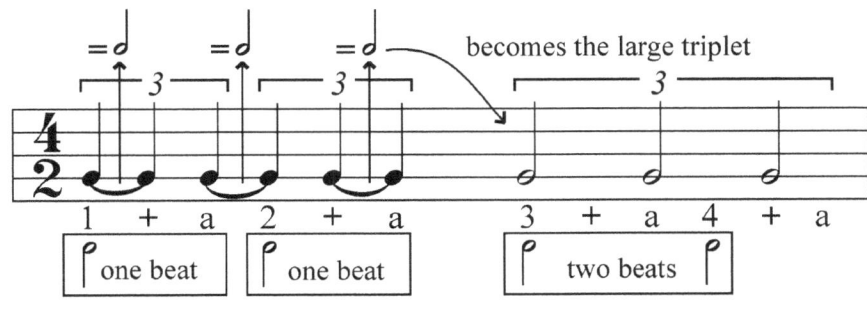

Example 1–32 shows the relationship between the note values of the small triplet (tied together in pairs) and those of the large triplet in $\frac{4}{4}$ time and in $\frac{4}{2}$ time. The counting and articulation for the large triplets in the example are as follows: 1 + a 2 ± a 3 + a 4 ± a (the underlined characters indicate the articulated notes for each group of tied durations and therefore each note of the large triplet).

Example 1–32: relating the note values of the small triplet to those of the large triplet

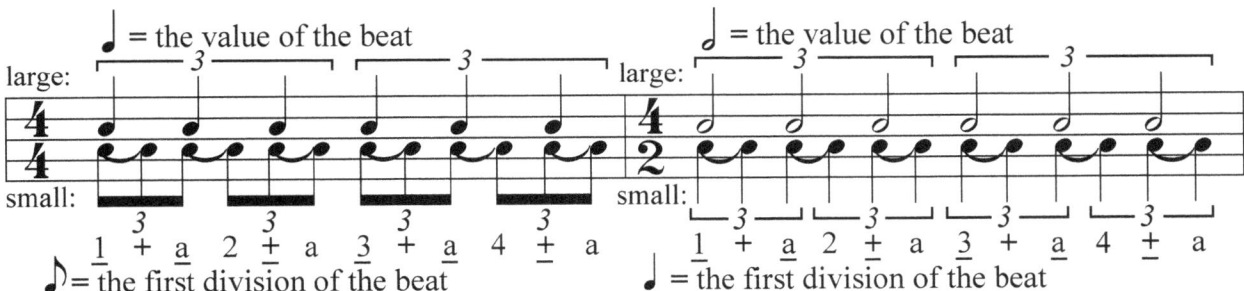

To summarize how the large triplet, the small triplet, and the micro triplet each relate the value of the beat and its potential divisions:
(1) the note value of any large triplet corresponds to the value of the beat for the meter in which the large triplet appears, substituting three notes for two notes at the level of the beat;
(2) the note value of any small triplet corresponds to the first division of the beat for the meter in which the small triplet appears, substituting three notes for two notes at the level of the first division;
(3) the note value of any micro triplet corresponds to the second division of the beat for the meter in which the micro triplet appears, substituting three notes for two notes at the level of the second division.

Duplets

A simple (two-part) division of the beat occurring in a compound meter is referred to as a duplet. When a compound meter borrows the first division of the beat from a simple meter, the first division carries the number 2 above the note group and is identified as a duplet. Example 1–33 shows how the duplet appears in the compound duple meter of ⁶⁄₈; the origin of the eighth-note duplet in ⁶⁄₈ can be traced to the first division of the beat in ²⁄₄ (the parallel duple meter of ⁶⁄₈). The example below displays two methods for counting the duplet in compound duple meter, in 2 and in 6. We shall explore further the formation of the duplet and its counting in examples 1–34 and 35.

Example 1–33: the duplet and its origin

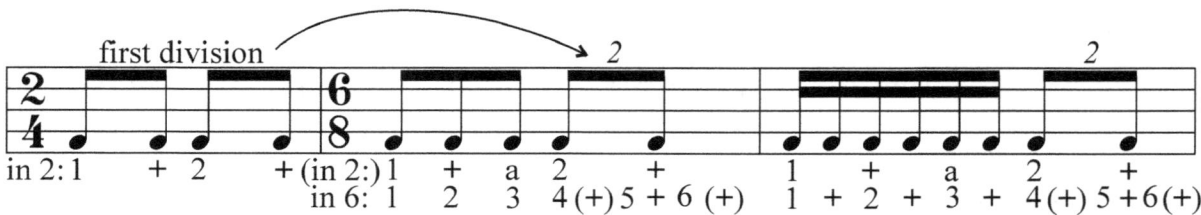

Although the duplet arises when a compound meter borrows the first division of the beat from a simple meter, the duplet can also be generated from within the compound meter itself. Example 1–34a illustrates the process by which six sixteenth notes of the second division in ⁶⁄₈ are tied together to produce two groups of three sixteenth notes (interpreting the meter in 2, see beat 1, stems up).

Each group of sixteenths is rewritten in example 1–34a as a dotted eighth note (beat 2, stems up), as a dotted eighth spans the same duration of time as three sixteenths. In effect, a duplet figure consisting of two dotted eighth notes arises from the tied sixteenths. Once the 2 is placed over that figure, as shown in 1–34b (and below the figure if the stems are down), the dot is no longer needed and the rhythm is counted just as it would be in the parallel duple meter, ²⁄₄ : 1 + 2 + . In compound meter, the duplet constitutes an irregular grouping of notes that conflicts with the normal three-part division of the beat.

Example 1–34: producing the duplet from within compound meter

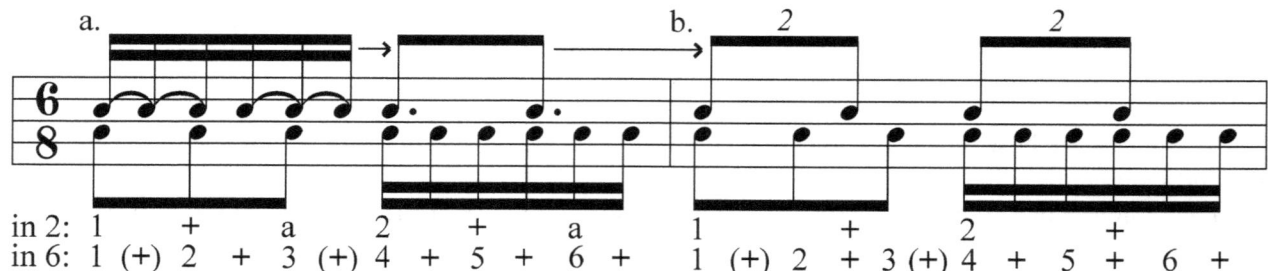

The duplet may also occur in simple meter. Example 1–35 presents the most common usage of the duplet within simple meter. The duplet in the second and third measures of the example transforms a simple triple meter (³⁄₄) into a simple duple meter (²⁄₄). Earlier in this chapter, we referred this type of transformation as the hemiola. Here, the duplet constitutes an irregular grouping of notes that conflicts with the normal three-part distribution of beats across the measure.

Example 1–35: using the duplet to transform simple triple meter into simple duple meter

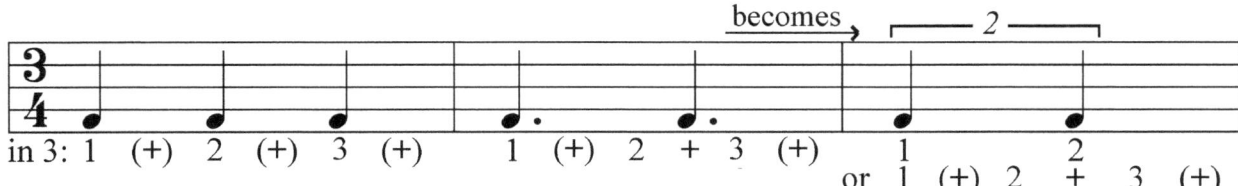

Asymmetrical Meter

We know that duple, triple, and quadruple meters are all considered to be symmetrical meters because they are divisible by either 2 or 3. Most of the time, a single, symmetrical meter will be used *consistently* throughout a piece of music. In other words, compositions that begin in, say, duple meter, usually remain in duple meter until the end. Sometimes, however, a piece of music might begin in one meter but subsequently change to another meter or a series of meters before the conclusion. Further, it is possible to have a meter with an odd number of beats per measure, a meter that is not divisible by either 2 or 3. Such meters are usually referred to as either **asymmetrical meters** or **odd meters**.

Let us consider a meter with five beats per measure. A meter "in 5" results when duple and triple meters are combined. There are a few ways in which to indicate a meter in 5. One method involves using two different time signatures in succession, such as the combination of $\frac{2}{4}$ and $\frac{3}{4}$ shown in example 1–36a. An alternative approach would be to place the two time signatures at the beginning of the composition and separate them with a plus sign, that is: $\frac{2}{4} + \frac{3}{4}$. If the bottom number for both time signatures represents the same note value, then the following option is available: $\frac{2+3}{4}$. In either instance, the person reading the music would understand that each pair of measures alternates between the two time signatures until the end or until a change in the metric structure occurs. This method avoids having to notate each measure of $\frac{2}{4}$ and $\frac{3}{4}$ throughout the entire composition.

The most common way to express a meter in 5, however, would be to simply consolidate $\frac{2}{4}$ and $\frac{3}{4}$ into $\frac{5}{4}$ time, as displayed in 1–36b. We classify $\frac{5}{4}$ time as a *simple* asymmetrical meter because dividing the number 3 into the top number of the time signature does not produce a whole number quotient greater than 4 (such as 5 or 7). Accordingly, the meter is simple rather than compound. The dotted line in 1–36b indicates what would otherwise be a measure of $\frac{2}{4}$ and a measure of $\frac{3}{4}$.

Again, combining duple and triple meters produces a meter in 5: either a measure of duple meter is followed by measure of triple meter ("two plus three") or a measure of triple meter is followed by a measure of duple meter ("three plus two"). Thus, a meter with five beats per measure can be subdivided and counted as either 1-2 1-2-3 (two plus three) or 1-2-3 1-2 (three plus two).

Example 1–36

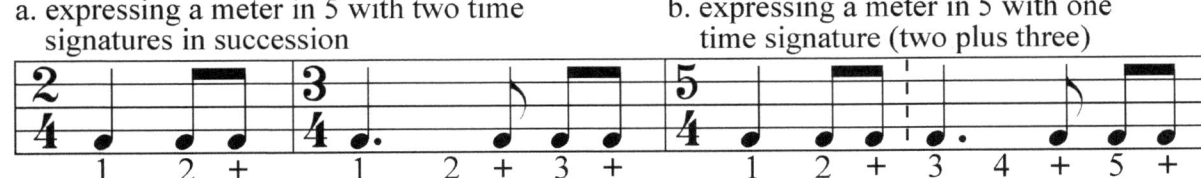

Example 1–37 displays three measures of $\frac{7}{8}$ time, an asymmetrical meter with seven beats per measure. The value of the beat is the eighth note. This asymmetrical meter can be classified as simple because dividing the number 3 into the top number of the time signature does not produce a quotient greater than 4. Each of the seven beats would be divided into two equal parts (or multiples of two). The first division of the beat occurs at the level of the sixteenth note. The subdivision of the meter is three plus two plus two; an alternative notation for 1–37 would be $\frac{3}{8} + \frac{2}{8} + \frac{2}{8}$ or $\frac{3+2+2}{8}$.

Example 1–37

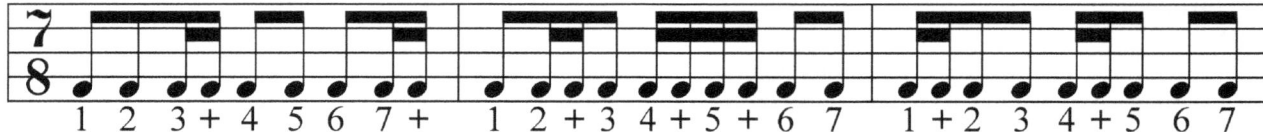

We conclude this chapter with one final asymmetrical meter, $\frac{15}{16}$ time, as shown in example 1–38. Dividing the number 3 into the top number yields a quotient of 5. This information tells us that the meter is compound asymmetrical with five beats per measure. To determine the value of the beat, we take the note value that the bottom number represents (the sixteenth note) and proceed to the note value that is one denomination higher (the eighth note), adding a dot to that note value. The value of the beat in $\frac{15}{16}$ time is a dotted eighth. The first division of the beat is the sixteenth.

Example 1–38

As for the subdivision of the meter, a grouping of three plus two begins to emerge only in the third measure of the example. We would need a few more measures of differentiated rhythms to confirm a clear subdivision of three plus two; for the pattern of notes could change to reveal a grouping of two plus three, a mixture of both possibilities, or an asymmetrical structure with no subdivisions at all beyond the basic five beats of the meter.

The fifteen notes of the first division in $\frac{15}{16}$ time could even be configured in such a way as to deny the five-beat implication of the time signature. For example, it is quite possible to arrange fifteen sixteenth notes into three groups of five notes each (five plus five plus five). Alternatively, we might encounter one group of seven notes and one group of eight notes (seven plus eight). Of course, within the context of $\frac{15}{16}$ time, these subdivisions could be viewed as irregular rhythmic patterns occurring at the level of the first division, a division that normally has three sixteenth notes for each dotted eighth.

Chapter 2 Pitch

An object moved by force produces vibrations that in turn create displacements throughout the surrounding area. The displaced area, which can be a liquid, a solid, or a gas, serves as a medium of transmission that carries the vibrations to the human ear. Functioning as a receptor, the ear perceives the vibrations as sound. The number of sound vibrations completed in one second of time is called **frequency**.

If the vibrating object produces a regular number of frequencies at a steady rate, then the sound will be heard as a musical tone. Such tones are referred to as pitches. The relative lowness or highness of any pitch corresponds to the rate of the vibrating frequency of the sound-producing object. Slower vibrating frequencies result in lower pitches, while faster vibrating frequencies produce higher pitches.

An inspection of the piano keyboard demonstrates the difference between lower and higher pitches. The standard 88-key piano, as represented in example 2–1, has 52 white keys and 36 black keys. Moving from the extreme left to the extreme right of the keyboard, each key produces a pitch that is incrementally higher and its equivalent frequency faster. From the lowest to the highest pitch, the frequencies range from 27.5 to 4186 vibrations per second. All of the pitches on the keyboard have names that correspond to the first seven letters of the alphabet, letters A through G. Every eighth pitch and letter repeats the first; this repetition is called an **octave**. Any two pitches of the same letter name that are one octave apart have a frequency ratio of 2:1. For example, the lowest A on the piano produces 27.5 vibrations per second; one octave above that A produces twice as many frequencies: 55 vibrations per second.

Musicians interpret the numerical relationship between pitches in spatial terms, using the word **interval** to describe the distance from one pitch to any other pitch. On the keyboard, the distance between any two immediately adjacent piano keys constitutes an increment in pitch called a **half step**, **semitone**, or **minor 2nd**. The half step is the smallest possible interval on the piano keyboard and in our Western tradition of music. There are twelve half steps within any single octave.

Example 2–1: the standard 88-key piano

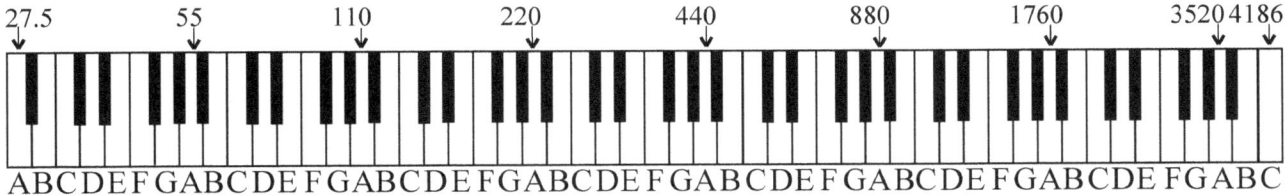

Study example 2–2 and notice the intervallic distances between both the white and black keys of the piano keyboard. The black keys are arranged in alternating groups of two and three with one intervening black key between each white key except from E to F and from B to C, the only two places within the octave where there are half steps between two adjacent white keys.

Example 2–2

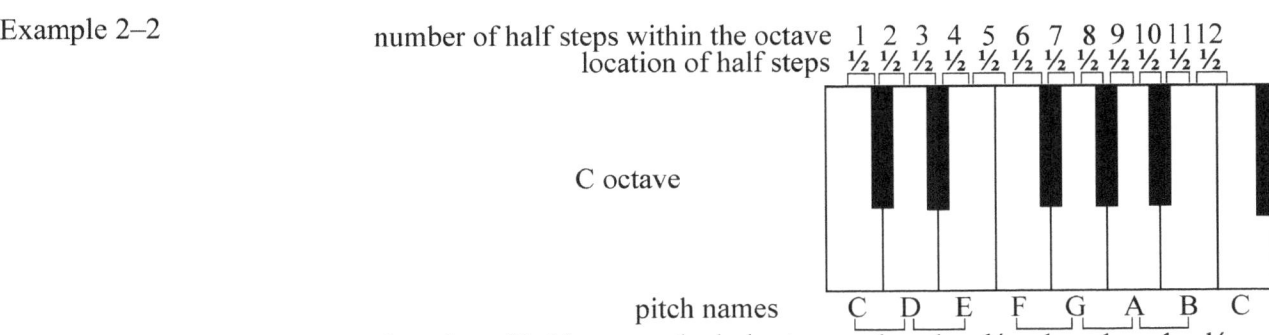

In all other places, two adjacent white keys produce two half steps because a black key separates each pair. Two consecutive half steps between any two piano keys comprise the interval of a whole step (sometimes referred to as a "step"). Thus, with the exception of E to F and B to C, the distance between white keys is always a whole step, also known as a **major 2nd**. With respect to the alternating groups of two and three black keys that extend across the piano keyboard, three half steps separate each group while a whole step spans the distance between black keys within each group (example 2–3).

Example 2–3

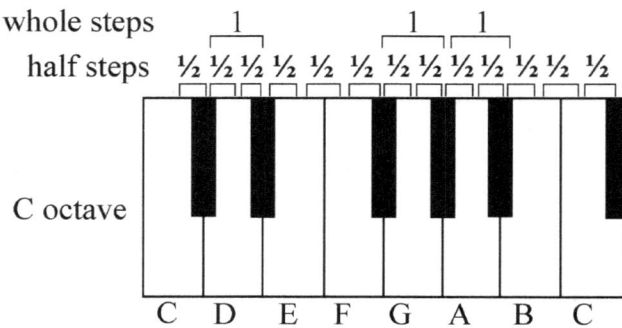

Accidentals and Enharmonic Equivalency

A conflict arises from the fact that twelve half steps fill the span of any octave but only seven alphabet letters are available to designate pitches. The conflict is more apparent than real because each of the seven pitch names can have more than one spelling of itself; that is to say, the seven pitch names can be modified with additional symbols called **accidentals**.

Accidentals raise or lower any of the seven pitch names. The names and the shapes of the accidentals are as follows: sharp (♯), flat (♭), double flat (♭♭), double sharp (𝄪), and natural (♮). The natural sign cancels any accidental used to raise or lower a pitch. Each pitch and its associated name can be raised one half step with the addition of a sharp or lowered one half step with the addition of a flat. In music notation, the accidental immediately *precedes* the pitch to which it applies. When speaking or writing about an accidental that is attached to a pitch, however, the symbol or the word for the accidental *follows* the pitch name, as for example: C♯ or C sharp.

Example 2–4 shows how the pitch C can be raised one half step on the piano keyboard with the addition of a sharp to become C♯ (pronounced C sharp). The pitch B can be lowered one half step with the addition of a flat to become B♭ (pronounced B flat). Raising the pitch from C to C♯ requires a move from the left to the right of the keyboard, whereas lowering the pitch from B to B♭ necessitates a move from right to left. In both cases, the move to C♯ and B♭ ends on one of the black keys. We shall soon see, however, that raising and lowering a pitch does not always involve using one of the black keys.

Example 2–4

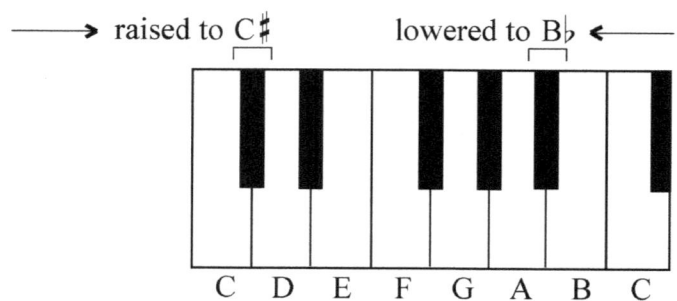

It is also possible to raise a pitch (and its name) two half steps with the addition of a double sharp and to lower it two half steps with the addition of a double flat. As illustrated in example 2–5, a move from C to C× (pronounced C double sharp) can be accomplished by raising the pitch from C to C♯ and then from C♯ to C× (example 2–5). Similarly, the move to B♭♭ (pronounced B double flat) can be made by lowering the pitch from B to B♭ and then from B♭ to B♭♭.

Raising C to C× takes us to the equivalent white key and pitch of D. If we lower B two half steps, the operation changes the white key and pitch of A into B♭♭. By using sharps, flats, double sharps, and double flats, at least two different letter names may be assigned to any single pitch. In fact, every pitch can have three different letter names except for G♯ and A♭ (see example 2–7 below). When we apply different letter names to the same pitch, the names are called **enharmonic equivalents**.

Example 2–5

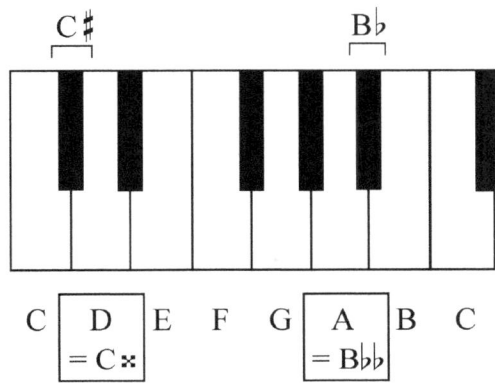

Example 2–6 demonstrates how the black piano key of C♯ can also be reinterpreted as D♭ if we lower D one half step. Hence, C♯ and D♭ are enharmonic equivalents. If F is lowered one half step to F♭, it falls on the white key of E. Raising D to D× brings us again to the white key of E, thereby producing three names for the same pitch: F♭, E, and D×.

Example 2–6

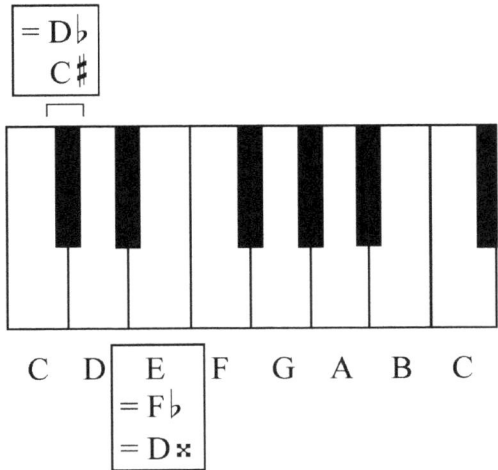

Example 2–7 locates all of the possible enharmonic equivalents within the C octave; the names of these pitches remain the same regardless of the octave in which they occur. Again, every pitch can have at least three different letter names except for G♯ and A♭.

Example 2–7

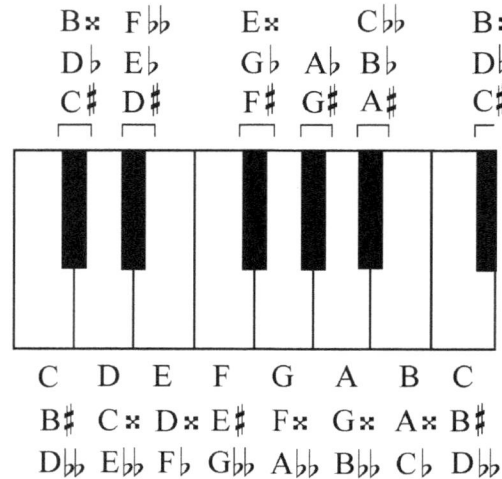

Chromatic and Diatonic Half Steps

In example 2–4, we saw how the pitch C could be raised one half step with the addition of a sharp. Raising C one half step requires a move to the immediate right on the keyboard from the white key of C to the adjacent black key of C♯ (example 2–8). When there is a half step between two different versions of the same letter name, the intervallic relationship between the two pitches is termed chromatic. In other words, the pitches C and C♯ constitute a **chromatic half step**. C♯ and C𝄪 is also a chromatic half step. The distance from B to B♭ is a chromatic half step, as is the distance from B♭ to B♭♭.

Chromatic half steps may be formed between all of the black and white keys of the piano and in two places where there are no intervening black keys, two white-key areas: from E to F and from B to C. However, in order to produce chromatic half steps without using black keys, we must respell F, E, C, and B enharmonically: F becomes E♯, E becomes F♭, C becomes B♯, and B becomes C♭. Thus, enharmonic respelling creates chromatic half steps from E to E♯, F to F♭, B to B♯, and C to C♭.

Example 2–8

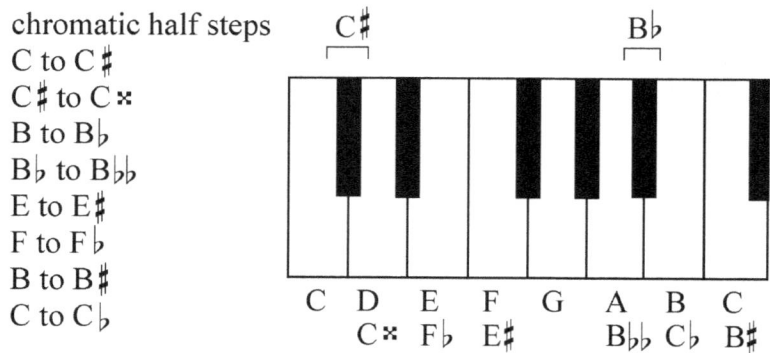

When there is a half step between two different letter names, the intervallic relationship between the two pitches is termed diatonic. If we respell C♯ enharmonically as D♭, then the pitches C and D♭ constitute a **diatonic half step** (example 2–9). Re-evaluating B♭ as A♯ produces a diatonic half step between A♯ and B. The only two places within the octave where diatonic half steps may occur without an enharmonic respelling to produce two different letter names are from E to F and from B to C.

Example 2–9

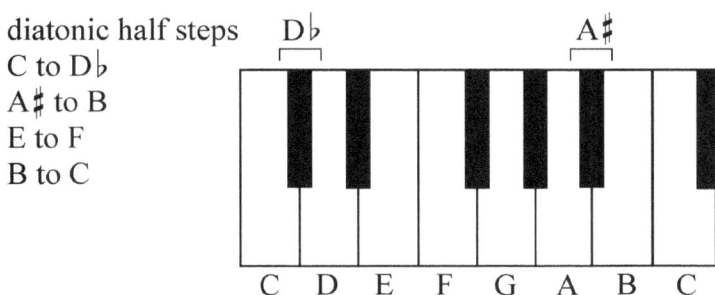

The Great Staff and Clefs

As mentioned in Chapter 1, the staff consists of five lines and four spaces and is an integral component of most music notation. Example 2–10 displays two staffs, or staves (an alternate plural for staff), joined together by a bracket in the left margin known as a brace. This apparent two-staff ten-line configuration is referred to variously as the **great staff**, the **grand staff**, or the **piano staff**. The staff alone cannot represent pitches, however. Any set or range of pitches requires the use of a symbol called a clef sign. The two most common clefs are the **F clef** and the **G clef**.

Example 2–10 shows the location and appearance of both the F clef and the G clef on the great staff. The F clef is so named because the sign's two dots surround the line on which the pitch F is fixed. Another name for the F clef is the **bass clef**. The G clef takes its name from the swirl around the second line from the bottom, the line on which the pitch G is designated. Another name for the G clef is the **treble clef**.

Between the two staves of the great staff is an additional line called a **ledger line**. Here, the line designates a pitch called "middle C." Musicians use ledger lines to retain within a single clef pitches that exceed the limits of any single staff (see examples 2–15 and 3–9 below).

Example 2–10

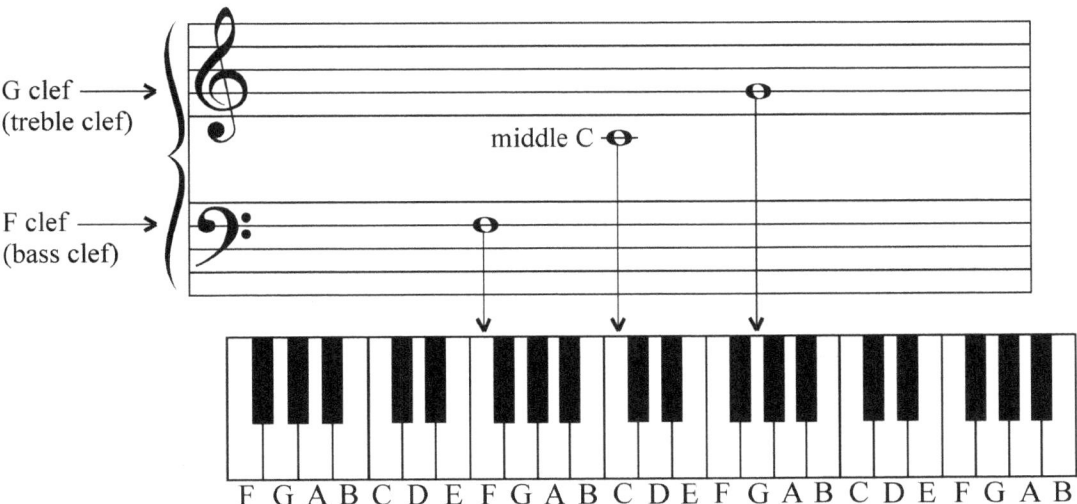

With F and G located on the staff by their respective clefs, it is possible to find the other pitches on the lines and spaces according to the letters of the alphabet (example 2–11).

Example 2–11

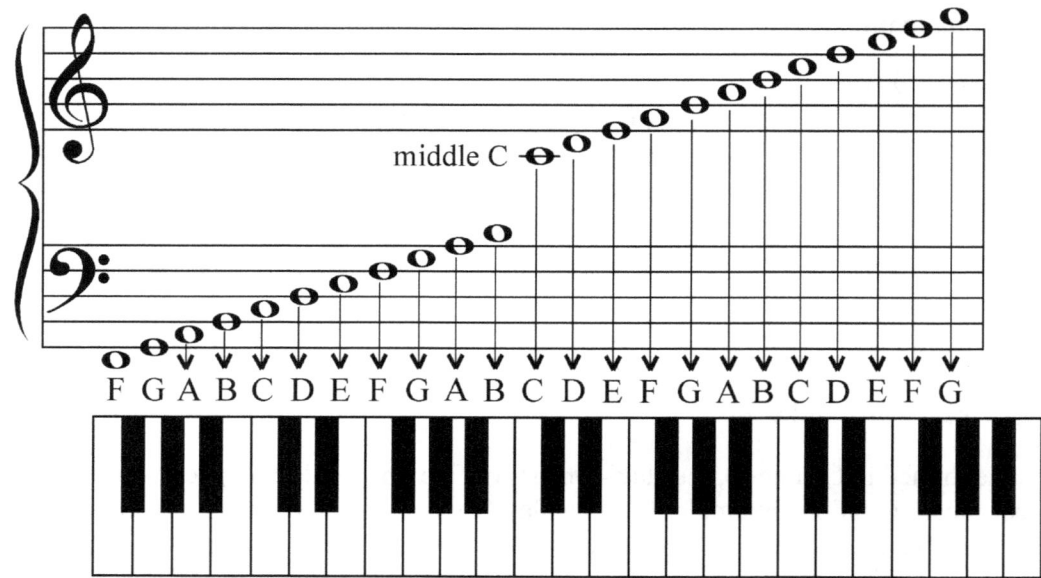

Traditionally, when learning the names of the lines and spaces on the F and G clefs, music teachers have provided students with helpful ways for remembering the location of the various pitches. For the five lines of the G clef, from the bottom to top, the pitch names are as follows: E, G, B, D, and F (example 2–12). An easy way to recall the names of these five lines is to associate them respectively with the first letter of each word of the sentence "every good boy does fine." The four spaces of the G clef, from bottom to top, spell the word "face."

For the lines of the F clef, from bottom to top, the pitch names are as follows: G, B, D, F, and A. These lines would read "good boys do fine always." The four spaces of the F clef, from bottom to top, read "all cows eat grass" for the pitches A, C, E, and G (or perhaps "all cars eat gas").

Example 2–12

Octave registers

In the previous sections of this chapter, we located the seven basic pitch names on the standard 88-key piano, introduced the five types of accidental signs, explained the concept of enharmonic equivalency, distinguished between chromatic and diatonic half steps, and explored the range of the great staff within the general context of the F and G clefs.

Initially, we used letters to represent the seven pitch names that span the seven octaves of the keyboard. Middle C, which is expressed on the great staff with the use of a single ledger line, is the fourth C from the extreme left of the keyboard. Below the first C are the two lowest pitches on the keyboard, A and B. As can be seen in example 2–13, the pitches A, B, and C occur eight times across the keyboard; D, E, F, and G appear seven times.

Example 2–13

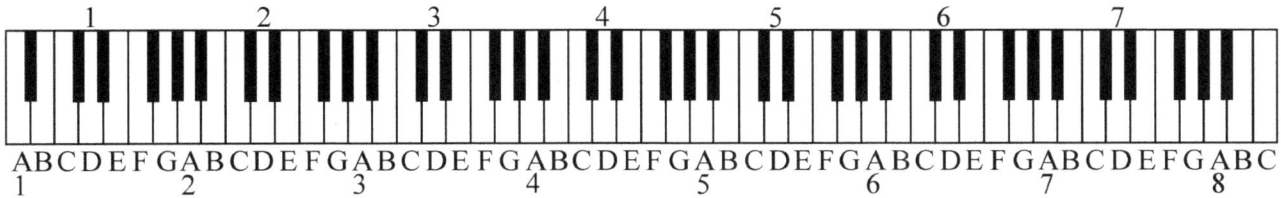

If we are referring to pitches in general terms, then there is no need to identify any given pitch within a specific octave register. But if we want to identify a pitch that occurs within a particular octave, then the problem of precise pitch location, or pitch register, arises—a problem for which a couple of different solutions have been put forward.

One solution for identifying a pitch within a specific octave register, shown in examples 2–14 and 15, divides the keyboard into seven segments of pitches with each segment beginning on C and ending on B. The first of the seven segments is preceded by the pitches A and B while the seventh segment is followed by the seventh repetition of C (C8).

The first C to the extreme left of the keyboard is designated as C1. Thus, the first D and G would be D1 and G1 respectively. The second C is C2. Middle C is C4. The highest C on the keyboard would be C8. The two lowest pitches on the keyboard, A and B, are sometimes referred to as A0 and B0. Example 2–15 shows all of the pitches on the great staff in relation to their location on the keyboard. (To compare this method of octave identification to its most common alternative, see my *Finding The Right Pitch: A Guide To The Study Of Music Fundamentals, Or An Introduction To Music Theory*.)

Example 2–14

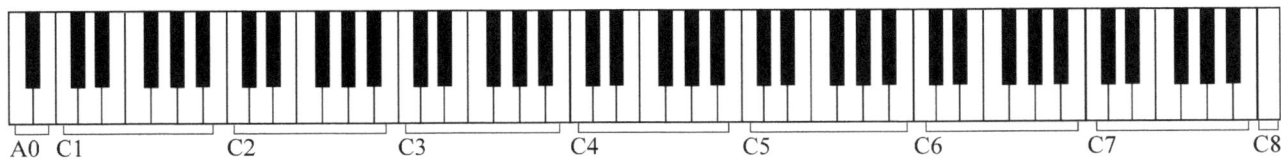

Example 2–15

C = middle C
A0B0C1D1E1F1G1A1B1C2D2E2F2G2A2B2C3D3E3F3G3A3B3C4D4E4F4G4A4B4C5D5E5F5G5A5B5C6D6E6F6G6A6B6C7D7E7F7G7A7B7C8
segment 1
segment 2
segment 3
segment 4
segment 5
segment 6
segment 7
A0B0C1D1E1F1G1A1B1C2D2E2F2G2A2B2C3D3E3F3G3A3B3C4D4E4F4G4A4B4C5D5E5F5G5A5B5C6D6E6F6G6A6B6C7D7E7F7G7A7B7C8

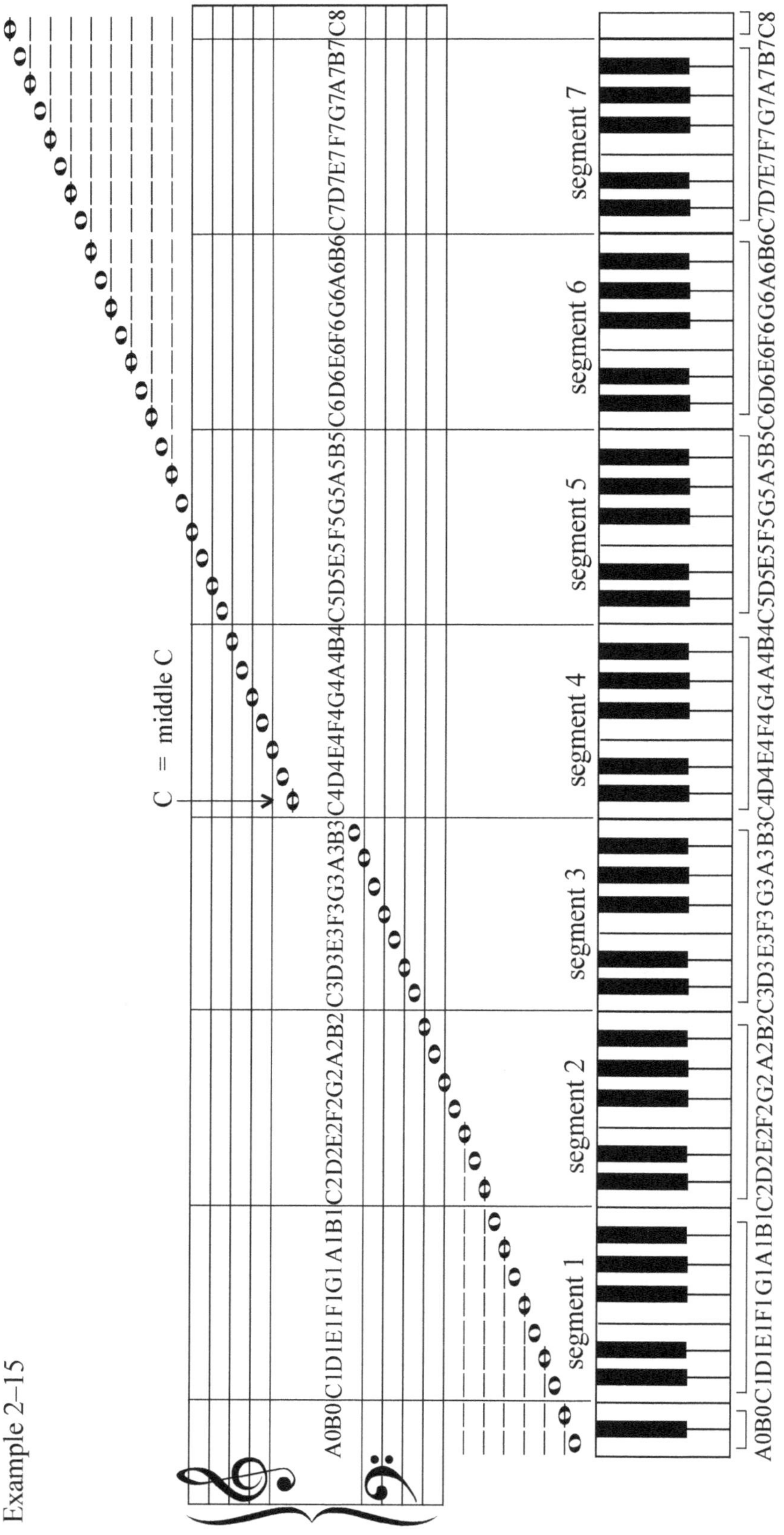

Octave Signs

In example 2–15 above, notice that it is possible to use up to six ledger lines in the F clef and nine ledger lines in the G clef to represent pitches that extend beyond the limits of the respective staves on which these clefs appear. However, reading music with too many ledger lines is very difficult. Fortunately, there is a sign that makes it possible to avoid or minimize some of the difficulties of reading ledger lines.

The sign, shown in example 2–16, is an abbreviation of the Italian expression *all'ottava* ("at the octave") and consists of the Arabic number 8 (or *8va*) followed by a dotted bracket. The *all'ottava* sign instructs the performer to play the pitches one octave higher than written when appearing in the G clef or one octave lower than written when appearing in the F clef. When used with the G clef, the sign usually appears above the staff and when used with the F clef, below the staff. In 2–16a, the octave sign indicates that the span of pitches in the F clef sounds one octave below the written register. In 2–16b, the octave sign indicates that the span of pitches sounds one octave above the written register.

Occasionally, the sign *8 bassa* or *8va bassa* is found in musical scores (often followed by a dotted bracket) instead of the *all'ottava* sign. The *8 bassa* sign means "at the octave below."

Example 2–16: the sign for *all'ottava*

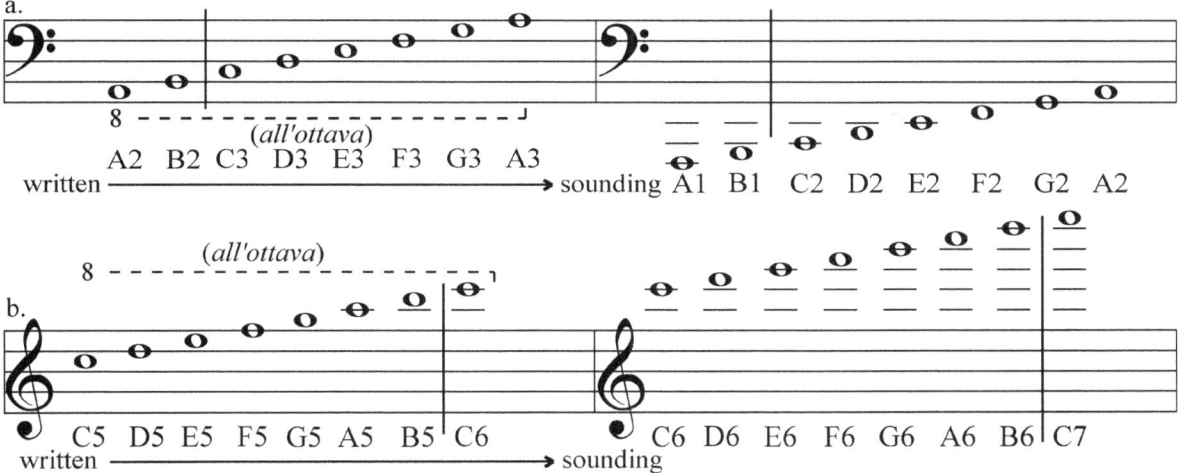

Chapter 3 The Major Scale

In Chapter 2, example 2–16 displayed octave spans on A and C in which eight pitches were arranged alphabetically in an ascending stepwise pattern. These octave configurations bring us to the concept of **scale**. The term scale derives from the Italian word *scala*, which means ladder. A scale is a ladder of tones: a representation of stepwise pitches running upwards or downwards. The tones of the scale are identified by the letter names of the alphabet.

The **chromatic scale**, as presented in example 3–1, divides the octave into twelve half steps. Sharps are generally used when the scale is notated in its ascending form, flats in its descending form. The chromatic scale contains pairs of pitches that involve two different versions of the same letter name: in the ascending form, C–C♯, D–D♯, F–F♯, G–G♯, and A–A♯ (3–1a); and in the descending form, B–B♭, A–A♭, G–G♭, E–E♭, and D–D♭ (3–1b).

Two exceptional areas of the chromatic scale have diatonic half steps, that is, two consecutive pitches with different letter names: E to F and B to C. In the examples below, the tones of the chromatic scale occur within the span of a single octave; however, the chromatic scale may be expressed in any register, starting on any of the seven alphabet names.

Example 3–1: the chromatic scale on C

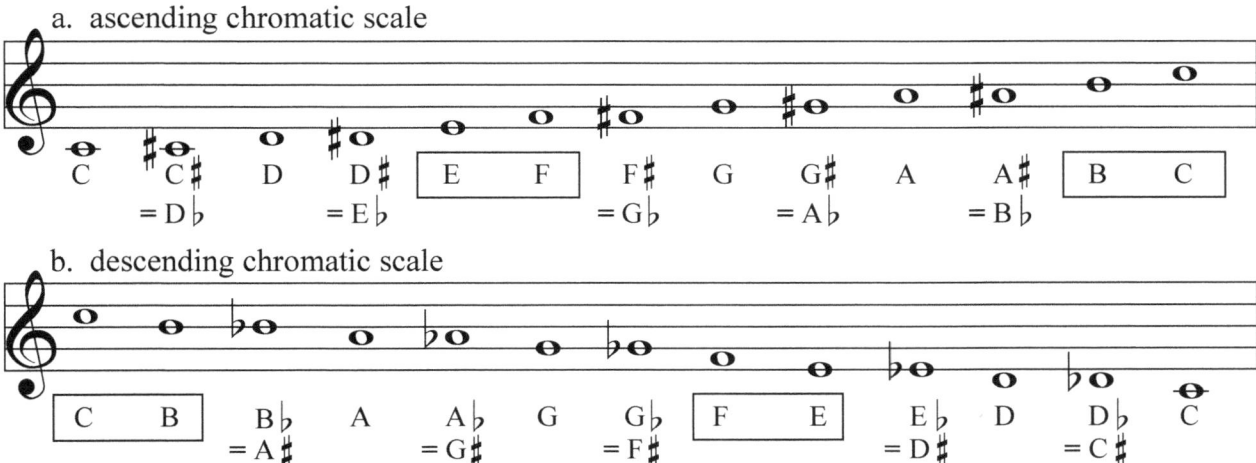

A scale having only one letter name for each of its seven pitches, spanning a single octave, and comprising five whole steps and two half steps is called a **diatonic scale**. The distribution of whole steps and half steps across the seven pitches of a diatonic scale can be found by examining the white keys of the piano within any octave of the keyboard. Example 3–2 shows a diatonic scale within the C octave.

Example 3–2

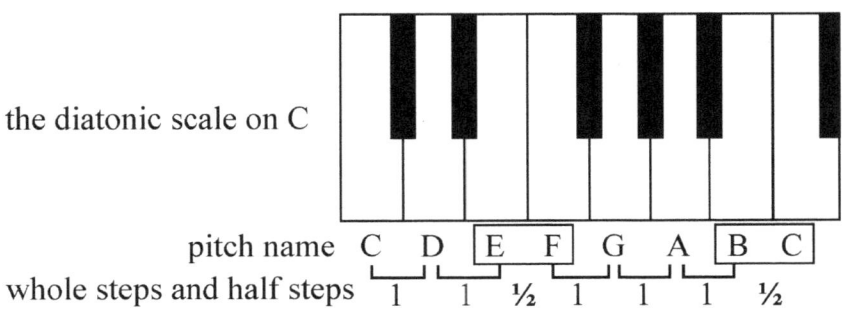

Chapter 3 The Major Scale

Each of the seven pitches of the diatonic scale is called a scale degree and assigned a number according to its relationship to the first pitch of the scale. Example 3–3 identifies C as scale degree 1 and D, E, F, G, A, and B as scale degrees 2, 3, 4, 5, 6, and 7 respectively. The octave duplication of C is 8, which is equivalent to scale degree 1. All diatonic scales can be divided into two four-note segments: from scale degrees 1 to 4 and 5 to 8. These segments are called **tetrachords**; they are usually separated by a whole step between scale degrees 4 and 5 (example 3–3).

The **major scale** on C occurs naturally on the white keys of the piano. The combined distribution of whole steps and half steps across the C-major octave creates, in this case, two matching tetrachords (whole step, whole step, half step from scale degrees 1 to 4 and whole step, whole step, half step from scale degrees 5 to 8). The *profile* of the complete scale consists of half steps between scale degrees 3 and 4 and scale degrees 7 and 8, with all other adjacent notes being whole steps.

Example 3–3

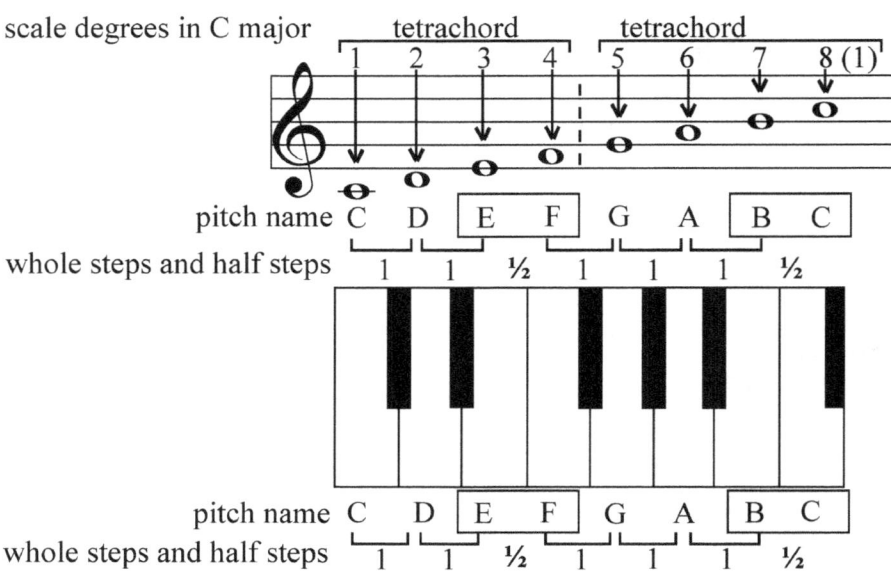

The pattern of half steps and whole steps in the major scale reflects two things, namely, **key** and **mode**. Key, which is also known variously as the **keynote** or **tonal center**, is that pitch to which all other pitches are related and toward which they ultimately move. If we play every pitch of the C-major scale in the numerical order of its scale degrees, starting with C as scale degree 1, the arrival of scale degree 7 confirms the strength of the key; for here, there is a compelling drive to complete the upward succession of pitches by ending on scale degree 8.

In addition to having an assigned number, each scale degree has a name. Scale degree 1 (or 8) is called the **tonic**, scale degree 2 the **supertonic**, 3 the **mediant**, 4 the **subdominant**, 5 the **dominant**, 6 the **submediant**, and 7 the **leading tone**. Later in this text, we shall add the term **subtonic** to our list of scale degrees (Chapter 6) and then discuss the reasons for all of the names (Chapter 7). For now, suffice it to say that the leading tone is so named because of its compelling drive to move upwards by a half step to the tonic.

The mode of a composition has a more direct relationship to the actual music than does the concept of scale, which is merely an alphabetical inventory of pitches derived from the music. Expressing certain characteristic patterns and configurations of pitches, the mode confirms and establishes the key of a musical work. Among the most important characteristic patterns of any mode is the arrangement of linear half steps and whole steps such as the one shown above in 3–3, which illustrates the C-major scale and mode. Indeed, its profile of half steps between scale degrees 3 and 4 and scale degrees 7 and 8 distinguishes the major mode from the profiles of other diatonic modes (see Chapters 6 and 8).

Moving the Major Scale to Octaves Other than C with the Addition of Sharps

Since there are twelve half steps and pitches within any octave, each pitch may have its own major mode and scale. It is therefore possible to move the C-major scale to any of the remaining eleven pitches within the octave. However, when moving the major scale to octaves other than C, its profile of half steps can be maintained only with the inclusion of one or more black keys of the piano.

Let us begin with the G octave. The first step is to start on C, scale degree 1 of C major, and go up to G, scale degree 5 of C major (example 3–4). Note carefully that the distance from C to G is 3½ steps (3½ steps is an abbreviation for three whole steps and one half step). Later, in Chapter 5, we shall refer to this distance as a **perfect 5th**.

Example 3–4

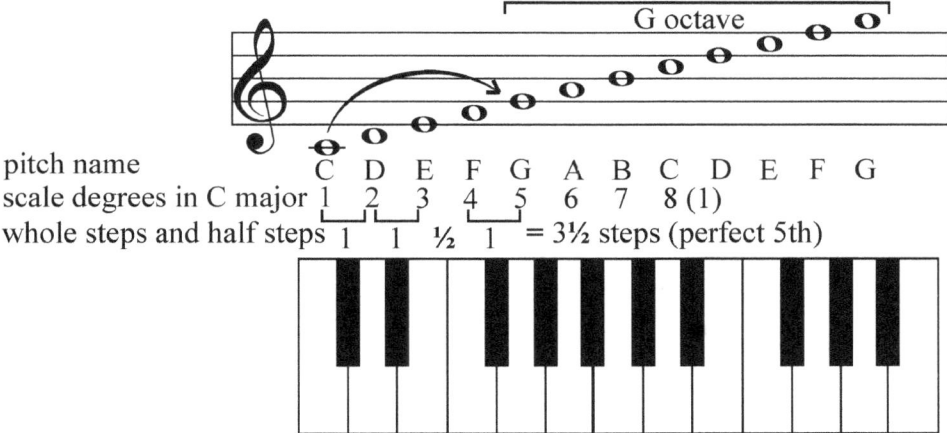

Once the G octave has been identified, C major's profile of half steps and whole steps must be preserved in G major. In order for the half steps to remain between scale degrees 3 and 4 and scale degrees 7 and 8, the tetrachord structure of the major mode has to be maintained (each tetrachord contains within its four-note span the following pattern: whole step, whole step, half step).

In example 3–5, we can see that the **lower tetrachord**, scale degrees 1 to 4, does not require the addition of black keys to preserve the four-note pattern of whole steps and half steps; however, the **upper tetrachord**, scale degrees 5 to 8, does. In order to establish a half step between scale degrees 7 and 8 and to maintain the tetrachord structure, it is necessary to raise the F one half step to F♯.

Example 3–5

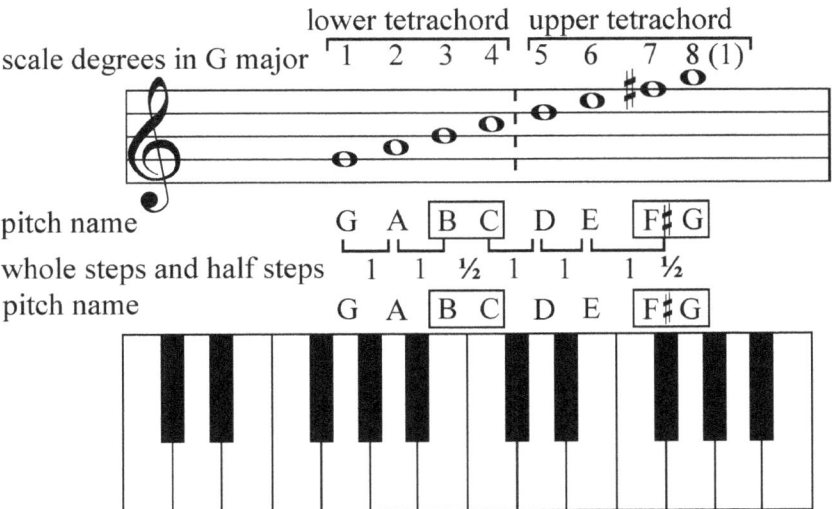

38   Chapter 3 The Major Scale

Moving upwards in 3½-step increments from C takes us through what is called the sharp side of major. The starting notes for the seven major scales on the sharp side consist of G, D, A, E, B, F♯, and C♯. *As long as the starting note of each scale is 3½ steps above the one that preceded it, all of the sharps added previously for each scale will be used in subsequent formations; and, each new scale will add one sharp to those that have been retained from previous formations.* As indicated in example 3–6, the additional sharp creates scale degree 7 within the upper tetrachord of each new scale (see the circled notes). (Notice that the starting notes D, E, B, and C♯ appear below rather than above the starting note of the previous scale. After counting upwards in 3½-step increments to find these notes in a higher register, transferring each of them down into a lower octave minimizes the use of ledger lines.)

Example 3–6: the sharp side of major

G major (3½ steps above C)

D major (3½ steps above G)

A major (3½ steps above D)

E major (3½ steps above A)

B major (3½ steps above E)

F♯ major (3½ steps above B)

C♯ major (3½ steps above F♯)

After C♯, the seventh scale, it is theoretically possible, though not practical, to locate the next octave in which to build a major scale by continuing upwards 3½ steps from C♯ to G♯ (example 3–7). The structure of G♯ major's lower tetrachord remains complete, as it incorporates the sharps from C♯ major (example 3–8). The upper tetrachord, however, requires the addition of an eighth sharp. Since all the pitches already have one sharp, a double sharp replaces the F♯ on scale degree 7. Hence, the half step between scale degrees 7 and 8 is established by raising F♯ one half step to F𝑥, the leading tone of G♯ major.

Again, building a major scale on G♯ is a useful theoretical exercise but not a practical one. We shall see that it is far more desirable to re-evaluate the G♯ enharmonically as A♭, and there construct a major scale that will require four flats rather than eight sharps.

Example 3–7

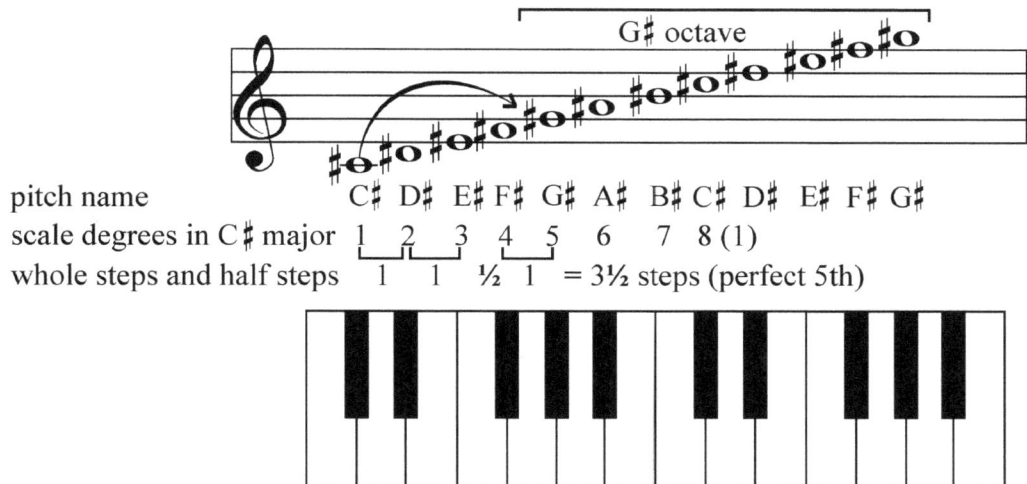

Example 3–8

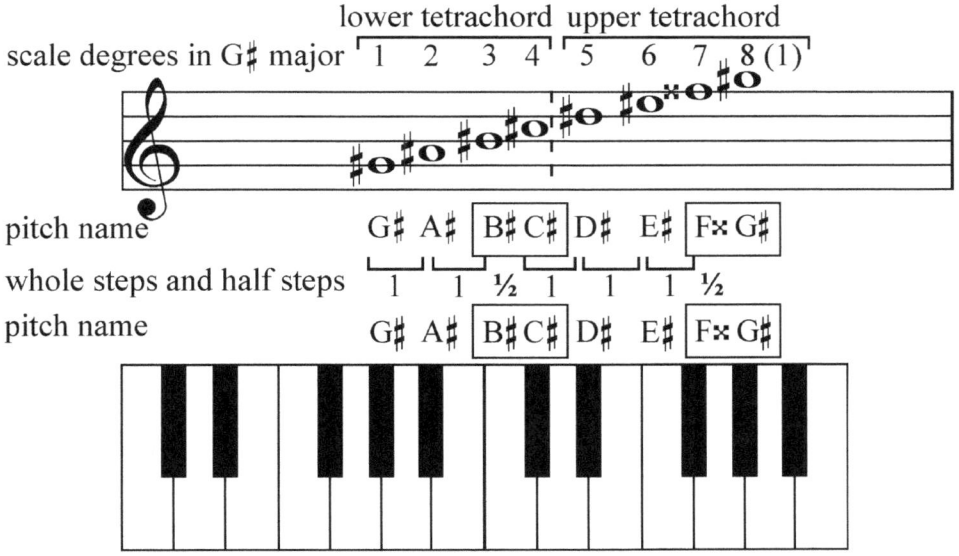

40   Chapter 3   The Major Scale

Moving the Major Scale to Octaves Other than C with the Addition of Flats

To find the starting notes and octaves for the seven scales on the flat side of major, count downwards 3½ steps from C (example 3–9). Moving downwards in 3½-step increments from C yields the following octaves: F, B♭, E♭, A♭, D♭, G♭, and C♭. The flat side of major may also be located by continuing upwards in 2½-step increments from C (example 3–11). Later, in Chapter 5, we shall refer to the distance of 2½-steps between pitches as a **perfect 4th**.

As demonstrated in example 3–9, counting upwards 2½ steps from C4 brings us to F4. Proceeding downwards 3½ steps from C4 leads to F3. Thus, the same pitch, though not the same register, can be reached by moving either up 2½ steps (a perfect 4th) or down 3½ steps (a perfect 5th) from any given tone.

Having located the F octave, let us build the F major scale. In order to preserve the half step between scale degrees 3 and 4, a B♭ must be added to the *lower tetrachord* to produce scale degree 4 (example 3–10). The upper tetrachord requires no changes, as a half step already exists between E and F, scale degrees 7 and 8.

Example 3–9

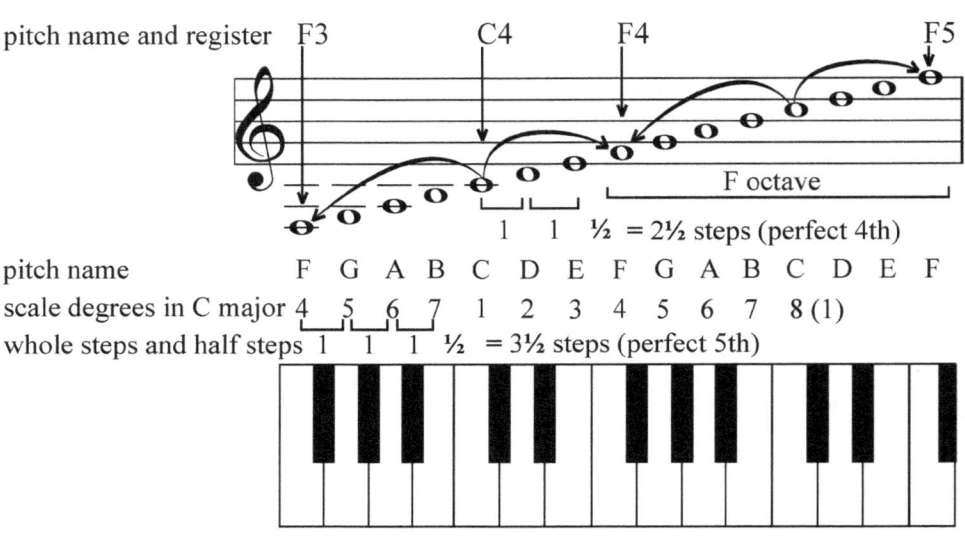

Example 3–10

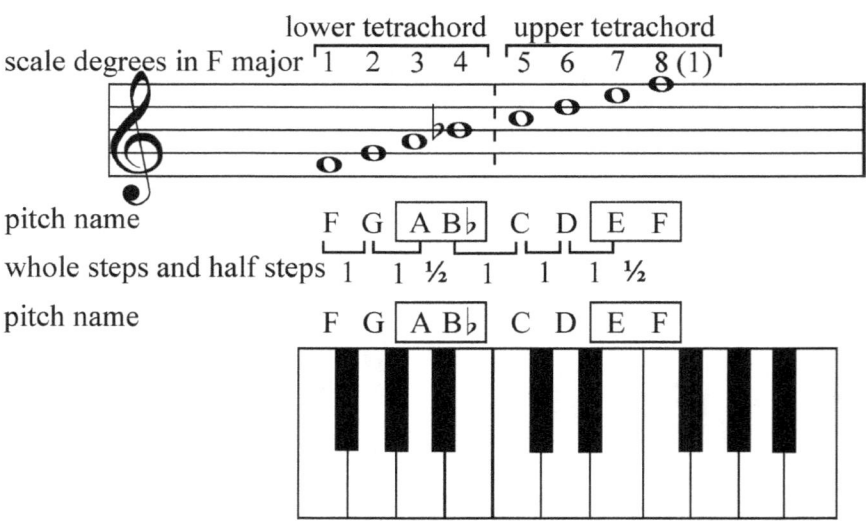

During our construction of the sharp side of major, we said that as long as the starting note of each scale is 3½ steps above the one that preceded it, all of the sharps added previously for each scale will be used in subsequent formations; and, each new scale will add one sharp to those that have been retained from previous formations. With respect to the construction of major scales with flats, the addition of each new flat will occur within the *lower tetrachord*, as long as the starting note of each scale is 2½ steps above the one that preceded it (or 3½ steps below the one that preceded it). As shown in example 3–11, for the flat side of major, the addition of a flat in the lower tetrachord occurs on scale degree 4 (see the circled notes).

Example 3–11: the flat side of major

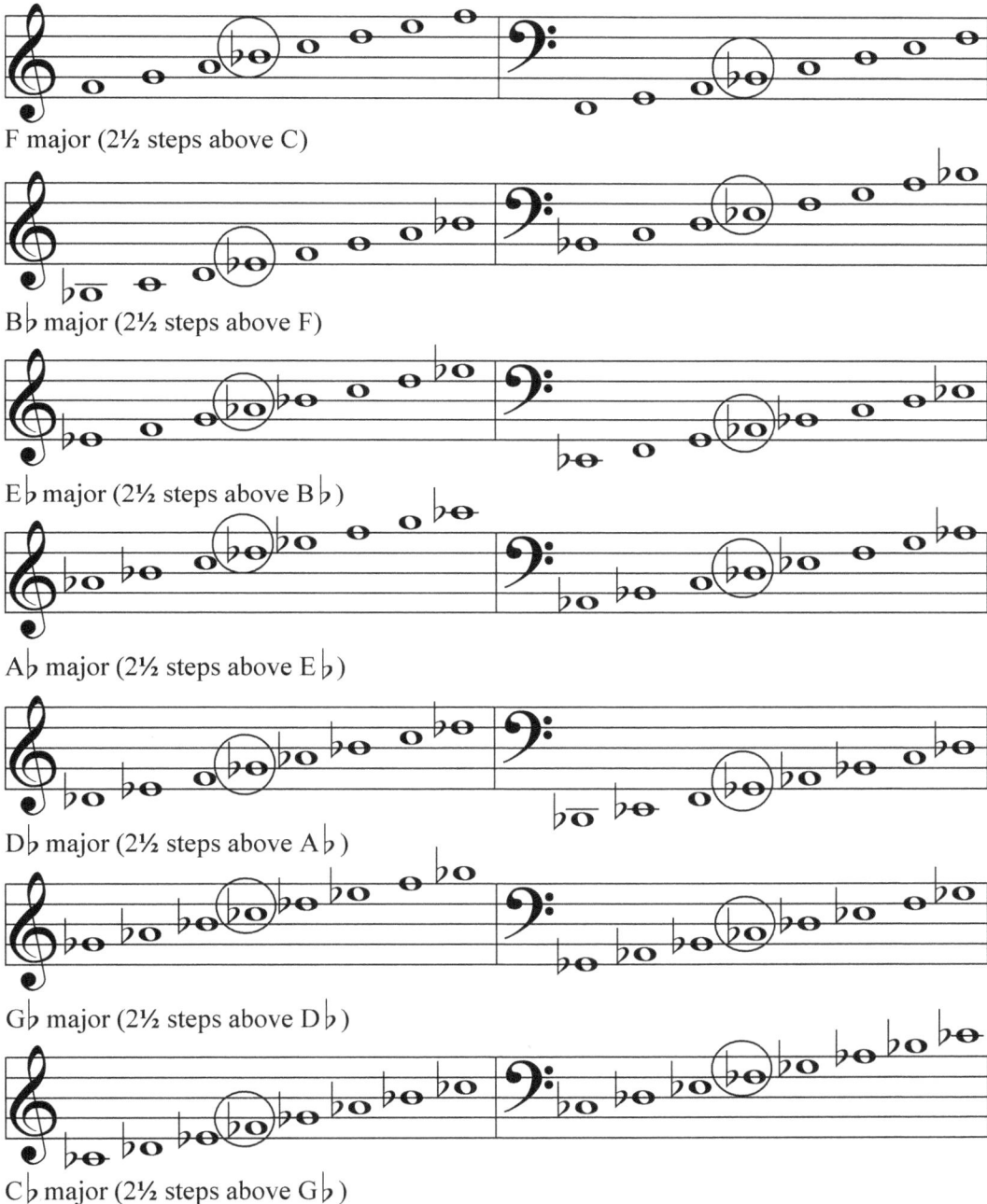

Chapter 4 Major Key Signatures

In Chapter 3, we learned that when moving the major scale to octaves other than C, the half steps between scale degrees 3 and 4 and scale degrees 7 and 8 can be maintained only with the inclusion of one or more black notes of the piano. It is, however, unwieldy to place all of the sharps or flats of the mode throughout the notated score of a music composition. Accordingly, the accidentals (sharps or flats) of any mode appear in a type of shorthand notation known as a **key signature**.

The key signature identifies the specific notes that are appropriate to the mode of a musical work. Before we investigate the construction and configuration of key signatures for the major mode, it would be well to reconsider how each major scale adds one sharp or flat to those that have been retained from previous scale formations.

As we have seen, there are two sides to the major mode: a flat side and a sharp side. We shall discuss these two sides presently and then find the connection between them in the next section, The Circle of 5ths. Starting on C and proceeding downwards in 3½-step increments (a perfect 5th) or upwards in 2½-step increments (a perfect 4th) brings us to the flat side of major. Each new scale formation adds one flat to those that preceded it. Example 4–1 shows the ascending or descending order of scales on the flat side of major: F, B♭, E♭, A♭, D♭, G♭, and C♭.

Example 4–1

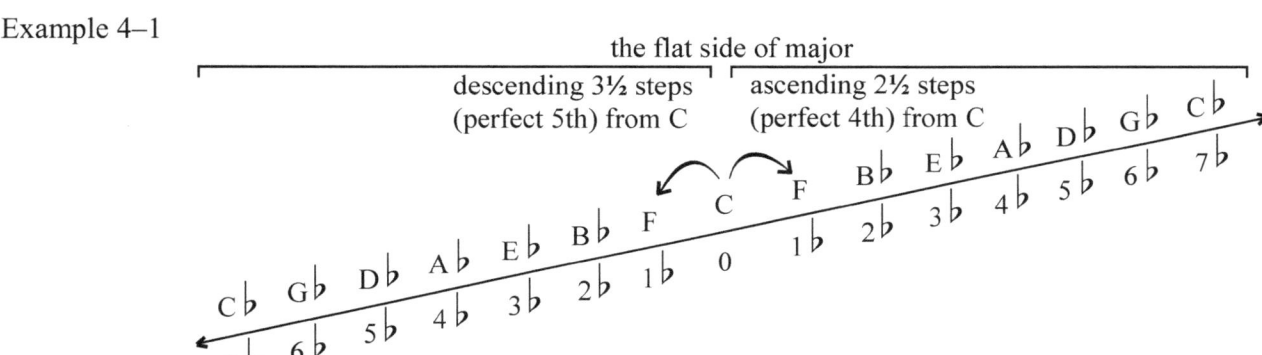

It is possible to apply the process of moving in either direction from C to the sharp side of major by continuing upwards in 3½-step increments or downwards in 2½-step increments. Each new scale construction adds one sharp to those that preceded it. Example 4–2 illustrates the ascending or descending order of scales on the sharp side of major: G, D, A, E, B, F♯, and C♯.

Example 4–2

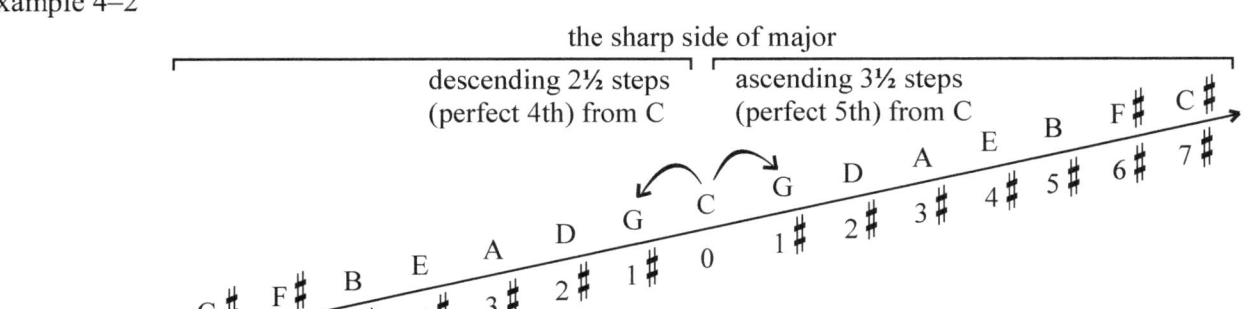

Example 4–3 combines the descending portion of example 4–1 and the ascending portion of example 4–2, with the sharp side of major rising 3½ steps above C and the flat side falling 3½ steps below C.

Example 4–3

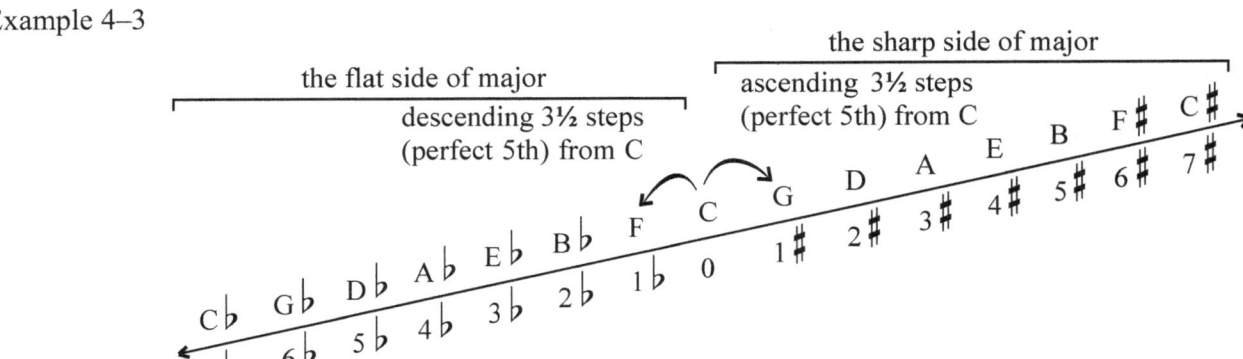

Look at the configurations of the key signatures for C♯ major and C♭ major as they appear on both the G clef (treble clef) and the F clef (bass clef). Examples 4–4a and 4b present the key signature as a collection of accidentals that appears between the clef sign and the time signature. The key signature forms a pattern that is logically designed to keep all of the accidentals within the limits of the staff and to facilitate reading.

The pattern for both sharp and flat keys is consistently maintained except in one place. Starting with F♯, the pattern for sharp keys is down a 4th and up a 5th, except for the A♯, which continues down another 4th before the pattern resumes. Determine the intervals of a 4th and 5th by counting each line and space on the staff. The key signature pattern for flat keys contains no irregularities: up a 4th and down a 5th.

Example 4–4

Consider what would have happened to the A♯ if the pattern of descending 4ths and ascending 5ths had been consistently observed. Both the A♯ and the B♯ would have required ledger lines and thereby exceeded the limits of the staff (example 4–5).

Example 4–5

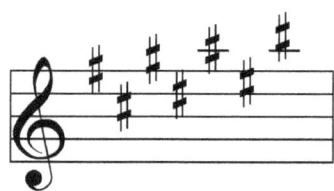

The Circle of 5ths

In example 4–3, we used C major as a starting point and ascended in perfect-5th intervals through G, D, A, E, B, F♯, and C♯, increasing by one the number of sharps for each successive key. Similarly, we descended from C in perfect-5th intervals through F, B♭, E♭, A♭, D♭, G♭, and C♭, increasing by one the number of flats for each successive key. Out of these formations, fifteen major keys emerge, seven with sharps, seven with flats, and C major, which has neither sharps nor flats.

As shown in example 4–6, the procession of ascending perfect 5ths on the sharp side of major and descending perfect 5ths on the flat side of major forms a circle, a **circle of 5ths**. Remember each key's position in the circle and you will be able to determine how many accidentals any given major key has.

For example, the third key from C on the sharp side, A major, has three sharps. The fourth key from C on the flat side, A♭ major, has four flats. Notice the three pairs of keys located on the lower portion of the circle, namely, D♭ and C♯, G♭ and F♯, and C♭ and B. Play the scales for these three pairs of keys on the piano and you will find that each pair sounds the same; they are **enharmonic keys**. The enharmonic keys close the circle of 5ths by bringing the sharp and flat sides of major together.

Example 4–6: the sharp and flat sides of major in the circle of 5ths

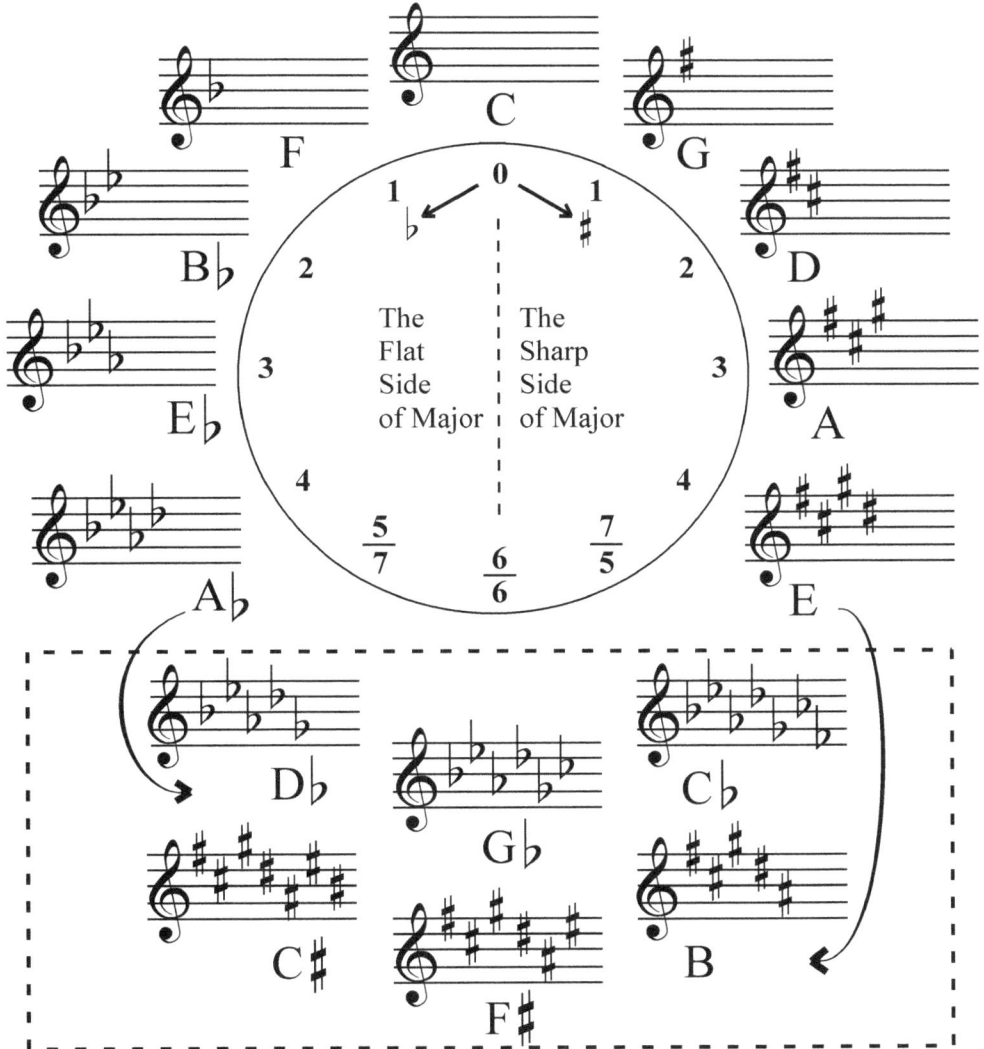

46   Chapter 4   Major Key Signatures

Examples 4–7a, 7b, 7c, and 7d show both the sharp and flat key signatures in their respective treble and bass clefs. As stated above, the arrangement for sharps is down a 4th and up a 5th, except for the A♯, which continues down another 4th before the initial pattern is resumed. For the flat keys, the pattern reverses the configuration of the sharp keys: up a 4th and down a 5th, with no irregularities.

A useful way to remember the order of sharps as they appear on the staff is to associate them respectively with the first letter of each word of the sentence "friends can go dancing at Ernie's bar." For flats, remember that the first four flats spell the word BEAD, followed by the letters GCF, which we could read as an abbreviation for "good cars fast."

Example 4–7

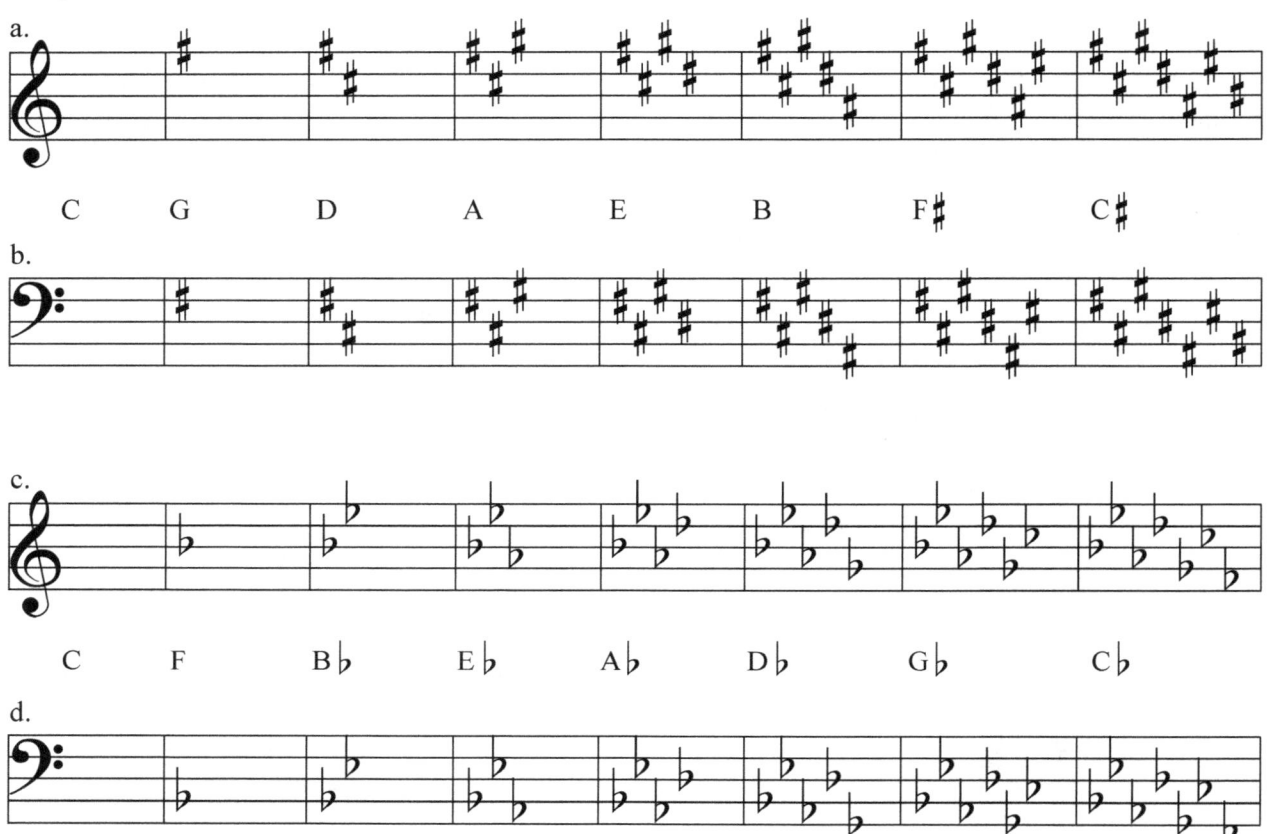

Example 4–8 illustrates some of the common mistakes that music students make when writing key signatures.

Example 4–8

Identifying Major Key Signatures

There is a paradox in the relationship between key signatures and the scales and modes they signify. The paradox involves the difference in the order of accidentals that appear in the construction of a scale versus the order of accidentals as they appear in that scale's key signature. Consider the scale construction for C♯ major (example 4–9a); here, the order of sharps is C♯, D♯, E♯, F♯, G♯, A♯, and B♯. Compare the sequence of sharps in the construction of the C♯-major scale to the order of sharps in the key signature (4–9b): F♯, C♯, G♯, D♯, A♯, E♯, and B♯.

The only common factor of significance between the order of accidentals in the construction of a scale with sharps and the order of accidentals in the scale's key signature is as follows: the last sharp added to the scale (not including scale degree 8, which is a duplication of scale degree 1) is scale degree 7, the leading tone; the last sharp of the key signature is also scale degree 7. In the case of C♯ major, scale degree 7 is B♯.

The fact that the last pitch of the key signature is scale degree 7 helps us to identify the keynote of any sharp key, as the note following scale degree 7 is scale degree 8, the keynote (see the upward arrow pointing to C♯ in 4–9b). And so, for all of the sharp key signatures, look at the last sharp and realize that the keynote is one half step above that last sharp.

Example 4–9: C♯ major

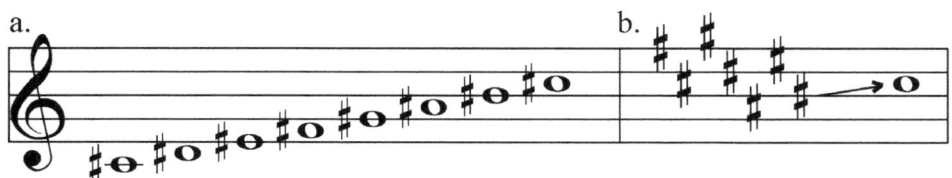

For flat keys, we find the same paradox in the relationship between key signatures and the scales and modes they signify (examples 4–10a and 10b); however, the last flat of the signature cannot help us identify the keynote. Rather, a different principle must be applied to acquire this information. If the flat key has two or more flats in its key signature, then the next-to-the-last flat will be the keynote. The key with one flat is F major and you will simply have to memorize this fact.

Example 4–10: C♭ major

Diatonicism, Chromaticism, Tonality, and Atonality

The terms diatonic and chromatic can be used in a variety of ways. In Chapter 2, we noted that a half step occurring between two pitches that involve two different consecutive letter names is referred to as a diatonic half step. A half step between two different versions of the same letter name is called a chromatic half step. In Chapter 3, we distinguished between diatonic scales and the chromatic scale, the former having one version only of the seven available pitch names and the latter dividing the octave into twelve half steps and consisting primarily of pairs of pitches that involve two different versions of the same letter name.

We also learned that the pattern of half steps and whole steps in the major scale reflects two things, namely, key and mode. The mode of a composition expresses certain characteristic designs that confirm and establish the key. The key is that pitch to which all other pitches are related and toward which they ultimately move. The key represents the **tonality** of the mode.

Tonality in music is analogous to the gravitational force exerted by the Sun upon any object that comes within its field of attraction. Tonality is a system of pitch organization that establishes its own field of attraction around one central tone. All of the other tones of the mode seek to revolve around and gravitate toward this central tone in a hierarchical order.

The tonic, as the principal tone of this hierarchy, exerts its gravitational force upon all of the other tones of the mode, each of which assumes a position of relative strength and stability within the tonic's field of attraction. In other words, within the framework of the key and mode, some tones have a stronger relationship to the tonic than others. We shall explore further the hierarchical relationships of tonal music in Chapter 7.

In broad terms, the concepts of key, mode, and tonality bring us to a consideration of the principles of **diatonicism** and **chromaticism**. The study of music fundamentals deals largely with diatonic usages in music. Perhaps the best way to understand diatonicism is to recognize that every mode (including those that we have yet to examine) has certain tones that represent its unique profile of half steps and whole steps. The tones that are specific and appropriate to the mode are diatonic elements; these tones are part of the key's orbital system.

In most cases, the diatonic elements will be reflected in the key signature. However, the key signature may not represent all of the pitch content of a music composition. The tones that are neither native to the mode nor reflected in the key signature are referred to as chromatic pitches. Chromaticism, if used extensively in a musical work, can not only undermine both the key and mode, it can eliminate them altogether. In the early twentieth century, certain composers began creating music that expressed no key at all, generally referred to as **atonality**.

Atonal music is based upon a system of pitches, either strictly or loosely organized, in which all tones are of equal importance—there is no key center toward which other tones seek to move, no tonal hierarchy. Moreover, in atonal music, there is no distinction between something known as **consonance** and **dissonance**. We shall encounter consonance and dissonance again in the next chapter.

Chapter 5   Intervals

In Chapter 2, the term interval was introduced to describe the distance from one pitch to any other pitch. It is possible to measure the numerical distance between two pitches by counting the letter names from the lower pitch to the higher pitch or from the higher pitch to the lower pitch. For example, C to D, is called a 2nd, C to E a 3rd, C to F a 4th, C to G a 5th, C to A a 6th, and C to B a 7th (example 5–1a). When speaking of the numerical distance from C to C (the second C is a duplication of the first in a higher register), we use the term octave rather than the number 8. The abbreviation for octave is 8ve.

When two or more musicians perform the same pitch in the same register, the terms unison or prime are used to designate the interval. If two pitches occur simultaneously, then the interval is called a **harmonic interval**. Example 5–1a illustrates some of the harmonic intervals that may exist within the range of a single C octave; intervals no larger than an octave are called **simple intervals**.

Example 5–1b demonstrates what happens if the upper pitch of each pair of simple intervals is moved into the next higher octave; this action produces what are referred to as **compound intervals**, intervals exceeding the span of an octave. To determine the numerical designation for a compound interval, add the number 7 to its simple intervallic counterpart: 2+7 becomes a 9th, 3+7 a 10th, 4+7 an 11th, 5+7 a 12th, 6+7 a 13th, 7+7 a 14th, and 8+7 a 15th. Since the top pitch of the octave duplicates the bottom pitch, we add 7 rather than 8 to the simple interval in order to avoid counting the same pitch twice.

Example 5–1: harmonic intervals

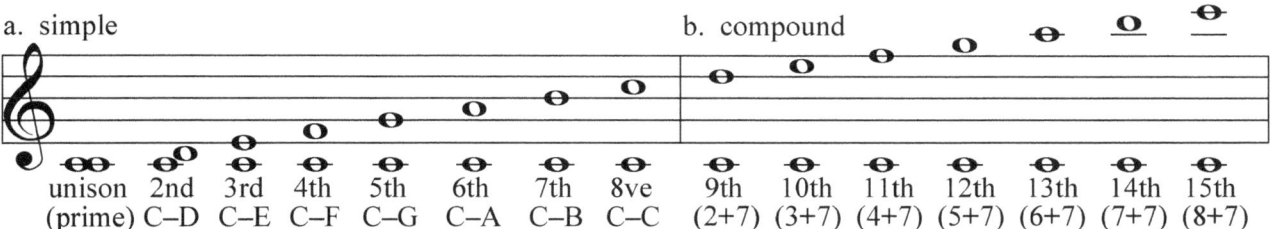

Example 5–2 shows the appearance on the staff of various harmonic intervals irrespective of clef but with the bottom note placed on either a space or a line (except for the unison, which has no bottom note). Notice that with the unison, 3rd, 5th, and 7th, both notes of the interval are placed on either spaces or lines. With the 2nd, 4th, 6th, and octave, however, one note of the interval will always be on a line and the other note will be on a space.

Example 5–2: harmonic intervals on the staff

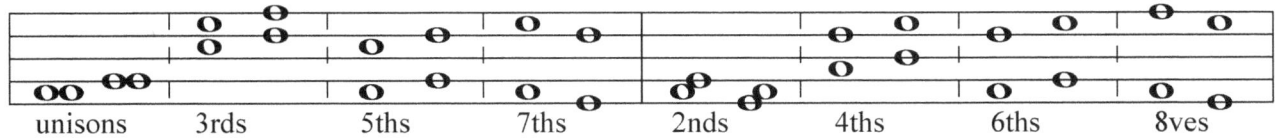

If two pitches occur in succession, then the interval is called a **melodic interval**. Example 5–3 demonstrates two different types of melodic succession between adjacent pitches, namely, **conjunct motion** and **disjunct motion**. Conjunct motion involves movement between pitches that are either a half step or whole step apart, whereas disjunct motion occurs when movement between pitches is greater than a whole step. Another term for conjunct motion is **melodic motion**. In Example 5–3, the distance between the bottom C and the upper pitches of each melodic interval becomes increasingly larger until the octave is reached.

Example 5–3: melodic intervals

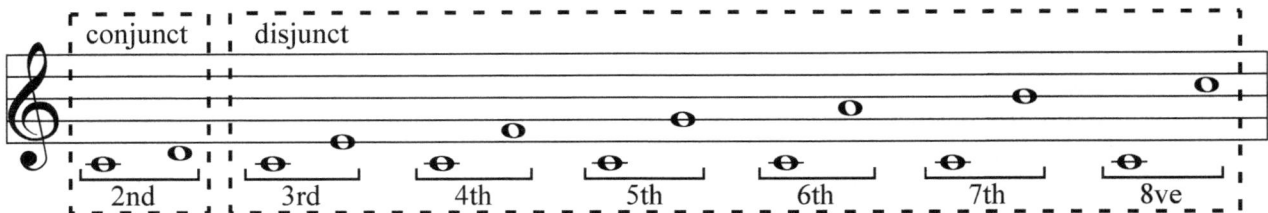

The Essential Diatonic Intervals of Major

In order to recognize and calculate the exact distance between two pitches, you must understand the intervallic relationships between scale degree 1 and all of the other scale degrees of the major mode. As stated above, the numerical size of an interval in major can be determined by counting the pitch names between the bottom note and each note above it.

Intervals can be measured not only in terms of their numerical value but also according to their quality. "Perfect," "major," "minor," "diminished," "doubly diminished," "augmented," and "doubly augmented" are all qualitative descriptions applied to the distance between two pitches. Doubly diminished and doubly augmented intervals are far less common than the other five varieties; however, you will encounter them if your study of music theory continues beyond the purview of music fundamentals and basic harmony.

In C major, the intervals formed between scale degree 1 and the diatonic scale degrees that occur above scale degree 1 are described as either major or perfect. Major and perfect intervals are the two categories of "essential diatonic intervals" from which all invervallic relationships are determined; and when we move these intervals to keys other than C major, such as G major, the same numerical and qualitative relationships are preserved.

If, as shown in example 5–4, the interval's numerical distance from scale degree 1 is a 2nd, 3rd, 6th, or 7th, *and* if the top note of the interval is part of the scale (and therefore part of its key signature), then the quality of the interval is always major in a major mode. Moreover, the term major can be applied only to 2nds, 3rds, 6ths, and 7ths.

If the interval's numerical distance from scale degree 1 is a 4th, 5th, octave, or even a unison, *and* if the top note of the interval is part of the scale, then the quality of the interval is always perfect in a major mode (a perfect unison, however, does not have a top note since both pitches of the interval are identical). The term perfect can be applied only to 4ths, 5ths, octaves, and unisons.

Example 5–4: the essential diatonic intervals in C major

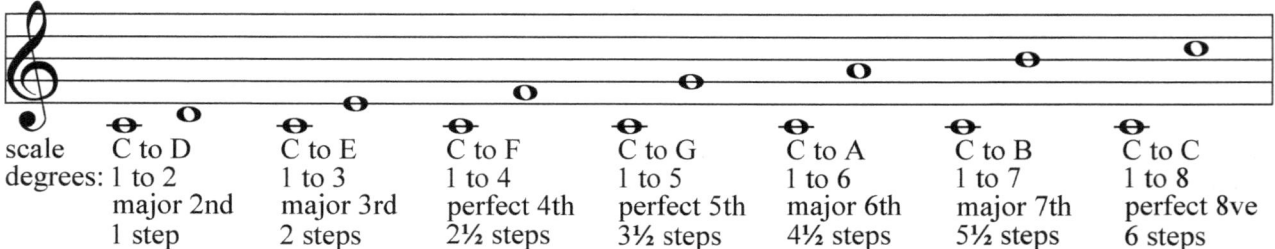

Study the essential diatonic intervals as they appear in example 5–5; for here we have the major scale and mode transposed to G, which requires the addition of F♯ to maintain the correct profile of half steps between scale degrees 3 and 4 and scale degrees 7 and 8. As long as the mode's half-step profile is preserved, the same intervallic relationships found in C major above scale degree 1 will be found also in G major above its scale degree 1.

Example 5–5: the essential diatonic intervals in G major

| scale degrees: | G to A
1 to 2
major 2nd
1 step | G to B
1 to 3
major 3rd
2 steps | G to C
1 to 4
perfect 4th
2½ steps | G to D
1 to 5
perfect 5th
3½ steps | G to E
1 to 6
major 6th
4½ steps | G to F♯
1 to 7
major 7th
5½ steps | G to G
1 to 8
perfect 8ve
6 steps |

Example 5–6 summarizes the two categories of essential intervals found above scale degree 1 in the major mode.

Example 5–6

Perfect Intervals	Major Intervals
unison	2nd
4th	3rd
5th	6th
8ve	7th

Two Principles for Recognizing and Constructing the Qualities of Intervals

In the foregoing section, we stated that if the bottom note of an interval is scale degree 1 of a major scale and if the top note of the interval coincides with a diatonic scale degree of the scale, then the quality of the interval is either major or perfect. The coincidence of the top note of the interval with a diatonic scale degree is the *first principle* for recognizing and constructing the qualities of intervals.

The *second principle*, referred to here as the re-sizing principle, is applied when the top note does not appear as a diatonic scale degree above scale degree 1. As demonstrated in example 5–7 below, the re-sizing principle uses the following qualitative terms: minor, diminished, doubly diminished, augmented, and doubly augmented. Accordingly,

(1) decreasing the size of a perfect interval by one half step produces a diminished interval (5–7a);
(2) reducing the size of diminished interval by one half step gives us a doubly diminished interval;
(3) a perfect interval increased in size by one half step becomes an augmented interval;
(4) expanding the size of any augmented interval by one half step results in a doubly augmented interval;
(5) decreasing the size of a major interval by one half step yields a minor interval (5–7b);
(6) reducing the size of a minor interval by one half step creates a diminished interval; and,
(7) a major interval increased in size by one half step becomes an augmented interval.

Example 5–7: the re-sizing principle

a. re-sizing perfect intervals (principle two)

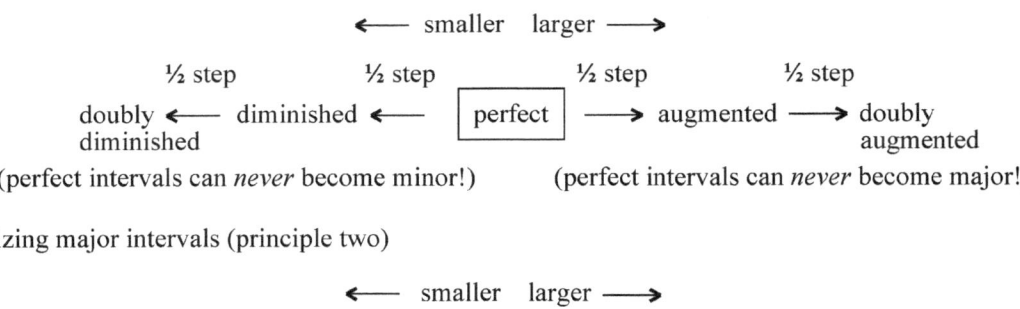

b. re-sizing major intervals (principle two)

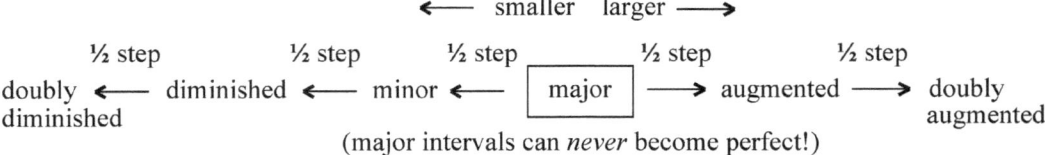

And so, to calculate the quality of an interval, evaluate the lower note as scale degree 1 of a major mode, if the top note coincides with a diatonic scale degree of that mode (based upon the mode's half-step profile and key signature), then according to principle one, the quality is either major or perfect. If, however; the top note does not constitute a diatonic scale degree of a major mode, then determine the quality according to the re-sizing principle as put forward in 5–7 above.

The diagrams in examples 5–8a and 8b show how to use the re-sizing principle to visualize the decrease or increase in the size of an interval without the benefit of a piano keyboard, clef, or pitch names as references.

Example 5–8

a. decreasing the size of perfect and major intervals by one half step

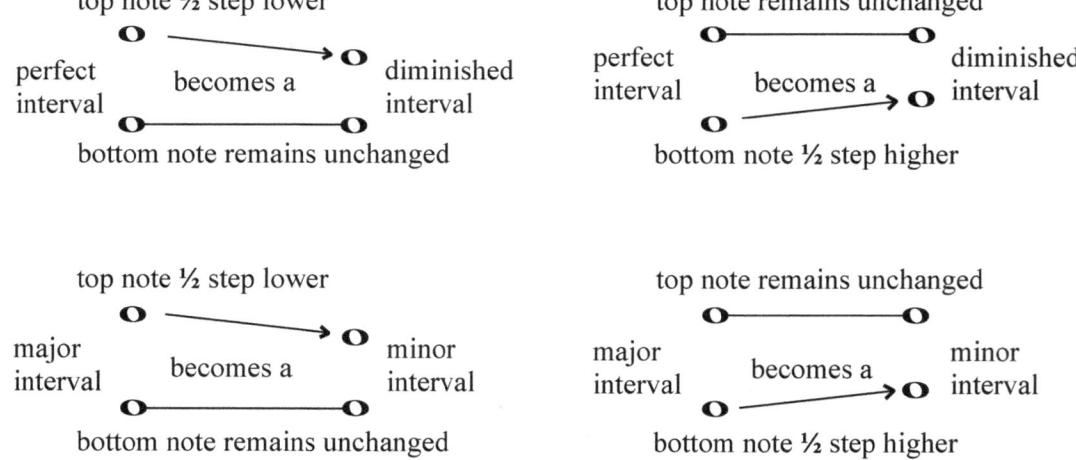

b. increasing the size of perfect and major intervals by one half step

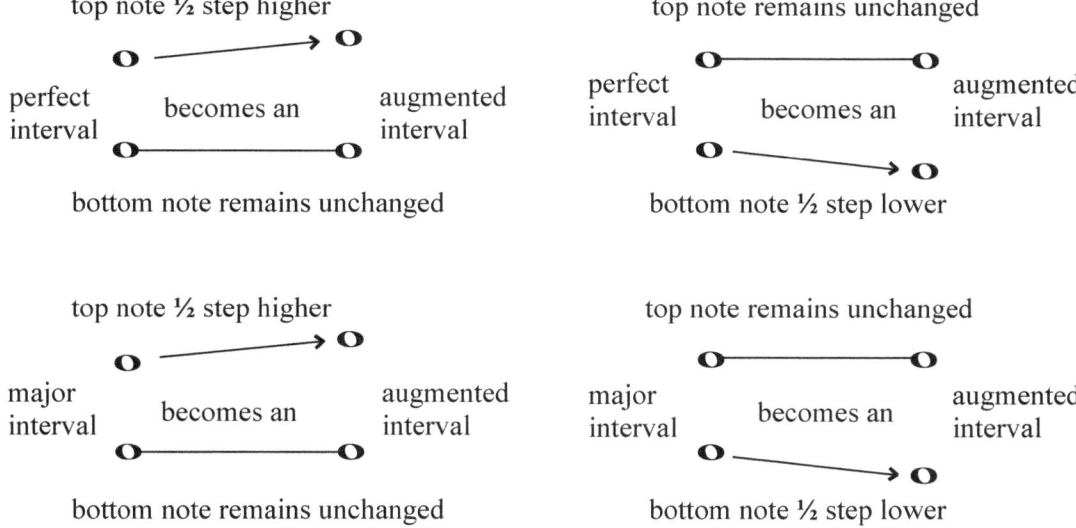

In examples 5–8a and 8b above, the diagrams demonstrate how perfect and major intervals may be decreased or increased in size by moving one of the two notes of the interval up or down one half step while the other note remains stationary. It is possible, however, to keep one note stationary while moving the other note two half steps, a move equivalent to that of one whole step. Indeed, as we saw in examples 5–7a and 7b, decreasing the size of a perfect interval by two half steps produces a doubly diminished interval, while increasing its size by two half steps results in a doubly augmented interval. Decreasing the size of a major interval by two half steps produces a diminished interval, while increasing its size by two half steps results in a doubly augmented interval.

Example 5–9 demonstrates another option for changing the size of an interval by two half steps; here, both notes move from their original position:

Example 5–9: decreasing or increasing the size of perfect and major intervals by two half steps

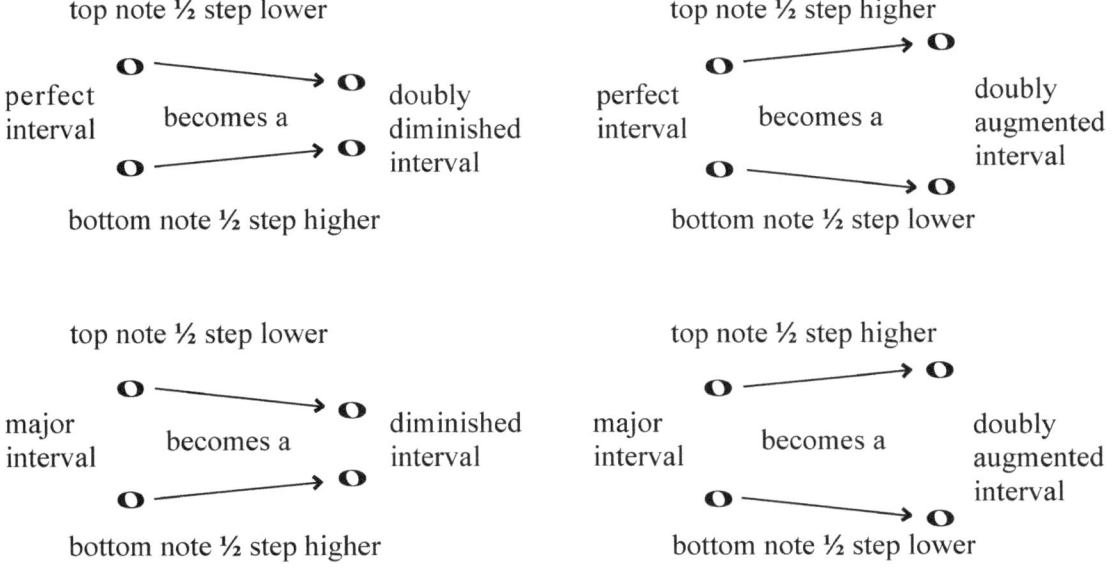

Let us return to our reference key and mode of C major and consider some of the intervals that may occur when the diatonic pitches above scale degree 1 are either raised or lowered by one half step with the addition of either a sharp or flat. You will notice that these alterations produce minor, diminished, and augmented qualities (example 5–10).

All qualitative descriptions of intervals take the following abbreviations: major as M, minor as m, diminished as d, and augmented as A. Uppercase and lowercase letters are used to distinguish between intervallic qualities. The filled-in note heads without stems in the example do not represent specific durational values.

Example 5–10: producing minor, diminished, and augmented intervals above C

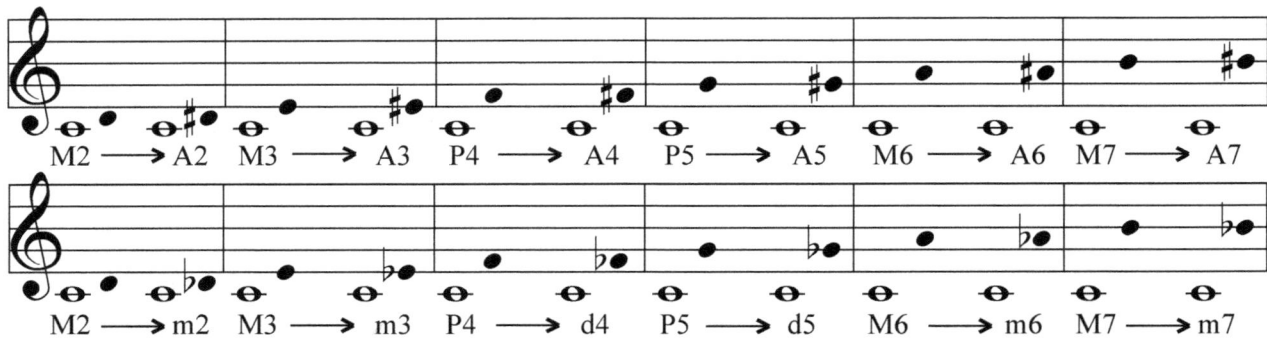

When the Bottom Pitch of the Interval Is Not Scale Degree 1 of C Major

Recognizing or calculating the numerical distance and quality of an interval is a relatively simple task when the bottom pitch is scale degree 1 of C major. But when the bottom pitch is not scale degree 1 of C major, we are confronted with a new set of challenges and one central fact: the key signatures that arise from the fourteen transpositions of the C major scale and mode must be committed to memory; for our study of music fundamentals cannot progress without meeting this requirement.

The following examples will focus on the difficulties that underlie these challenges. We begin with the problem of building intervals above pitches other than C. Example 5–11a starts with the pitches F and B♮ (natural). Our knowledge of key signatures tells us that F major takes one flat, B♭. Therefore, B♮ is not a diatonic member of F major. Counting the pitch names, we can determine that the numerical distance between F to B♮ (counting F as 1) is a 4th. Since B♭ is native to F major, F to B♭ must be a perfect 4th (i.e., P4), one of the essential diatonic intervals of F major.

If F to B♭ is a perfect 4th, then what interval is produced when the B♭ becomes B♮? Visualize the perfect 4th from F to B♭ without reference to a clef or staff and ask yourself if the interval becomes larger or smaller when the B♭ becomes a B♮ (5–11b).

Example 5–11

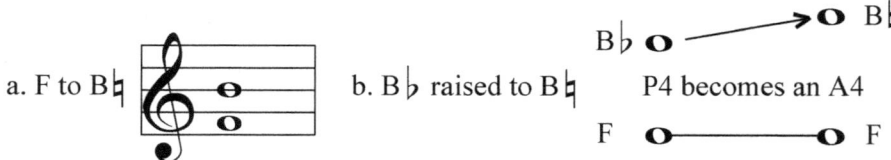

The question posed in the preceding paragraph may well be the most difficult one to address because finding the correct answer requires you to understand that the move from B♭ to B♮ constitutes a raising of the pitch by one half step. Remember that when we proceed from left to right on the piano keyboard, each piano key produces a pitch that is incrementally higher and its equivalent frequency faster (see above, p. 25).

Once you are able to recognize that B♮ is one half step higher than B♭, it should be clear that F to B♮ is one half step larger than F to B♭. *If the size of a perfect interval is increased by one half step, then the quality changes from perfect to augmented*; hence, F to B♮ is an augmented 4th (A4). An inspection of the piano keyboard reveals that F to B♮ is the *only* place within the octave where the interval of an augmented 4th occurs between white keys. Committing this fact to memory now will help significantly to calculate the qualities of certain intervals and chords later.

Before we consider some of the more complex issues associated with interval recognition and construction, it would be well to look at a few examples in which the bottom pitch of the interval carries an **inflection**, in other words, a note that has been altered with the addition of an accidental. In example 5–12a, both the bottom and top pitches of the interval are inflected, that is, C♯ and A♯.

In order to identify the exact quality of the interval, our first question should be: "what is the numerical distance between these two notes?" Counting the pitch names between C♯ and A♯ (counting C♯ as 1), we find that A♯ is 6 steps away from the bottom pitch; hence, the numerical distance is a 6th. (The interval of the 6th can *never* be associated with the term perfect because only 4ths, 5ths, octaves, and unisons belong to the category of perfect intervals.)

Secondly: "in C♯ major, is there an A♯?" If you have memorized the key signatures for the fourteen transpositions of C major, then you will determine quite easily that A♯ is a diatonic member of C♯ major because C♯ major has seven sharps, one of which is A♯. Since the interval here is a 6th, the qualitative description is major because A♯ is part of the C♯-major scale. And so, the interval would be called a major 6th (M6).

Example 5–12

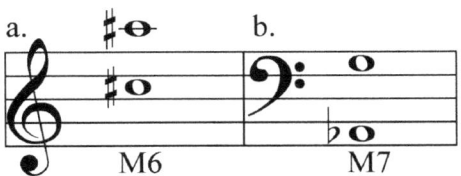

The interval in 5–12b above presents a slightly different challenge in that only one of its two pitches has an accidental, namely, A♭. Once you have asked and answered the question of the numerical distance between A♭ and G and determined that the interval is a 7th, you must call upon your memory to tell you that A♭ major has four flats, none of which involve G. However, it is important to recognize that G, C, and F are all native to A♭ major, despite the fact that none of these pitches carry a flat. Indeed, except for C♯ major and C♭ major, there will be pitches in the key signature that are not inflected with an accidental. Since G is scale degree 7, the leading tone of A♭ major, the interval between A♭ and G is a major 7th (M7).

In example 5–13a, the interval from B♭ to D♯ consists of two different types of accidentals, a flat and a sharp. As before, the first question we address is the numerical distance between the two pitches. Since the distance between B♭ and D♯ is a 3rd, the interval can never be described as perfect. The next step is to determine if D♯ is a diatonic scale degree of B♭ major. Drawing upon our knowledge of key signatures, we know that B♭ major has two flats and no D♯. Therefore, the quality of the 3rd cannot be major. If the pitches had been B♭ to D, then the interval would have been a major 3rd because D is scale degree 3 of B♭ major. (If the pitches had been B♭ to D♭, then the interval would have been a minor 3rd.)

And so, what is B♭ to D♯? Once again, the challenge is recognizing that D♯ is one half step higher in pitch than D and that the distance from B♭ to D♯ is one half step larger than the distance from B♭ to D. If the size of a major interval is increased by one half step, then the quality changes from major to augmented; hence, B♭ to D♯ is an augmented 3rd (A3). The diagram to the right of 5–13a will help you to visualize the change in the size of the interval.

Example 5–13

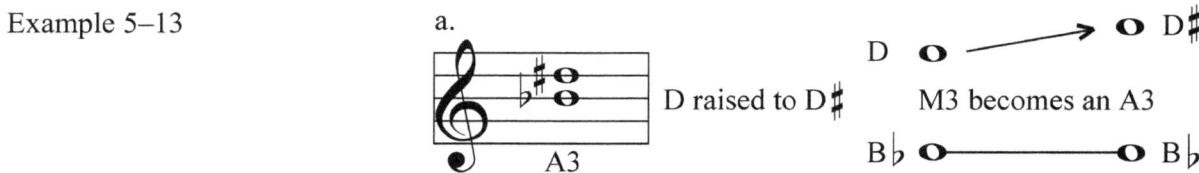

The next interval is built on C♭ and contains an E♭♭ as its upper component (example 5–13b). The numerical distance between the pitches C♭ and E♭♭ is a 3rd; but is there an E♭♭ in C♭ major? We know that C♭ major has seven flats, one of which is E♭ rather than E♭♭. Therefore, C♭ to E♭ constitutes a diatonic major 3rd. If E♭ is lowered to E♭♭, is the interval larger or smaller? The diagram to the right of 5–13b illustrates the change in size that occurs when E♭ is lowered to E♭♭, a change in size that produces a minor 3rd (m3); for *when the size of a major interval is decreased by one half step, the quality changes from major to minor.*

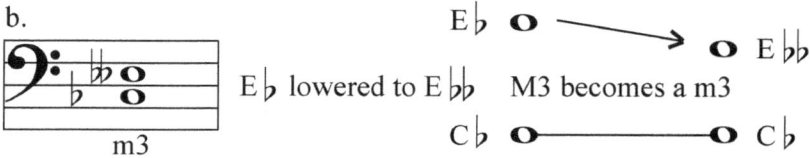

Counting the letter names from the F♯ to the E♭ in 5–13c confirms the numerical distance to be a 7th. But now we want to know if there is an E♭ in F♯ major. Since F♯ major has six sharps, the answer is no. The sixth sharp of F♯ major's key signature is E♯. E♯ is scale degree 7; therefore, the quality from F♯ to E♯ is a major 7th, one of the essential diatonic intervals of major. If we lower E♯ to E, does the interval get larger or smaller?

Study the diagram to the right of 5–13c and notice that the move from E♯ to E decreases the size of the interval by one half step. When a major interval (F♯ to E♯) is reduced in size by one half step, the quality changes from major to minor (F♯ to E♮). Let us move the E to E♭, recognizing that the interval has now decreased in size another half step. If the size of a minor interval is reduced by one half step, then the quality becomes diminished; thus, F♯ to E♭ is a diminished 7th (d7).

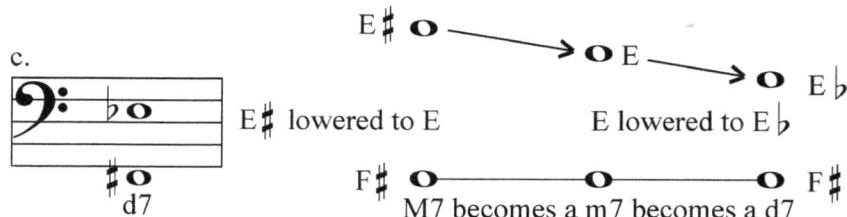

When the Bottom Pitch Does Not Correspond to One of the Fourteen Transpositions of C Major

In the examples 5–12 and 13, we assumed the bottom pitch of the interval to be scale degree 1 of the major mode and then used the two principles for recognizing and calculating the qualities of intervals to determine the exact distance between the two pitches. Thus, if the bottom note represents C major or corresponds to one of its fourteen transpositions (G, D, A, E, B, F♯, C♯, F, B♭, E♭, A♭, D♭, G♭, or C♭), then identifying the top note as a diatonic scale degree is a relatively simple task. On the other hand, if the top pitch is not a diatonic scale degree, then we can derive the quality of the interval according to the re-sizing principle.

But as we shall see presently, not all intervals have bottom pitches that correspond to one of the fourteen transpositions of C major. Consider example 5–14a, an interval consisting of F𝄪 and B♯. We can see from counting the letter names that the interval is some kind of 4th; however, there is no F𝄪 major key signature to use as a reference. Consequently, we must employ some alternative strategies to find the exact distance between the two pitches, to find the quality of the interval. Since the problem is with the F𝄪, simply remove the double sharp as well as the sharp attached to the B, evaluate the interval with no inflections (as F♮ to B♮), re-introduce the sharps, and then, apply principles one and two as needed.

(1) Starting with F♮ as the bottom note and assuming it to be scale degree 1 of F major, does its key signature have a B♮? The answer is no. F major has a B♭; therefore, B♮ is not a diatonic scale degree. The distance from F♮ to B♭ constitutes a perfect 4th.
(2) If we raise B♭ to B♮, the interval is one half step larger and as such becomes an augmented 4th.
(3) Raising the F♮ to F♯ makes the interval one half step smaller and brings us again to a perfect 4th.
(4) At this point, add back the sharp attached to the B; the move from B♮ to B♯ expands the perfect 4th by one half step and creates an augmented 4th (F♯ to B♯).
(5) Finally, re-introducing the double sharp to the bottom note contracts the augmented 4th by one half step and produces a perfect 4th. F𝄪 to B♯ is a perfect 4th.

Example 5–14

The diagram in 5–14b presents an alternative view of the five-step process outlined above.

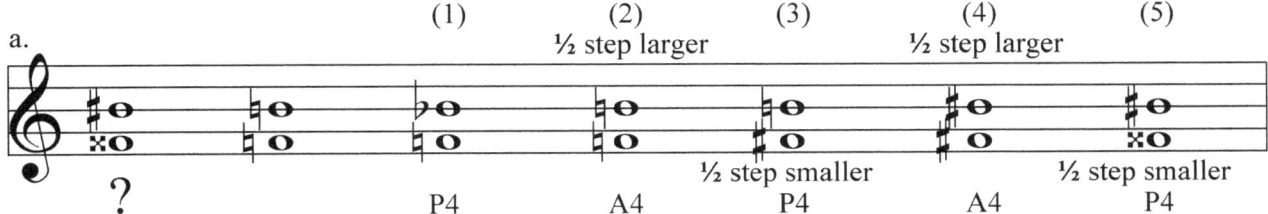

The Principle of Like Inflection

Although the foregoing exercise provides reliable results for recognizing the quality of an interval, it involves too many steps. This section will demonstrate how to streamline the process. Skipping the move to the perfect 4th between F♯ and B♮ eliminates the third re-sizing step displayed in example 5–14.

But what principle would allow us to bypass one of the steps outlined above? As example 5–15a shows, once we determine that F♮ to B♮ is an augmented 4th, inflecting both F♮ and B♮ with a sharp does not change the augmented quality of the 4th. Example 5–15a skips the perfect 4th from F♯ to B♮ and proceeds directly to the augmented 4th between F♯ and B♯. Raising the F♯ to F𝄪 produces a perfect 4th from F𝄪 to B♯.

We can conclude from this observation that *if both pitches of an interval are inflected equally in the same direction, upwards or downwards, then the quality of the interval does not change*. This phenomenon may be referred to as "the principle of like inflection." The only aspect of the interval that does change is that it occurs at a higher or lower pitch level depending on whether sharps or flats are used. Example 5–15b illustrates this fact.

Example 5–15: using the principle of like inflection to identify intervals

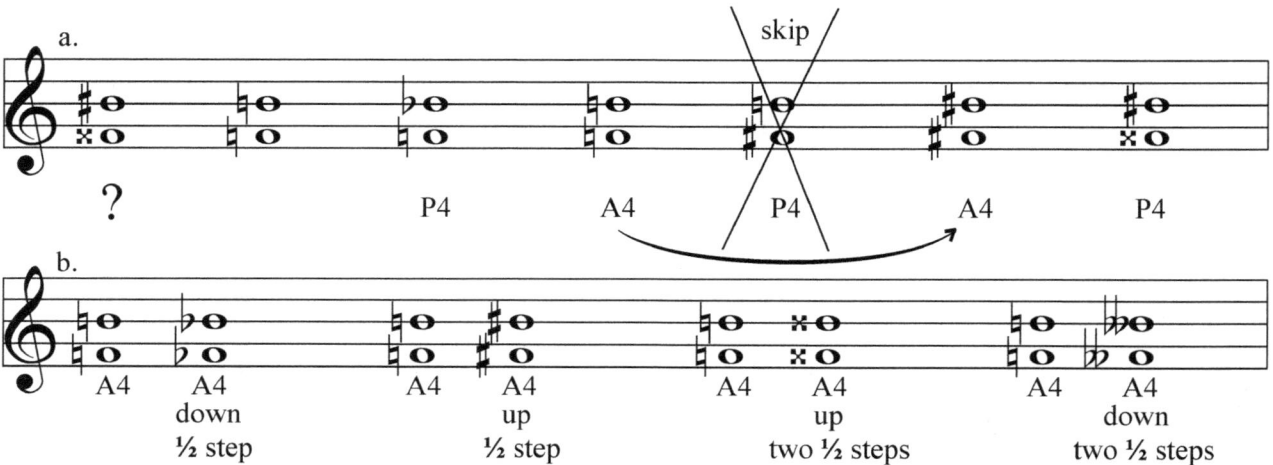

There is a simpler way to identify an interval with a complicated spelling, such as the one in 5–14, if you use your knowledge of enharmonic equivalency to re-interpret the pitch inflections. As directed in example 5–16, respell the F𝄪 and B♯ as G and C respectively. The numerical distance remains unchanged, as the interval is still a 4th; therefore, assume that G is scale degree 1 of the major mode and draw upon your knowledge of key signatures to determine if C is a diatonic component of G major. C is, in fact, native to G major which means that the 4th between the two pitches is perfect. Once you have identified the quality of the re-interpreted interval, simply reinstate the original spelling (in this case, G as F𝄪 and C as B♯).

Example 5–16

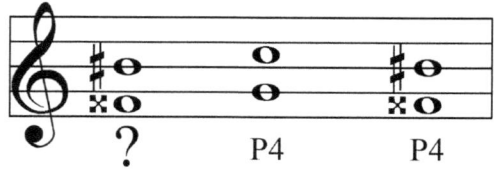

Compound Intervals

At the outset of this chapter, we noted that intervals may exceed the span of an octave. As shown in example 5–17b, the numerical designation for a compound interval is determined by adding the number 7 to its simple intervallic counterpart: 2+7 becomes a 9th, 3+7 a 10th, 4+7 an 11th, 5+7 a 12th, 6+7 a 13th, 7+7 a 14th, and 8+7 a 15th. Since the top pitch of the octave duplicates the bottom pitch, we add 7 rather than 8 to the simple interval in order to avoid counting the same pitch twice.

Although the numerical designation of a compound interval changes, its qualitative description does not. All minor intervals remain minor in their compound forms, major intervals remain major, perfect intervals remain perfect, diminished intervals remain diminished, and augmented intervals remain augmented. Thus, a major 2nd becomes a major 9th, a major 3rd becomes a major 10th, a perfect 4th becomes a perfect 11th, a perfect 5th becomes a perfect 12th, a major 6th becomes a major 13th, a major 7th becomes a major 14th, and a perfect octave becomes a perfect 15th.

Example 5–17

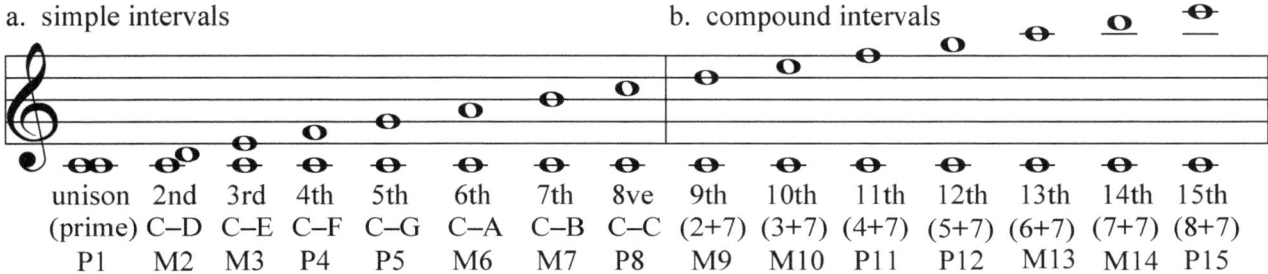

Consider the compound interval in example 5–18. To identify the numerical distance of the compound interval in its simple form, move either the top note of the compound interval down one octave or the bottom note of the interval up one octave: move C4 down to C3 or A2 up to A3. Either adjustment will confirm the numerical distance to be a 3rd; therefore, adding 7 to that 3rd reveals the interval from A2 to C4 to be a 10th.

With the numerical distance identified as a 10th (or as a 3rd), determine the quality of the interval according to principles one and two (see above, pp. 51–54). Since there is a C♯ in A major rather than a C♮, the quality of the interval is minor; hence, the interval in its compound form is a minor 10th (m10). Had the C carried a sharp, the interval would have been a major 10th.

Example 5–18

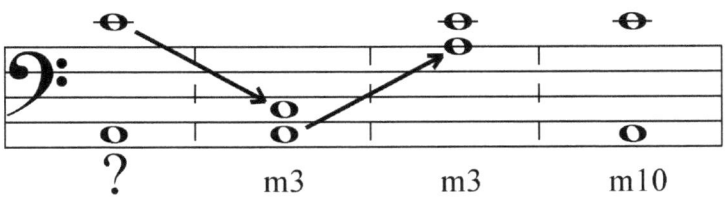

Interval Inversion

In 5–18 above, we identified the numerical distance of a compound interval in its simple form by shifting either the top note of the interval down one octave or the bottom note of the interval up one octave. It is important to recognize that despite these adjustments, the bottom note of the interval remains an A and the top note of the interval remains a C; in other words, the basic identity of the interval is unchanged.

Moreover, the interval's qualitative description remains intact, as the quality of the interval is minor in both its simple and compound forms. To be sure, interpreting a compound interval as a simple interval changes the numerical distance by at least one octave (in this case, a 10th becomes a 3rd); but again, the A retains its status as the bottom note and the C retains its status as the top note. In fact, the minor 10th in 5–18 can also referred to as a compound minor 3rd.

But what happens to the numerical distance and quality of a simple interval when its two pitches are turned upside down or flipped, that is, when either the bottom note of the simple interval is placed one octave higher to become the top note or the top note is moved one octave lower to become the bottom note? Intervals that undergo this type of alteration are said to be inverted. As we shall see, interval inversion changes the numerical distance of the two pitches and *frequently* the quality of the interval.

Using C major as our reference key and mode, let us consider the inversions of intervals in example 5–19a. Notice that when C4 is moved one octave higher into the C5 register, the unison (or prime) becomes an octave, the 2nd a 7th, the 3rd a 6th, the 4th a 5th, the 5th a 4th, the 6th a 3rd, the 7th a 2nd, and the octave a unison. If you add the pair of numbers that the interval and its inversion represent, the sum is always nine: 1+8=9, 2+7=9, 3+6=9, 4+5=9, 5+4=9, 6+3=9, 7+2=9, and 8+1=9. As indicated in 5–19b, perfect intervals (P) remain perfect upon inversion, whereas major intervals (M) become minor (m).

Example 5–19

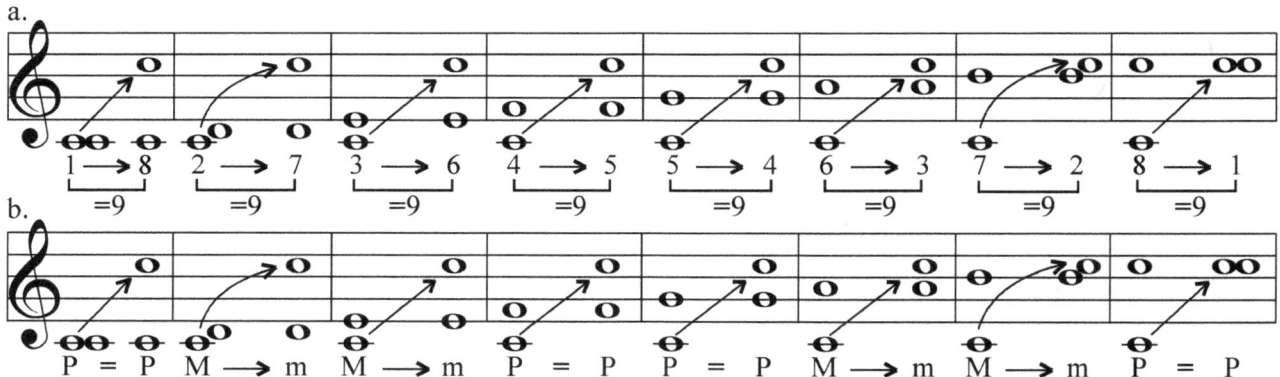

Example 5–20 summarizes the numerical and qualitative changes that occur when an interval is inverted. Note carefully that upon inversion, diminished intervals become augmented and augmented intervals become diminished.

Example 5-20

Upon inversion:

the unison (prime) becomes an octave	1 ⟶ 8 (= 9)
the 2nd becomes a 7th	2 ⟶ 7 (= 9)
the 3rd becomes a 6th	3 ⟶ 6 (= 9)
the 4th becomes a 5th	4 ⟶ 5 (= 9)
the 5th becomes a 4th	5 ⟶ 4 (= 9)
the 6th becomes a 3rd	6 ⟶ 3 (= 9)
the 7th becomes a 2nd	7 ⟶ 2 (= 9)
the octave becomes a unison	8 ⟶ 1 (= 9)

Therefore, upon inversion:

P1 ⟶ P8 ⟶ P1
M2 ⟶ m7 ⟶ M2
M3 ⟶ m6 ⟶ M3
P4 ⟶ P5 ⟶ P4
P5 ⟶ P4 ⟶ P5
M6 ⟶ m3 ⟶ M6
M7 ⟶ m2 ⟶ M7
P8 ⟶ P1 ⟶ P8

A4 ⟶ d5 ⟶ A4
d5 ⟶ A4 ⟶ d5

Upon inversion:

perfect intervals remain perfect	P = P
major intervals become minor	M ⟶ m
minor intervals become major	m ⟶ M
diminished intervals become augmented	d ⟶ A
augmented intervals become diminished	A ⟶ d

Consonance and Dissonance

The distinction between consonance and dissonance in music is a means by which intervals are classified according to whether they are perceived by listeners as either stable or unstable. Consonant intervals exhibit a feeling of rest, while dissonant intervals exude a sense of tension. Dissonant intervals usually seek to form connections to consonant intervals in a process known as resolution. Traditionally, dissonances resolve to consonances. When a dissonant interval is resolved to a consonance, a feeling of relaxation is produced. Resolutions of dissonance endow most of the tonal music of the Western tradition with a sense of forward motion, as the alternation between tension and relaxation propels the music ever forward.

There are two classes of consonant intervals, perfect consonances and imperfect consonances. The perfect consonances are the unison, the perfect octave, the perfect 5th, and *sometimes the perfect 4th*. The imperfect consonances consist of both major and minor 3rds and 6ths. The dissonant intervals include 2nds, 7ths, the augmented 4th, diminished 5th, and *sometimes the perfect 4th*.

The diminished 5th and the augmented 4th are notable for their sound and construction. Both intervals are often referred to as the **tritone** because each of its forms consists of three whole tones (i.e., three whole steps). The tritone stands exactly in the middle of the octave, dividing it in half. The sound of the tritone remains the same when it inverts because it always consists of three whole tones. The only change that occurs with the inversion of the tritone is within the context its numerical size: 4ths always invert to become 5ths and *vice versa*.

Of all the consonant and dissonant intervals, the status of the perfect 4th, depends on its position within the musical texture. If the perfect 4th occurs between the lowest note of the musical texture, called the **bass** (pronounced bās), and an upper note, then the interval is treated as a dissonance (example 5–21a). If, however, the perfect 4th does not occur between the bass and an upper note, then the interval is consonant (5–21b).

Therefore, the consonant perfect 4th is a 4th that occurs between two pitches above the bass; neither of the two upper pitches form the interval of a 4th with the bass. Example 5–21 illustrates the difference between the consonant and dissonant 4th. The brackets show the two pitches that form the interval of the perfect 4th. Notice that both the consonant and the dissonant 4th can appear as either a simple or compound interval (a perfect 11th).

Example 5–21

Example 5–22 demonstrates how dissonant 7ths, 4ths, 2nds, and tritones are usually treated. The conventional way for dissonant intervals to resolve is by either a whole step or by a half step, in other words, by conjunct motion. All of the resolutions in 5–22 are conjunct. The numerical distances of the intervals shown here are given below the staff, except for the augmented 4th (A4) and the diminished 5th (d5), which are also identified according to quality (5–22e and 22f). The examples below shows how the tritone interval is typically used: as an augmented 4th, it expands to a 6th; as a diminished 5th, it contracts to a 3rd. (The principle of stem direction mentioned on p. 1 does not apply when two individual melodic lines appear simultaneously on one staff.)

Example 5–22

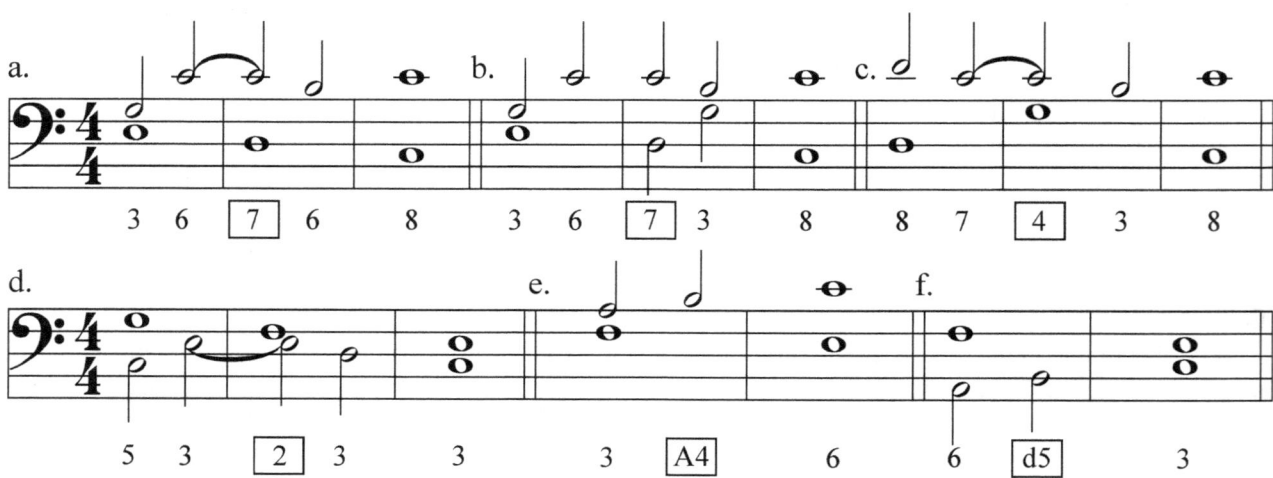

The Suspension

Examples 5–22a, 22b, 22c, and 22d in particular illustrate a special use of consonance, dissonance, and syncopation known collectively as the **suspension**. The suspension has three parts:
  (1) the suspension is *prepared*, usually as a consonance (but sometimes as a dissonance, see 5–22c);
  (2) the preparation is held, or *suspended*, as the opposing line (usually the bass) moves to form a dissonance with the suspension (a consonant suspension is also possible); and finally,
  (3) the suspended line moves down by step to *resolve* to a consonance.

An essential feature of the suspension is the degree of metric stress each part of the operation receives. First and foremost, the resolution must be metrically weaker than the suspension itself. The initial preparation, however, can be made from either a strong or weak position.

In three of the four examples of the suspension in 5–22, notice that the second half note of measure 1 is tied into the first half note of measure 2. Although the tie is the most common means for executing the suspension, it should be understood that an actual tie between two note values is not required to employ this technique, as a repeated pitch also produces the same result. That result is to lengthen the duration of the second half note of measure 1.

Normally, without either tying or repeating the pitch, the second half note of measure 1 would be weaker than the first half note. By increasing its duration, however, the second half note becomes stronger than the first half note, resulting in syncopation. As stated in Chapter 1, *syncopation makes strong that which is otherwise weak.*

Here is a brief description of the suspensions in 5–22:
  (1) In 5–22a, the suspension is prepared on the second half note of measure 1 with a consonant 6th (E/C). In the next measure, the dissonant 7th (D/C) resolves to a 6th (D/B); the bass remains stationary during both the suspension and resolution (D/C to D/B).
  (2) In 5–22b, the suspension is once again prepared on the second half note of measure 1 with a consonant 6th (E/C). However, this time the resolution of the dissonant 7th (D/C) produces a 3rd (G/B) instead of a 6th because the bass moves with the resolution instead of remaining stationary (D/C to G/B). Notice also that the suspended pitch (C) is repeated rather than tied.
  (3) As in 5–22a, the suspension in 5–22c takes place over a stationary bass; but here, the preparation is a dissonant 7th (D/C) and the suspended dissonance is a 4th (G/C) resolving to a consonant 3rd (G/B).
  (4) In 5–22d, we have another kind of suspension. In this example, the operation is inverted; for the top line remains stationary while the bass produces the preparation (E/G), the suspension (E/F), and the resolution (D/F). A dissonant 2nd resolves to a consonant 3rd.

Chapter 6   The Minor Mode

The major mode is not the only mode in music that has a tonal center; however, as mentioned in Chapter 3, its profile of half steps and whole steps distinguishes major from the profiles of other diatonic modes. In this chapter, we shall learn about the properties of the minor mode and discover the ways in which it resembles and differs from the major mode.

In major, certain scale degrees are relatively stable, while other scale degrees are relatively unstable. That is to say, some scale degrees seek to move to other scale degrees, while some scale degrees have less of a tendency to move. Scale degrees 1, 3, 5, and 8 are comparatively stable and can be referred to as **rest tones**. The scale degrees between the rest tones, scale degrees 2, 4, 6, and 7, are unstable; the unstable scale degrees seek to move to one of the more stable rest tones. The unstable scale degrees shall be called **active tones**.

Scale degree 2 usually moves to either scale degrees 1 or 3, scale degree 4 to either 3 or 5, and scale degree 6 to either 5 or 7. If scale degree 6 proceeds to 7, the leading tone, then the motion frequently continues upwards to the tonic note (8). It is important to understand the relatively unstable nature of active tones because their tendency to attach themselves to the more stable rest tones accounts for some of the melodic patterns that occur in both the major and minor modes. In this text, we refer to the major and minor modes collectively as the **major-minor tonal system**.

The Natural Minor Mode

The minor mode has three forms, the harmonic minor, the melodic minor, and the natural minor, which is also known as the pure minor and the Aeolian mode (for a discussion of the Aeolian mode and the other modes that have Greek names, see Chapter 8). The natural minor can be located on the piano keyboard by finding the A octave in any register. As shown in example 6–1, the natural minor in the A octave consists of white keys only; no black keys are involved and no pitches inflected. Since the pitches E to F and B to C constitute the only two places within the octave where there are half steps between two adjacent white keys, the combined distribution of whole steps and half steps across the A octave produces a profile of half steps between scale degrees 2 and 3 and scale degrees 5 and 6.

Example 6–1

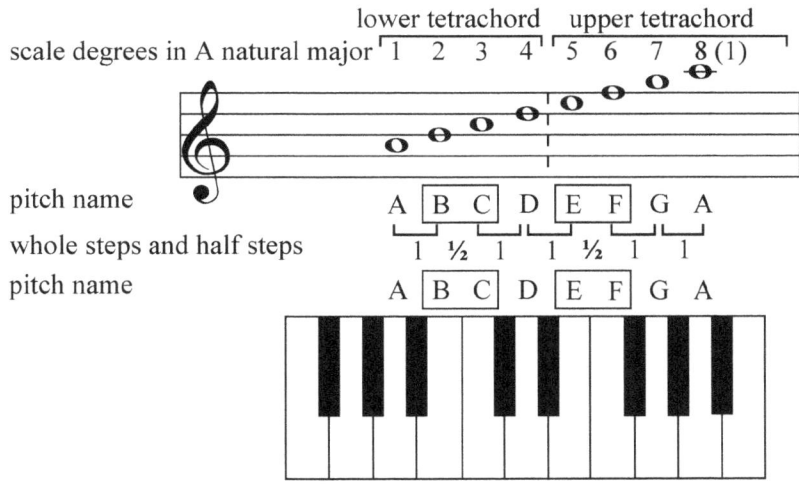

The natural minor takes from the major mode the names of the tonic, supertonic, mediant, subdominant, dominant, and submediant to designate scale degrees 1, 2, 3, 4, 5, and 6 respectively. Scale degree 7, however, is a special case. Unlike the major mode, the natural minor contains a whole step rather than a half step between scale degrees 7 and 8. Scale degree 7 of the natural minor is called the subtonic in order to distinguish it from the leading tone of the major mode. The natural minor does not share the major mode's compelling drive to move upwards by half step from scale degree 7 to scale degree 8. It is therefore more difficult to define and hear the tonic of the natural minor. The presence of the subtonic note may well be the natural minor's most distinctive feature. (In Chapter 8, however, we shall encounter other modes that also have the subtonic scale degree.)

The natural minor contains two tetrachords, each of which is separated by a whole step (see example 6–1 above). Unlike the major mode, the tetrachords for the natural minor are non-matching; in other words, the profile of half steps and whole steps for the lower tetrachord from scale degrees 1 to 4 (whole step, half step, and whole step) does not match the profile of half steps and whole steps for the upper tetrachord from scales 5 to 8 (half step, whole step, whole step).

Following the method introduced in Chapter 5 for describing major and minor intervals, we use lowercase letters when referring to the tonic of any minor mode. Therefore, the minor mode in the A octave will be written as "a minor" rather than as "A minor" (and pronounced as ā minor, not ă minor). On the other hand, major keys such as C major, F♯ major, and D♭ major use uppercase letters.

The Relative Minor

Since no black keys are involved in the construction of a minor, its key signature is identical to that of C major. Having neither sharps nor flats, both modes possess exactly the same pitch content and therefore *share the same key signature* (example 6–2). The principal differences between C major and a minor are their tonics and ranges. C major's scale degree 1 is C; its range extends across the C octave. Scale degree 1 of a minor is A; its range falls within the A octave.

Despite these differences, the common pitch content between C major and a minor constitutes an important *relationship* between the two modes. Indeed, within the context of C major, a minor is described as the **relative minor** key area of C major. The relative minor key area always occurs on scale degree 6 of the corresponding major mode.

Example 6–2

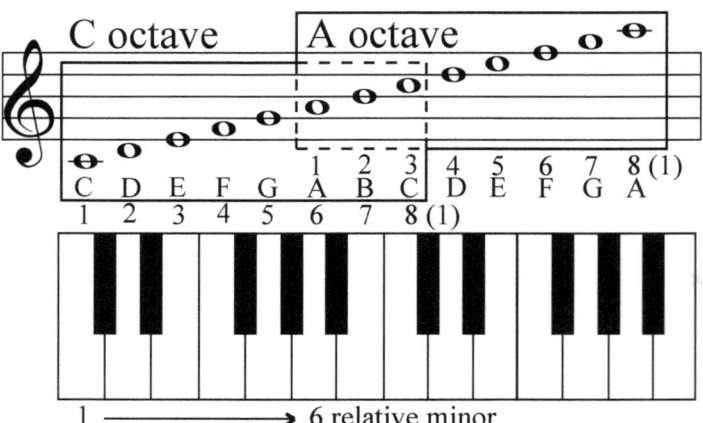

Each of the fourteen transpositions of C major has a relative minor. To find the relative minor of any transposed major mode, transpose the relationship between C major and a minor. In other words, locate scale degree 6 of any transposed major mode and that pitch will be the relative minor key area. For example, what is the relative minor key of G major? Scale degree 6 of G major is E. Therefore, e minor is the relative minor of G major; and both modes have one sharp (F♯) in their key signatures.

Another way to find the relative minor of any transposed major mode is to recognize that scale degree 6 is always a major 6th above the tonic note. Also, remember that the inversion of a major 6th is a minor 3rd (see example 5–20 above); accordingly, we can find the relative minor of any major mode by proceeding either up a major 6th *or* down a minor 3rd from the tonic note. Either direction from scale degree 1 leads to scale degree 6 (example 6–3).

What is the relative minor of F major? A major 6th above (or a minor 3rd below) F is D; thus, d minor is the relative minor of F major. Both F major and d minor have one flat (B♭). What is the relative minor of E major? A minor 3rd below (or a major 6th above) E is C♯; and so, c♯ minor has four sharps (F♯, C♯, G♯, and D♯)—the same sharps that occur in E major.

Example 6–3

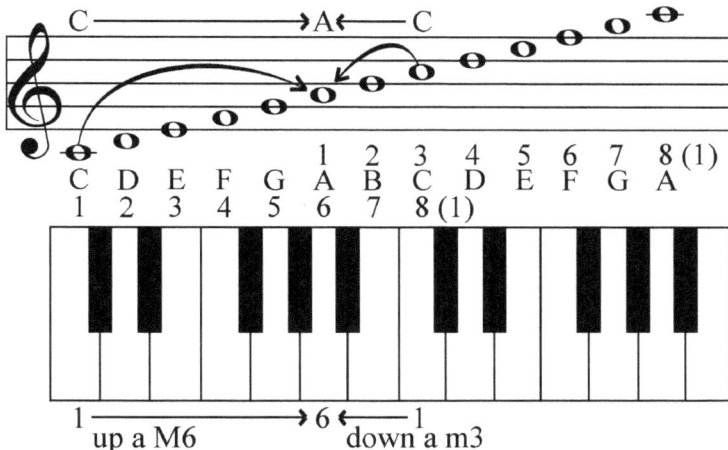

The Parallel Minor and the Parallel Major

In the foregoing paragraphs, we saw how major and minor modes standing in a relative relationship to one another share the same key signature (and therefore the same pitch content) but always have different tonics and different ranges. Another type of modal relationship involves two modes that have different key signatures but share the same tonic and the same range. Because both modes have the same tonic note, they are considered to be *parallel* to one another. Every major mode has a **parallel minor** mode, every minor mode a **parallel major**. Using C as scale degree 1, examples 6–4a and 4b illustrate the differences and the similarities between two parallel modes.

Example 6–4

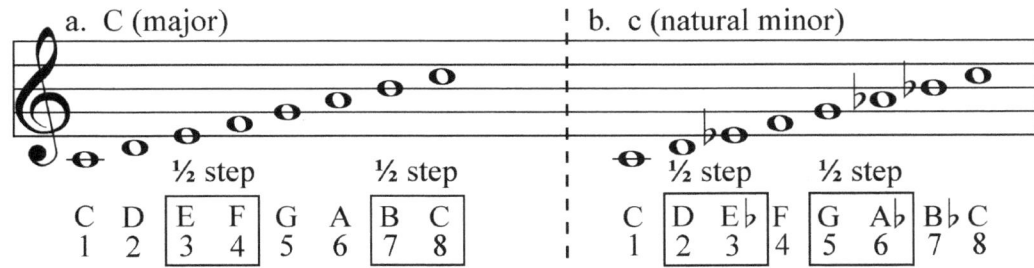

As we have observed, the major mode contains half steps between scale degrees 3 and 4 and scale degrees 7 and 8, whereas the natural minor has half steps between scale degrees 2 and 3 and scale degrees 5 and 6. When the major mode and the natural minor are parallel, having the same tonic and range, the pitch content between them will be different; specifically, their scale degrees 3, 6, and 7 cannot be the same.

Example 6–4b above presents the scale formation for the natural minor within the C octave. Since C is the tonic, the mode must include an E♭, A♭, and B♭ (scale degrees 3, 6, and 7) in order to preserve the profile of half steps between scale degrees 2 and 3 and scale degrees 5 and 6. On the other hand, C major maintains its profile of half steps with E♮, A♮, and B♮.

The Relative Major

Although it is possible to construct the scale for the natural minor on any pitch and add the appropriate accidentals to preserve its half-step profile, there is a faster and easier way to find the accidentals that comprise the key signature for the minor mode. In the preceding section, we noted that every major mode has a parallel minor and every minor a parallel major. And just as every major mode has a relative minor, every minor mode has a **relative major**.

To find the relative major, proceed to scale degree 3 of the minor mode by counting up a minor 3rd from the minor mode's tonic pitch. Once you have located the relative major, its key signature will provide the pitch content and the key signature for the natural minor (see example 6–5b, A up to C is a minor 3rd).

Let us clarify this point with a few practice questions. What is the relative major of b♭ minor? Counting up a minor 3rd from B♭ brings us to D♭; since D♭ major has five flats (B♭, E♭, A♭, D♭, and G♭), the same five flats are found in the key signature of b♭ minor. What is the relative major of e minor (count up a minor 3rd)? G is the relative major of e minor. The key signature of G major has one sharp; accordingly, e minor has one sharp. What is the relative major of d minor? The answer is F major. Thus, the key of d minor has the same key signature as F major: one flat.

Examples 6–5a and 5b show the various options for finding relative major and minor key areas. We know that the relative minor of a major mode can be found by counting either up a major 6th or down a minor 3rd from the major mode's tonic pitch (6–5a). Similarly, it is possible to locate the relative major key area of any minor mode by counting either down a major 6th *or* up a minor 3rd from the minor mode's tonic pitch (6–5b).

Example 6–5

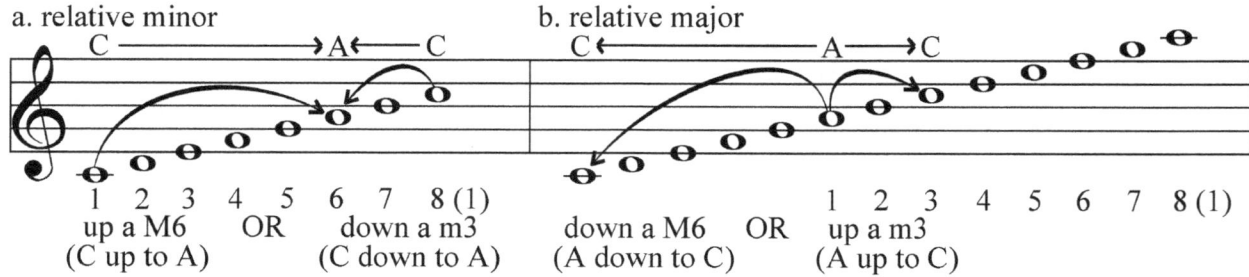

To summarize parallel and relative modal relationships: any two modes that stand in a parallel relationship to one another will share the same tonic pitch and range but have different key signatures. Any two modes that stand in a relative relationship to one another will share the same key signature but have different tonics and different ranges. Scale degree 6 of the major mode is the relative minor key area. Scale degree 3 of the natural minor is the relative major key area.

The Circle of 5ths for Minor

In Chapter 4, we assembled a group of ascending and descending perfect 5ths to form a circle of 5ths for the major mode (see example 4–6 above), a circle that has a sharp side of ascending perfect 5ths and a flat side of descending perfect 5ths. Three of the keys located in the lower portion of the circle (D♭ and C♯, G♭ and F♯, and C♭ and B) constitute enharmonic keys that close the circle of 5ths and bring the sharp and flat sides of major together.

The minor mode also has a circle of 5ths (example 6–6) and it is organized in exactly the same way as the circle of 5ths for the major mode. As with the major mode, the minor mode has fifteen key and scale formations, seven with sharps, seven with flats, and the key of a minor, which has neither sharps nor flats.

On the sharp side of minor, the circle begins with a minor and ascends in perfect 5ths through the keys of e, b, f♯, c♯, g♯, d♯, and a♯, increasing by one the number of sharps for each successive key. Similarly, on the flat side of minor, the circle begins on a minor and descends in perfect 5ths through d, g, c, f, b♭, e♭, and a♭. Three pairs of enharmonic keys located in the lower position of the circle, namely, b♭ and a♯, e♭ and d♯, and a♭ and g♯, close the circle of 5ths and bring the sharp and the flat sides of minor together.

Example 6–6: the sharp and flat sides of minor in the circle of 5ths

70 Chapter 6 The Minor Mode

Example 6–7 places all of the major keys next to the minor keys in order to show the relationship between each pair of relative major and minor modes (uppercase letters represent major keys, while lowercase letters signify minor keys). Notice that moving clockwise two perfect 5ths from a minor and C major brings us to b minor and D major—both of which have two sharps in their key signatures. The relative major of b minor is D major; D major's relative minor is b minor. Proceeding counterclockwise four perfect 5ths from a minor and C major, we arrive at f minor and A♭ major—both of which have four flats in their key signatures. The relative major of f minor is A♭ major; A♭ major's relative minor is f minor.

Example 6–7: the sharp and flats sides of major and minor in the circle of 5ths

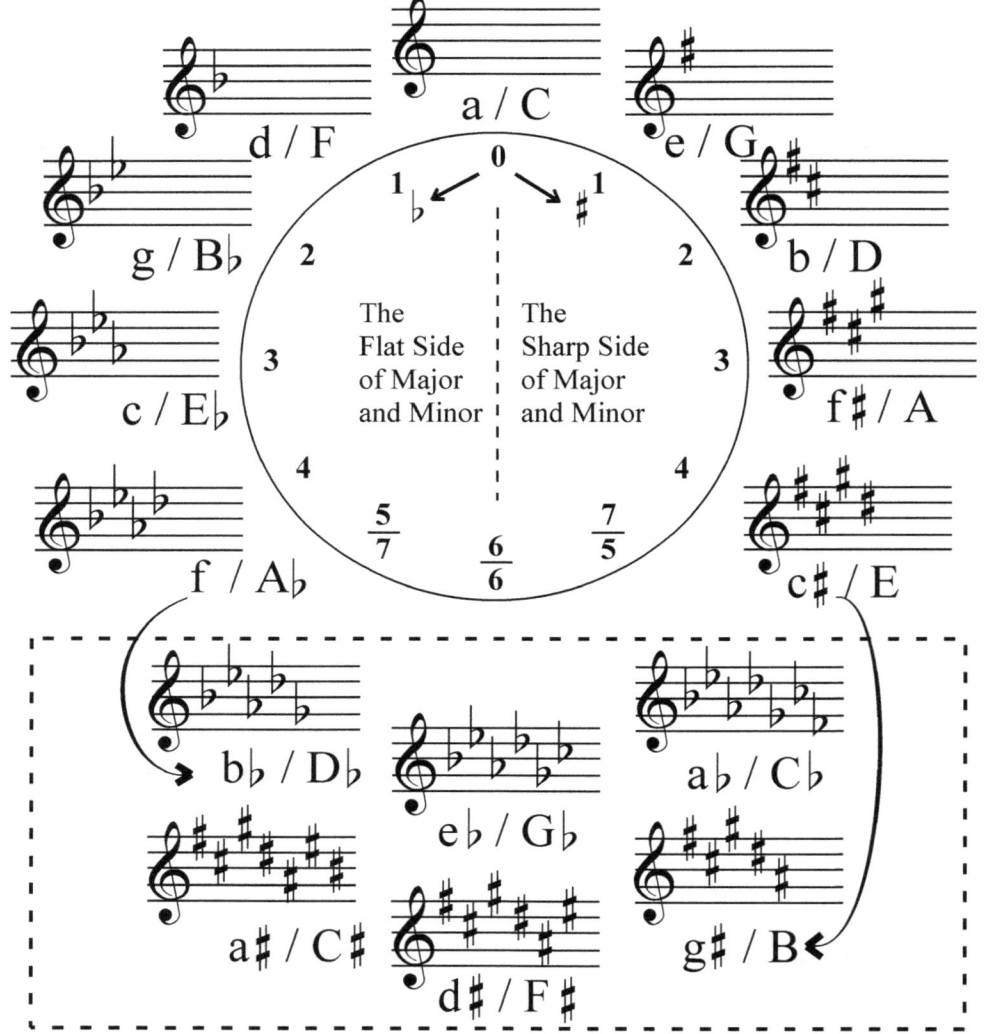

The Harmonic Minor Mode

The harmonic minor and the natural minor are almost identical—except for one *very* important difference. The natural minor employs the subtonic, which is one whole step below the tonic. The harmonic minor, on the other hand, borrows the leading tone from the parallel major; which in effect raises the subtonic by one half step and produces a half step between scale degrees 7 and 8 (examples 6–8a and 8b).

The harmonic minor's use of the leading tone (instead of the natural minor's subtonic scale degree) intensifies the melodic motion upwards to the tonic note. Moreover, the drive upwards by half step from scale degree 7 to scale degree 8 helps to firmly establish the key center. Conversely, the subtonic scale degree lacks the leading tone's compelling drive to move upwards by half step to the tonic; thus, as we have said, the key center is more clearly defined in those modes that employ the leading tone and more difficult to hear in modes that have subtonics, such as the natural minor.

Example 6–8: the harmonic minor and its parallel major

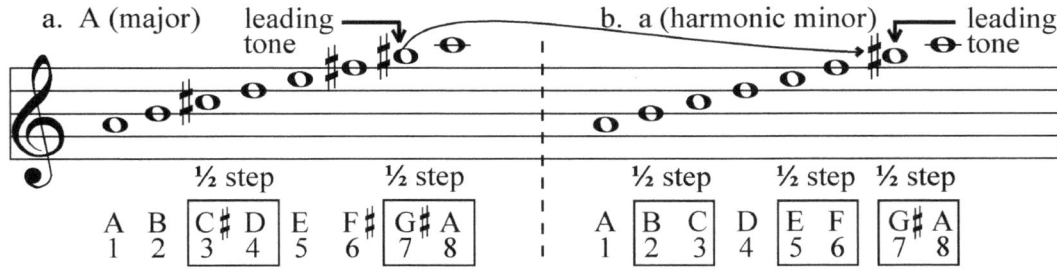

As shown in examples 6–9a and 9b, the harmonic minor retains all of the pitch content of the natural minor *except* for the incorporation of the major mode's leading tone. This one difference, however, produces a very unusual mode and scale. First, the harmonic minor has half steps between scale degrees 2 and 3, scale degrees 5 and 6, and scale degrees 7 and 8—a mode and scale with three pairs of half steps. Secondly, by raising the subtonic one half step to produce a half step approach to scale degree 8, an augmented 2nd (1½ steps) is created between scale degrees 6 and 7. The augmented 2nd is far more difficult to sing than either the major or minor 2nd.

Finally, the leading tone of the harmonic minor is never indicated in the key signature for the minor mode. Notably, both the harmonic minor and the melodic minor (to be discussed below) base their key signatures on the pitch content of the natural minor, despite the fact that both modes have tones that do not occur in the natural minor.

Example 6–9

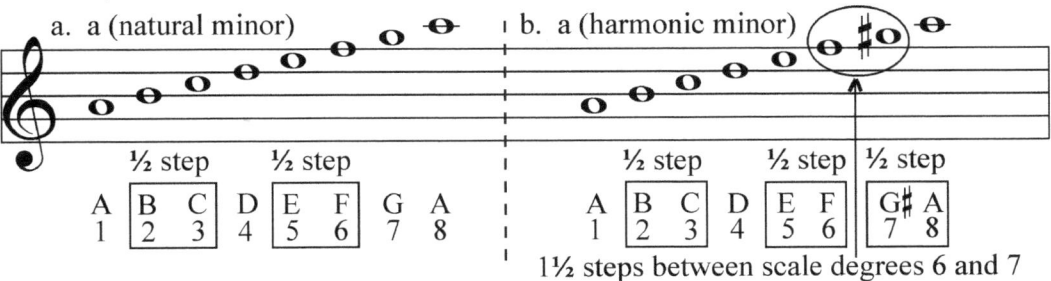

The Melodic Minor Mode

The melodic minor contains elements of the major mode and the natural minor. The melodic minor arises from two important factors:
(1) the inherent tendency of active tones to move to more stable rest tones; and,
(2) the preference of composers to create conjunct (i.e., stepwise) melodic structures that avoid awkward intervals such as the augmented 2nd.

The Ascending Form of the Melodic Minor

When a melody in the harmonic minor moves upwards towards scale degree 8, composers usually raise scale degree 6 by one half step in order to eliminate the augmented 2nd that would otherwise occur between scale degrees 6 and 7 (example 6–10).

Example 6–10

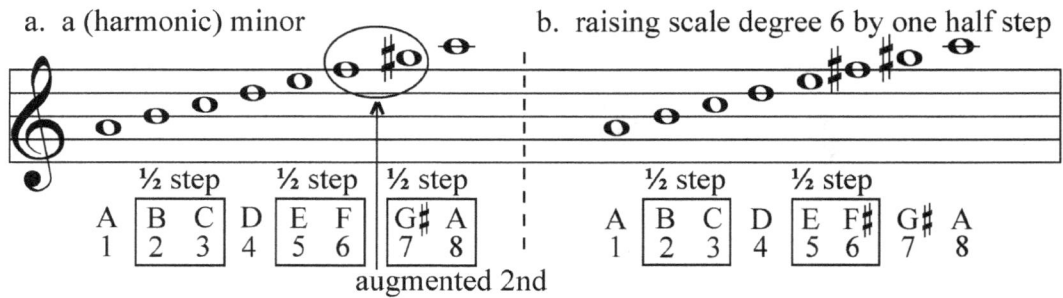

Raising scale degree 6 by one half step to avoid the augmented 2nd of the harmonic minor results in an upper tetrachord with a profile of half steps and whole steps that is identical to the upper tetrachord of the major mode, that is: whole step, whole step, half step (example 6–11). Borrowing the upper tetrachord of the major mode produces what is referred to as the "ascending" form of the melodic minor. Whenever the melodic activity of a composition written in the minor mode moves upwards in the direction of scale degree 8, the ascending form of the melodic minor is usually preferred.

Notice that the key signature for c minor in the second measure of example 6–11 has three flats but that an A♮ (rather than an A♭) is used to avoid the augmented 2nd that would occur in the harmonic minor between scale degrees 6 and 7. Henceforth, we refer to scale degrees 6 and 7 as "raised 6" and "raised 7" when the ascending melodic minor is used. The symbols for raised 6 and raised 7 are ♯6 and ♯7.

Example 6–11: borrowing the upper tetrachord of major to produce the ascending melodic minor

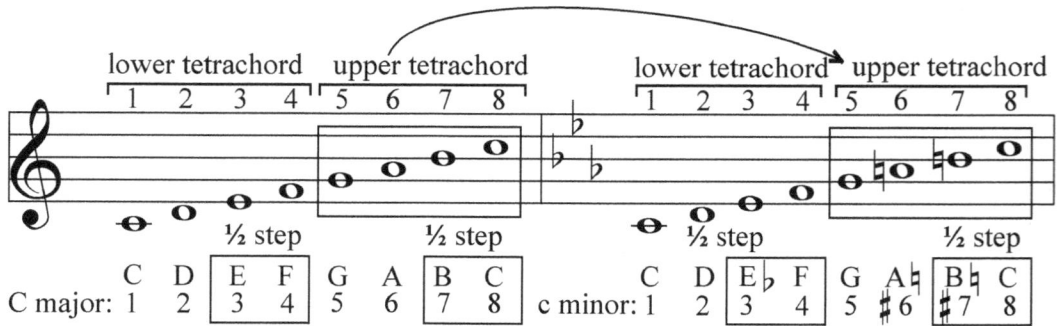

The use of the sharp (♯) in front of the number does not necessarily mean that the pitch itself carries a sharp. Indeed, in 6–11 above, the pitches for ♯6 and ♯7 are A♮ and B♮. (The reason for not referring to the leading tone of the harmonic minor as raised 7 will be explained below.)

It is central to our understanding of the minor mode to recognize that scale degrees ♯6 and ♯7 are not reflected in the minor key signature. If, therefore, a composition is written in a key such as c minor, which has three flats in its key signature (B♭, E♭, and A♭), the music will probably also include an A♮ and/or a B♮, particularly when the melody moves upwards towards scale degree 8. And so, when reading music in the minor mode, it would be well to expect that tones representing scale degrees ♯6 and ♯7 are likely to appear and that their presence will contradict the implied pitch content of the key signature.

The Descending Form of the Melodic Minor

If the minor mode descends towards scale degree 5, scale degrees 6 and 7 are each lowered by one half step from their raised counterparts, scale degrees ♯6 and ♯7. Lowering scale degrees 6 and 7 produces what is called the "descending" melodic minor (example 6–12). We call the lowered forms of scale degrees 6 and 7 "lowered 6" and "lowered 7" to distinguish them from their raised counterparts, scale degrees ♯6 and ♯7. The symbols for lowered 6 and lowered 7 are ♭6 and ♭7. Notably, the pitch content of the descending form of the melodic minor is identical to that of the natural minor.

Let us consider the key of c minor in example 6–12 to see how the process of lowering scale degrees 6 and 7 works. The ascending form of the melodic minor in the key of c minor shows A♮ and B♮ as scale degrees ♯6 and ♯7. But when the c-minor scale moves down in the direction of scale degree 5 (G) in the descending form of the melodic minor, both the A♮ and B♮ are lowered by one half step to A♭ and B♭.

Example 6–12: the ascending and descending forms of the melodic minor

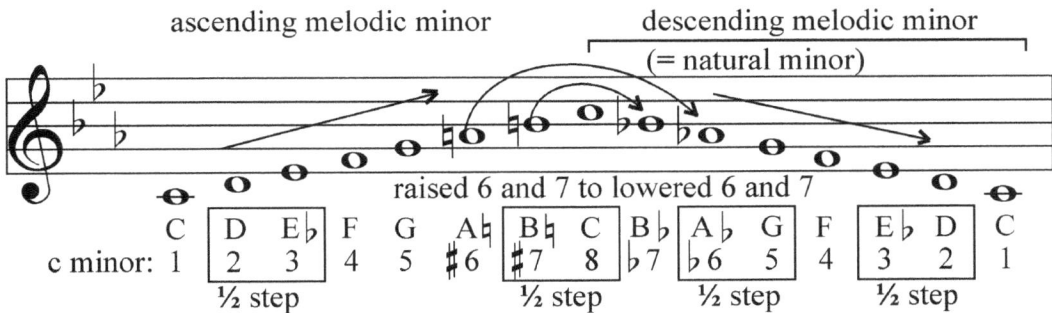

The use of scale degrees ♭6 and ♭7 intensifies the melodic motion downwards to scale degree 5 by creating a half-step approach from scale degree ♭6 to scale degree 5. We term scale degrees 6 and 7 raised or lowered and apply symbols to them (either ♯ or ♭) because on each of these scale degrees, the melodic minor has two different versions of the same letter name. For example, in c minor, scale degrees 6 and 7 may be either A♮ or A♭ and B♮ or B♭, according to whether the tones are either raised or lowered. The sharp or flat in front of the number merely indicates that there are two pitches with the same letter name and that one pitch is either raised or lowered *in relation to the other pitch*.

Having two versions of the same letter name, scale degrees 6 and 7 are *variable* tones in the melodic minor; we therefore refer to scale degrees 6 and 7 as "variable scale degree 6" and "variable scale degree 7." A more complete and specific verbal description of the variable scale degrees in the melodic minor would be as follows: "variable scale degree raised 6," "variable scale degree raised 7," "variable scale degree lowered 6," and "variable scale degree lowered 7."

It is important to understand that the flat (♭) in front of the number 6 and 7 does not necessarily mean that the pitch itself carries a flat. For example, compare the keys of c minor and a minor. In c minor (6–12 above), the lowered variables happen to take flats (A♭ and B♭), whereas in the key of a minor (example 6–13), the lowered variables do not carry flats (F♮ and G♮).

Example 6–13

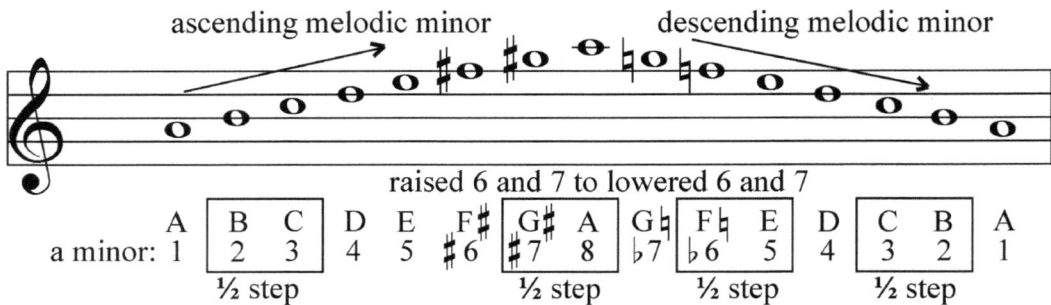

The foregoing examples 6–11, 12, and 13 demonstrate that the sharp or flat in front of the number only means that the variable scale degree is either raised or lowered by one half step; the act of raising or lowering the pitch by one half step could be indicated just as easily with an arrow pointing upwards or downwards in front of the scale degree.

Finding the Variable Scale Degrees of the Melodic Minor

Variables ♯6, ♯7, ♭6, and ♭7 may be located in any key according to the following guidelines:
  (1)   ♭6 is one half step above scale degree 5 (and a minor 6th above scale degree 1).
  (2)   ♭7 is one whole step below scale degree 1 (and a minor 7th above scale degree 1).
  (3)   ♯6 is one whole step above scale degree 5 (and a major 6th above scale degree 1).
  (4)   ♯7 is one half step below scale degree 1 (and a major 7th above scale degree 1).
  (5)   ♭6 and ♭7 are one half step lower than ♯6 and ♯7.
  (6)   ♯6 and ♯7 are one half step higher than ♭6 and ♭7.
  (7)   ♯6 and ♯7 are *never* included in the key signature of the minor mode.
  (8)   ♭6 and ♭7 are *always* included in the key signature of the minor mode.
  (9)   ♯6 and ♯7 correspond to scale degrees 6 and 7 of the parallel major mode.
  (10) The pitch content of the descending melodic minor is exactly the same as the natural minor.
  (11) Since ♯6 and ♯7 of the melodic minor correspond to scale degrees 6 and 7 of the parallel major mode, ♯6 and ♯7 can be found easily if you know the key signature of that minor key's parallel major mode. For example: what are variables ♯6 and ♯7 in the key and mode of a minor?
     (a) The parallel major of a minor is A major, which has three sharps (F♯, C♯, and G♯).
     (b) Scale degrees 6 and 7 in A major are F♯ and G♯.
     (c) Therefore, variables ♯6 and ♯7 in the key and mode of a minor are also F♯ and G♯.

Comparing the Three Forms of Minor

The key signature of all three forms of the minor mode is derived from the pitch content of the natural minor (again, despite the fact that both the harmonic minor and the melodic minor have tones that do not occur in the natural minor).

In the natural minor, the harmonic minor, and the melodic minor, scale degrees 1, 2, 3, 4, and 5 are all invariable tones with one pitch name only for each mode's five respective scale degrees. For all three forms of minor, the profile of half steps and whole steps from scale degrees 1 to 5 is the same; therefore, all three forms of minor have the same pitch content for their invariable tones.

With respect to the melodic minor, if all of its pitch content is taken into account, then strictly speaking, the mode is not a seven-tone diatonic scale. On the other hand, the harmonic minor is diatonic to the extent that it has one pitch name only for each of its seven scale degrees; as a consequence, the term leading tone is sufficient to describe its scale degree 7. Since the harmonic minor does not have a lowered 7 scale degree, there is no need to refer to the leading tone as raised 7.

Example 6–14 shows all three forms of minor together in order to facilitate comparison; additionally, each mode appears untransposed in the key of a minor and then transposed to the key of c minor. Attaching the accidentals directly to the notes rather than using key signatures underscores both the differences and the similarities between the three forms.

Example 6–14

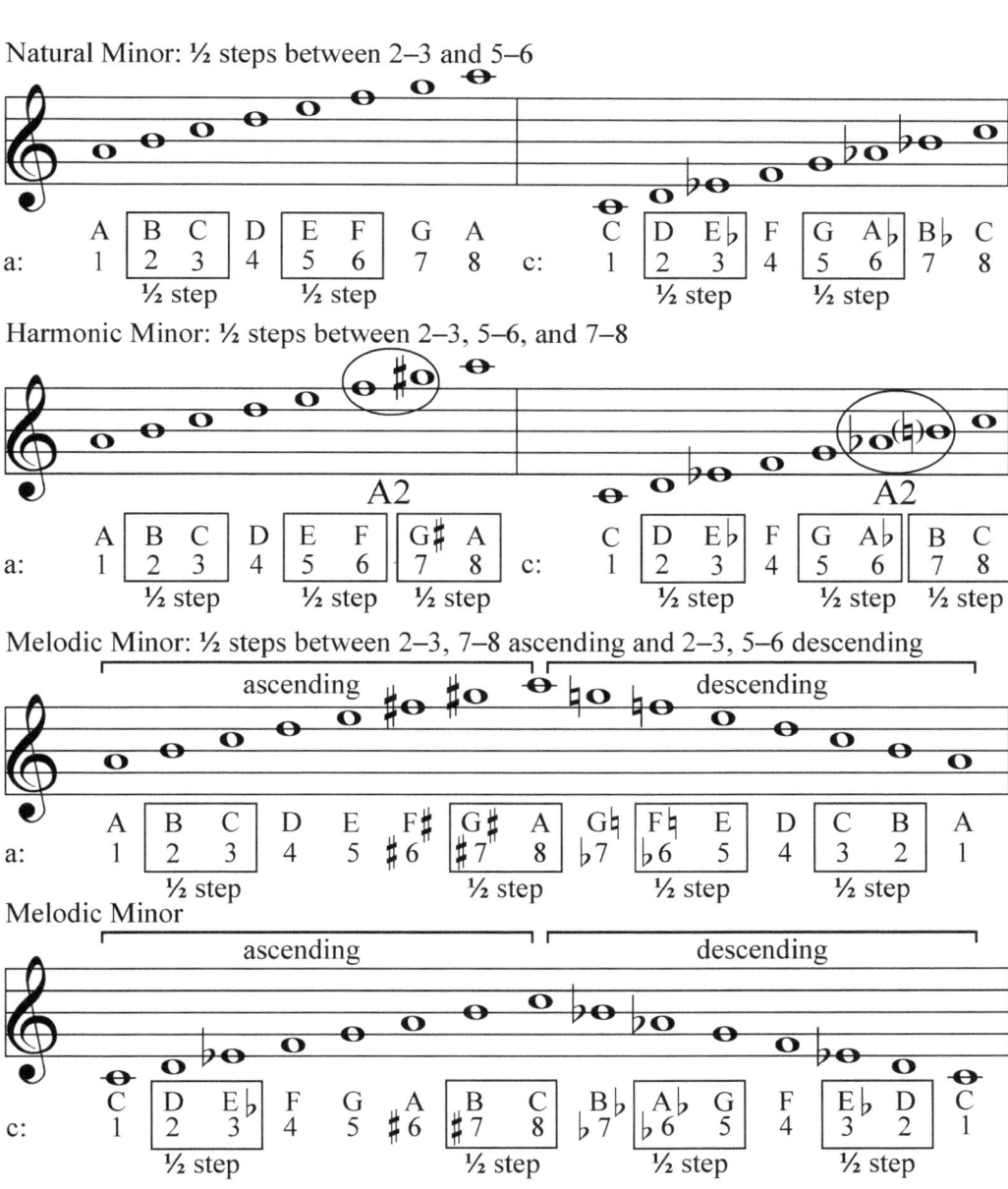

A comparison of the three forms of minor shown above in 6–14 reveals that the natural minor and the harmonic minor do not share all of the same pitches and that the melodic minor contains all of the pitches found in both the natural minor and the harmonic minor. Since the pitch content of the melodic minor exceeds that of the natural and harmonic forms of minor and therefore presents the most complete inventory of pitches, we shall prefer the melodic minor for the purpose of demonstrating the formation of triads in Chapter 7.

Chapter 7 Triads

Since the ninth century of the Common Era in Western Europe, music makers have combined two or more musical tones together, creating sounds that are either pleasing or displeasing to the ear. The perception of what constitutes a good or bad combination of musical tones at any point in history changes over time. Moreover, the many diverse cultures of the world do not necessarily share the same musical values and therefore may have different opinions and beliefs regarding the qualities of musical sounds.

For example, someone accustomed to listening to the music of the Western European tradition might have difficulty appreciating the performance of *ganga* songs found in the mountainous regions of Bosnia and Herzegovina, which exhibit close combinations of tones, particularly the interval of the 2nd. The performers of *ganga* songs consider the sounds of 2nds to be pleasing to the ear; conversely, we in the West are more accustomed to the perceived richness of 3rds.

In Chapter 5, we learned that when two pitches occur simultaneously, the resulting sound is a harmonic interval. Any time two or more pitches occur simultaneously, it produces an effect known as **harmony**. When three or more *different* pitches sound simultaneously, the resulting harmony is called a **chord**.

Examples 7–1a, 1b, and 1c demonstrate three forms of harmony that assume chord status; in each instance, the chord has five different pitches and at least four intervals. The first type of chord, shown in 7–1a, is **secundal**; a secundal chord results from a combination of major and/or minor 2nds. (Although secundal harmonies must contain major and/or minor 2nds, they may also have 3rds.) Example 7–1b illustrates **quartal** harmony, a chord formation consisting of 4th intervals.

The most common harmonic construction to appear in the music of the Western European tradition and the one with which we are concerned here is **tertian** harmony. As illustrated in 7–1c, tertian chords have two or more superimposed 3rds. When notated on the staff, secundal and quartal harmonies involve a combination of spaces and lines. On the other hand, tertian harmonies (when positioned in a close structure on a single staff) are placed on either spaces or lines, rather than a combination of both. The tertian harmony in 7–1c displays intervals of the 3rd, 5th, 7th, and 9th above the lowest pitch of the chord; so constructed, we have a chord of the ninth, or ninth chord (C E G B D). Removing the ninth produces a chord of the seventh, or seventh chord (C E G B).

Example 7–1

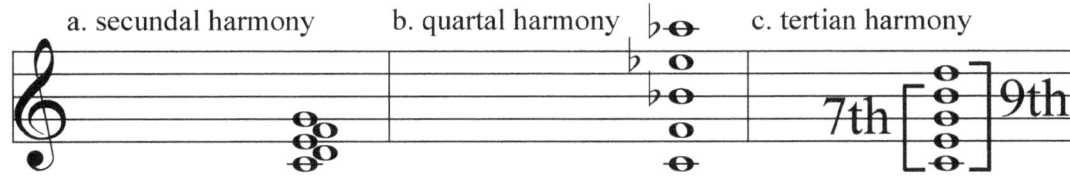

The pitches of a chord may be performed either simultaneously or in succession. A chord given a simultaneous performance of its pitches is called a **block chord** (example 7–2a). Successive presentation of some or all of a chord's pitches is described variously as **arpeggio**, **arpeggiated chord**, or **broken chord** (7–2b).

Example 7–2

Tertian harmony has been an important component of Western music for more than five hundred years. As early as the fifteenth century, people in Western Europe began to have a decided preference for the interval of the 3rd and its inversion, the 6th. Today, chords built from the interval of the 3rd are still favored in nearly every style of music in the Western world.

When a tertian harmony consists of three different pitches and two intervals of the 3rd, the chord is referred to as a triad. The triad in example 7–3 contains the pitches C, E, and G and has two 3rds formed above C, the lowest pitch of the musical texture and the foundation of the chord.

Example 7–3: the triad

The lowest pitch upon which the other two pitches of the triad are built is called the root. In example 7–4, C is identified as the root of the triad (R). The remaining tones of the triad, E and G, are known as the third (3) and the fifth (5) because they are located at the intervals of a 3rd and a 5th above the root. The triad in 7–4 is said to be in **root position** because the root is positioned as the lowest pitch of the musical texture.

Example 7–4: the components of the triad

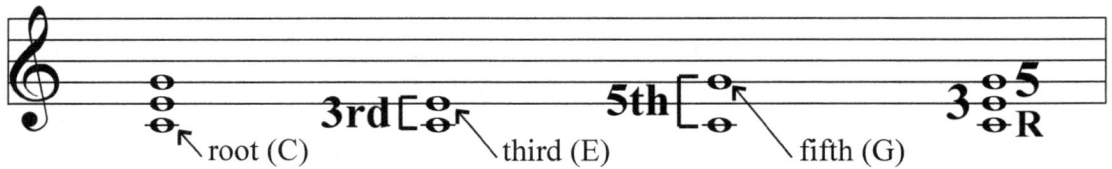

The triad derives its name from the root. For example, if the triad is built on the subdominant scale degree of the major mode (scale degree 4), then the chord would be termed the subdominant triad. Since there are seven tones in a major key and scale, it is possible to build a triad on each of these seven tones. Example 7–5 shows how each of the root-position triads occurring in C major receives the name of the scale degree with which it is associated.

Example 7–5: root-position triads in the key of C major

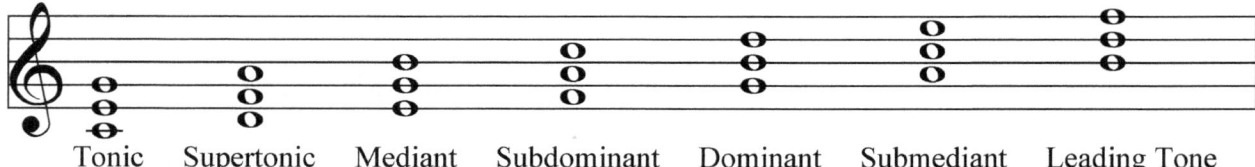

The root-position triads exhibited in 7–5 fall into two groups based upon their respective locations on either the lines or the spaces of the staff: triads of the tonic, mediant, dominant, and leading tone on the one hand and those of the supertonic, subdominant, and submediant on the other. When triads from either group are formed above each tone of the major scale, their placement on the staff is determined by the position of the tonic note on the staff.

If the tonic note begins on a line, then the first group of triads (tonic, mediant, dominant, and leading tone) uses lines, the second group (supertonic, subdominant, and submediant) spaces. Thus, with C4 as the starting note of the major mode (see example 7–5 above), the tonic, mediant, dominant, and leading-tone triads occupy lines on the staff, whereas the supertonic, subdominant, and submediant triads are placed on spaces. Starting the tonic one octave lower on C3 (a space) would put the first group on spaces and the second group on lines.

In example 7–6, the C-major scale is transposed to D major. All of the pitches that make up the triads are diatonic elements of the key and mode and therefore include the addition of F♯ and C♯. With D4 as the starting note of the scale, the tonic, mediant, dominant, and leading-tone triads occur on spaces instead of lines, whereas the supertonic, subdominant, and submediant triads utilize the lines of the staff instead of spaces. Starting the tonic one octave lower on D3 (a line) would put the first group on lines and the second group on spaces.

Example 7–6: root-position triads in the key of D major

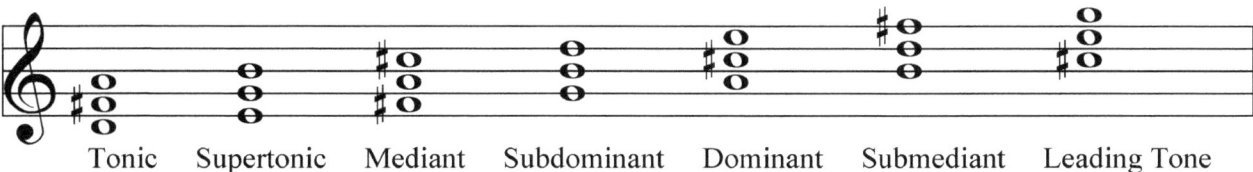

Tonic   Supertonic   Mediant   Subdominant   Dominant   Submediant   Leading Tone

Triad Quality

Triads, like intervals, may be classified according to their quality. There are four types of triad qualities: the **major triad** (MT), the **minor triad** (mt), the **diminished triad** (d°t), and the **augmented triad** (A+T). The quality of a triad is based upon the intervallic distance between the root and the third, the third and the fifth, and the root and the fifth.

Example 7–7 illustrates the configuration of intervals for the four triad qualities, all of which share the common tone C as the root. R – 3 represents the distance from the root to the third, 3 – 5 the distance from the third to the fifth, and R – 5 the distance from the root to the fifth. The superscript circle in the chord symbol d°t is a conventional sign for indicating diminished quality; it can be used with diminished chords and with diminished intervals (e.g., 5° or °5 = diminished 5th). The plus sign in the A+T chord symbol is the traditional designation for showing augmented quality; it appears in connection with augmented chords and with augmented intervals (e.g., 5+ or +5 = augmented 5th).

Example 7–7: the configuration of intervals for the four triad qualities rooted on C

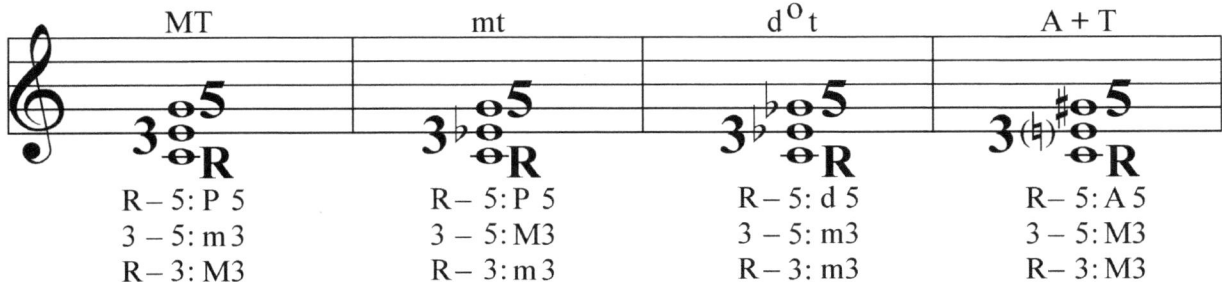

MT	mt	d°t	A+T
R – 5: P 5	R – 5: P 5	R – 5: d 5	R – 5: A 5
3 – 5: m 3	3 – 5: M 3	3 – 5: m 3	3 – 5: M 3
R – 3: M 3	R – 3: m 3	R – 3: m 3	R – 3: M 3

The major triad in example 7–8a contains a major 3rd from the root to the third (C to E) and a minor 3rd from the third to the fifth (E to G). Additionally, the chord has a perfect 5th from the root to the fifth (C to G). The minor triad, shown in 7–8b, has a minor 3rd from the root to the third (C to E♭), a major 3rd from the third to the fifth (E♭ to G), and a perfect 5th from the root to the fifth (C to G).

Although both major and minor triads are made up of a combination of major 3rds and minor 3rds, the internal configuration of 3rds in the minor triad is the reverse of that of the major triad. The ordering of thirds up from the root of the major triad is: M3/m3. The ordering of thirds up from the root of the minor triad is: m3/M3.

The pitch that represents the third of the minor triad is one half step lower than the corresponding third of the major triad with the same root. Accordingly, changing the major triad C E G into a minor triad requires lowering the third of the major triad one half step, from E to E♭: C E♭ G. Conversely, changing the minor triad C E♭ G into a major triad involves raising the third of the minor triad one half step from E♭ to E(♮): C E G.

Example 7–8: root-position major and minor triads

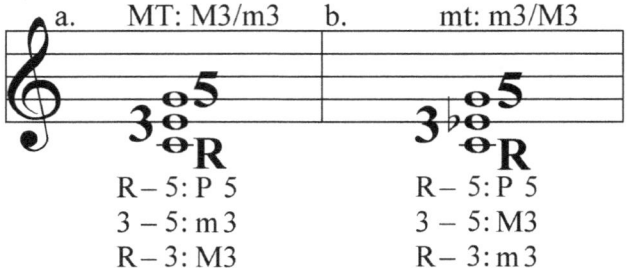

The diminished triad in example 7–9a bears a similarity to the minor triad in 7–9b in that it has a minor 3rd from the root to the third (C to E♭). Instead of having a perfect 5th from the root to the fifth, however, the diminished triad has a diminished 5th from the root to the fifth (C to G♭). From the third to the fifth, the diminished triad has a minor 3rd (E♭ to G♭). Thus, the ordering of thirds up from the root of the diminished triad is: m3/m3.

One way to build a diminished triad up from any given tone is to first construct a minor triad and then lower the fifth of the chord one half step. Remember, lowering the top note of a perfect 5th one half step produces a diminished 5th. For example, changing the minor triad C E♭ G into a diminished triad involves lowering the fifth of the minor triad one half step, from G to G♭: C E♭ G♭. Changing the diminished triad C E♭ G♭ into a minor triad necessitates raising the fifth of the diminished triad one half step from G♭ to G(♮): C E♭ G. (Musicians with either a commercial or jazz background often interpret the diminished triad as a minor triad with a lowered fifth.)

Example 7–9: root-position diminished and minor triads

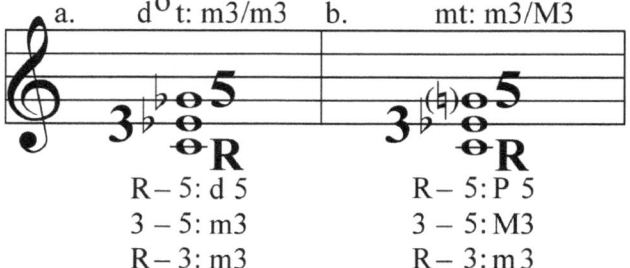

The augmented triad in example 7–10a, like the major triad shown in 7–10b, has a major 3rd from the root to the third (C to E). The distance from the root to the fifth of the augmented triad, however, is an augmented 5th (C to G♯), exceeding by one half step the perfect 5ths of the major and minor triads. From the third to the fifth, the augmented triad has a major third (E to G♯). The ordering of the thirds up from the root of the augmented triad is: M3/M3.

One way to construct an augmented triad up from any given tone is to form a major triad and then raise the fifth of the chord one half step to change the perfect 5th into an augmented 5th. Thus, changing the major triad C E G into an augmented triad requires raising the fifth of the major triad one half step, from G to G♯: C E G♯. Reversing the procedure by lowering the fifth of the augmented triad one half step from G♯ to G (♮) turns the chord into a major triad: C E G.

Example 7–10: root-position augmented and major triads

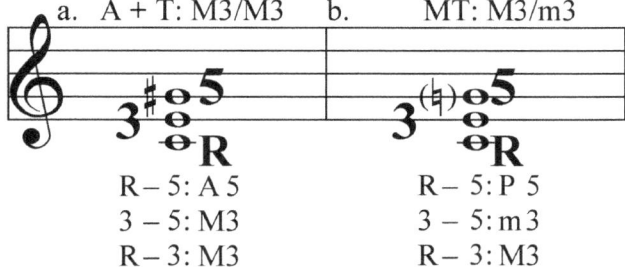

Triad Qualities In Major

In example 7–11, we return to the root-position triads constructed above each of the seven scale degrees of C major and identify the combinations of intervals in each chord. In C major, the major triad appears on the tonic (C E G), the subdominant (F A C), and the dominant (G B D), whereas the minor triad resides in the supertonic (D F A), the mediant (E G B), and the submediant (A C E). The diminished triad occurs in the leading tone (B D F).

Notice that the diatonic pitch content of C major cannot support the formation of the augmented triad; therefore, the augmented triad cannot exist in any transposition of C major. Later in this chapter, however, we shall see that the augmented triad can be formed in the minor mode.

Example 7–11: triad qualities in C major

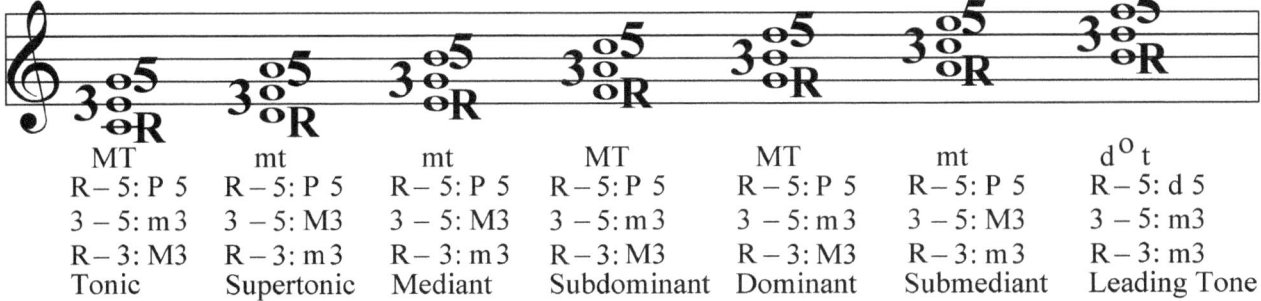

Inverting the Major Triad

Triads are created from combinations of intervals, intervals of the 3rd in particular. The 3rd can be transformed into the interval of the 6th by placing the bottom note of the 3rd one octave higher (example 7–12a) or by moving the top note of the 3rd one octave lower (7–12b).

Example 7–12: inverting the interval of the 3rd

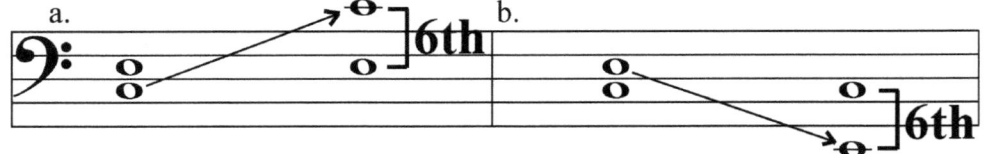

Example 7–13 shows how interval inversion changes the structure of the major triad in root position. Again, the two pitches of the triad standing above the root are referred to respectively as the third and the fifth because they are located at the intervals of a 3rd and a 5th above the root. In root position, *the bottom note of the interval of the 5th indicates the location of the root.*

Example 7–13a presents an alternative description for the intervallic structure of the root-position triad, designating the chord in "$\frac{5}{3}$ position." The Arabic numbers indicate the placement of certain intervals and pitches (in this case, E and G) above the lowest note of the musical texture (C); the numbers are referred to as **figured bass** ("figuring" means counting the intervals and pitches up from the bass note).

In 7–13b, the **first inversion** of the major triad is displayed. Shifting the root of the major triad into the next higher octave leaves the third of the chord (E) as the bass pitch. The figured bass for the first inversion of the triad is $\frac{6}{3}$, which means that the intervals of a 3rd (E to G) and a 6th (E to C) occur above the lowest note (E).

Example 7–13c illustrates the **second inversion** of the major triad. Moving the third component of the first-inversion triad up one octave leaves the fifth of the chord (G) in the bass. The figured bass for the second inversion of the triad is $\frac{6}{4}$, which means that the intervals of a 4th (G to C) and a 6th (G to E) occur above the lowest note (G).

The process of interval inversion alters the configuration of the triad by setting the root above the fifth. Inverting the triad transforms the interval of the 5th between the root and the fifth into the interval of the 4th from the fifth up to the root. Therefore, *when the triad inverts, the upper note of the 4th indicates the location of the root.* If the root is above the third and the fifth (third, fifth, root), then the chord is in $\frac{6}{3}$ position (7–13b). If, however, the root is in the middle (fifth, root, third), then the chord is in $\frac{6}{4}$ position (7–13c).

Example 7–13: the major triad in root position, first inversion, and second inversion

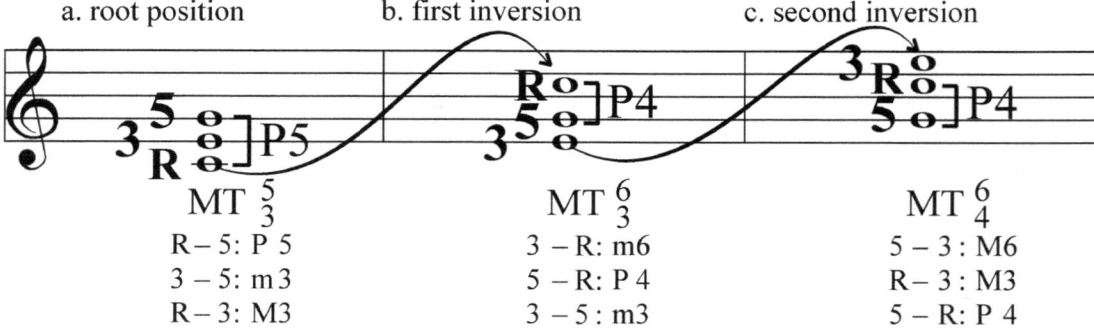

Before considering the inversions of minor, diminished, and augmented triads, let us compare the intervals that comprise the major triad in its root position, first inversion, and second inversion. We know that in root position (7–13a), the major triad has a major 3rd from the root to the third, a minor 3rd from the third to the fifth, and a perfect 5th from the root to the fifth.

In first inversion (7–13b), the perfect 5th from the root up to the fifth (C to G) is transformed into a perfect 4th from the fifth up to the root (G to C). The minor 3rd between the third and the fifth (E to G) remains unchanged from the root position because the two elements of the chord have not been inverted. However, the relationship between the root and the third does change, as the first inversion places the root above the third. The major 3rd between the root and the third (C to E) becomes a minor 6th between the third and the root (E to C).

In second inversion (7–13c), the fifth up to the root is, once again, a perfect 4th (G to C). A major 3rd remains between the root and the third (C to E). The fifth up to the third is a major 6th (G to E).

Inverting the Minor Triad

Earlier in this chapter, we said that the only difference between a major triad and a minor triad with the same root is the middle component of each respective chord, the third. In the minor triad, the third is one half step lower than the corresponding third of the major triad. Raising the third of the minor triad by one half step produces a major triad.

As shown in example 7–14a, the minor triad in root position has a perfect 5th between the root and the fifth (C to G). In first inversion (7–14b), a perfect 4th spans the distance from the fifth up to the root (G to C). The major 3rd between the third and the fifth (E♭ to G) remains unchanged from the root position because the interval has not been inverted. On the other hand, first inversion changes the relationship between the root and the third by placing the root above the third, leaving the latter element of the chord as the lowest note of the texture (E♭). The minor 3rd between the root and the third (C to E♭) becomes a major 6th between the third and the root (E♭ to C).

In second inversion, we find the root situated above the fifth of the chord (7–14c). As with the first inversion, the distance from the fifth up to the root constitutes a perfect 4th (G to C). The interval between the root and the third (C to E♭) remains a minor 3rd because the two elements of the chord have not been inverted. The fifth up to the third is a minor 6th (G to E♭).

Example 7–14: the minor triad in root position, first inversion, and second inversion

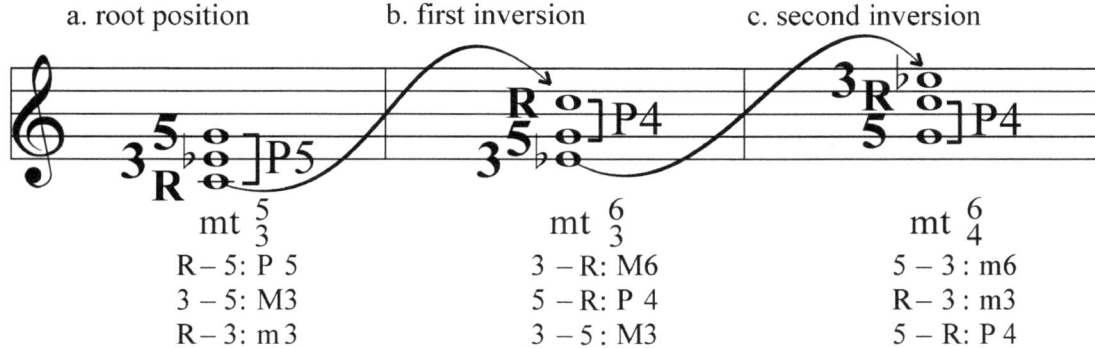

Inverting the Diminished Triad

The diminished triad (example 7–15a) has a diminished 5th between the root and the fifth (C to G♭). When the diminished triad inverts (examples 7–15b and 15c), the diminished 5th becomes an augmented 4th, as the root is placed above the fifth (G♭ to C). Two minor 3rds comprise the structure of the chord in root position. A minor 3rd occurs between the root and the third (C to E♭) and between the third and the fifth (E♭ to G♭).

In first inversion (7–15b), the third and the fifth retain their original relationship (a minor 3rd). The relationship between the root and the third, however, changes. Here, the root appears as an inverted tone above the third, producing a major 6th between the two elements of the chord (E♭ to C).

In second inversion (7–15c), the distance between the root and the third remains the same as it was in root position, a minor 3rd. The fifth up to the third is a major 6th (G♭ to E♭).

Example 7–15: the diminished triad in root position, first inversion, and second inversion

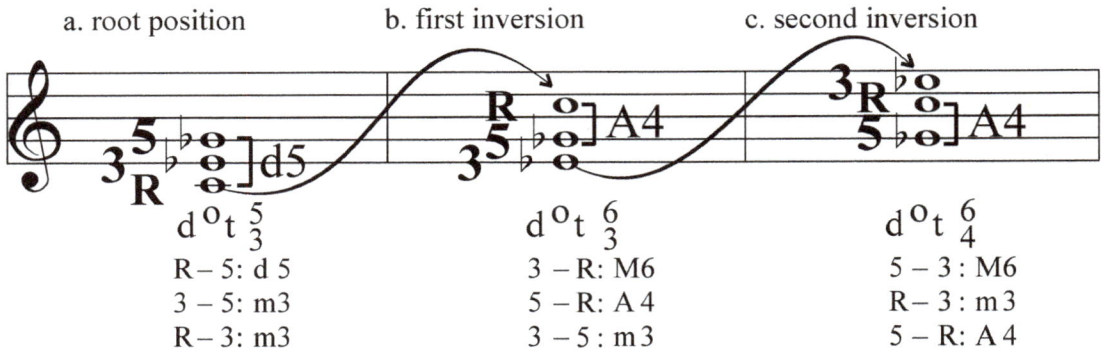

As indicated in examples 7–13, 14, and 15 above, when major, minor, and diminished triads invert, the root is situated above the fifth at the interval of the 4th. The inversions of these triads can be heard by locating the root as the upper note of the 4th among the three elements of the chord. Finding the position of the root within the texture tells us whether the third or fifth is in the bass. If the triad is inverted, do we hear the order of tones from the lowest to the highest pitch as third, fifth, and root (first inversion) or as fifth, root, and third (second inversion)?

Hearing the augmented triad as an inverted chord is impractical; for its unique combination of major 3rds projects the sound of a triad in root position, regardless of how the chord is written.

Inverting the Augmented Triad

Example 7–16 shows the augmented triad in root position, first inversion, and second inversion. In 7–16a, which illustrates the root position of the chord, we have two major 3rds, one between the root and the third (C to E) and the other between the third and the fifth (E to G♯). When the augmented triad inverts, as demonstrated in examples 7–16b and 16c, the root is placed above the fifth, changing the augmented 5th between the root and the fifth (C to G♯) into a diminished 4th (G♯ to C).

Example 7–16: the augmented triad in root position, first inversion, and second inversion

a. root position   b. first inversion   c. second inversion

$A^+T\,^5_3$ $A^+T\,^6_3$ $A^+T\,^6_4$

R – 5: A 5   3 – R: m 6   5 – 3 : m 6
3 – 5: M3   5 – R: d 4   R – 3 : M3
R – 3: M3   3 – 5 : M3   5 – R: d 4

    It should be understood that the diminished 4th between the fifth and the root of the augmented triad exists only within the *written context* of the chord because the *sound* of the diminished 4th is identical to that of another interval, the major 3rd. Therefore, the diminished 4th should be referred to properly as a **contextual interval**.

    Although the diminished 4th and the major 3rd are both identifiable within the written context, the major 3rd may also be classified as an **acoustic interval** because it has only one aural interpretation—the major 3rd cannot be heard as a diminished 4th. The acoustical major 3rd from the fifth up to the root gives the augmented triad a neutral-sounding profile that precludes hearing the chord as an inverted structure. Regardless of its written position, the augmented triad sounds like two superimposed major 3rds.

    In first inversion (7–16b), the third and the fifth (E to G♯) retain their original configuration (a major 3rd). The relationship between the root and third, however, changes. Since the inversion of the chord places the root above the third, the distance from the third up to the root is now a minor 6th (E to C). The diminished 4th from the fifth up to the root, G♯ to C, is enharmonically equivalent to the acoustical major 3rd, A♭ to C. With the diminished 4th producing the sound of a major 3rd from the fifth up to the root, the first inversion is heard as an augmented triad in root position, F♭ A♭ C (or perhaps E G♯ B♯), instead of as an inverted chord consisting of E G♯ C.

    In second inversion (7–16c), the distance between the root and the third remains a major third (C to E). Since the second inversion finds the third above the fifth, the interval from the fifth up to the third becomes a minor 6th (G♯ to E). With the diminished 4th producing the sound of a major 3rd from the fifth up to the root, the second inversion is heard as an augmented triad in root position, A♭ C E, rather than as an inverted chord consisting of G♯ C E.

Triad Qualities in Minor

As we have said, the augmented triad cannot be formed in the major mode, nor can it appear in the natural minor. All four qualities of the triad do occur, however, in the other two forms of minor: the harmonic minor and the melodic minor. Since the melodic minor has the most complete inventory of pitches of all three forms of minor, we use the melodic minor to demonstrate the formation of triads in the minor mode.

    Before constructing triads in the minor mode, let us review the pitch content and half-step profile of the melodic minor in the key of C, as presented in example 7–17. Remember that the symbols ♯6 and ♯7 indicate the raised variable scale degrees of the ascending melodic minor and that ♭6 and ♭7 represent the lowered variable scale degrees of the descending melodic minor.

Example 7–17

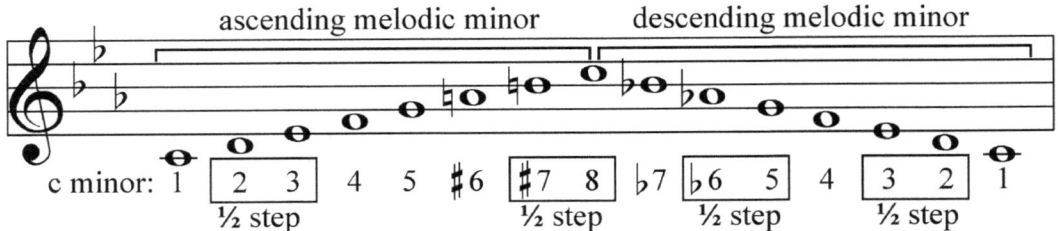

Example 7–18 shows the triads that occur in the ascending melodic minor. With the exception of the tonic triad (C E♭ G), all of the triads in the ascending melodic minor have either variable ♯6 or variable ♯7 within their chord structures. The filled-in note heads in 7–18 designate the variable scale degrees as the root, third, or fifth of the triad.

Using ♯6 (A) as the fifth of the chord, a minor triad (D F A) is formed in the supertonic area. An augmented triad (E♭ G B) occurs in the mediant, with ♯7 (B) as the fifth of the chord. Variables ♯6 and ♯7 appear as third components of two major triads: the subdominant (F A C) and the dominant (G B D). Variables ♯6 and ♯7 constitute the roots of two diminished triads: the submediant (A C E♭) and the leading tone (B D F).

Example 7–18: ascending melodic minor

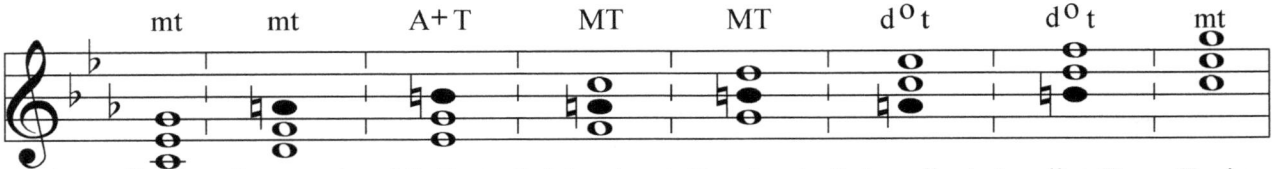

On the descending side of the melodic minor, as displayed in example 7–19, variable ♭7 (B♭) serves as the root of the major triad in the subtonic (B♭ D F) and as the fifth of the major triad in the mediant (E♭ G B♭); variable ♭6 (A♭) forms the root of the major triad in the submediant (A♭ C E♭). Excluding the tonic triad (C E♭ G), the descending melodic minor has two other minor triads, both of which contain a variable scale degree as an element of their chord structures. Variable ♭7 appears as the third of the minor dominant triad (G B♭ D); variable ♭6 constitutes the third of the minor subdominant triad (F A♭ C). Finally, variable ♭6 occurs as the fifth of the diminished supertonic triad (D F A♭).

Example 7–19: descending melodic minor

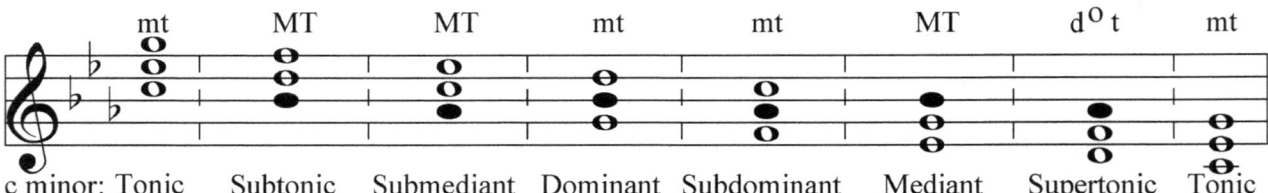

Example 7–20 incorporates elements of both the ascending and descending forms of the melodic minor into a single ascending scale that projects various chord qualities in each of its seven scale degree areas for a total of thirteen triads. Comparing the number and qualities of triads available in the melodic minor with the triad content of both the natural minor and the harmonic minor, as presented in examples 7–21 and 22, we can see that the melodic minor yields a much richer vocabulary of chords than either the natural minor or harmonic minor.

Example 7–20: the thirteen triads of the melodic minor

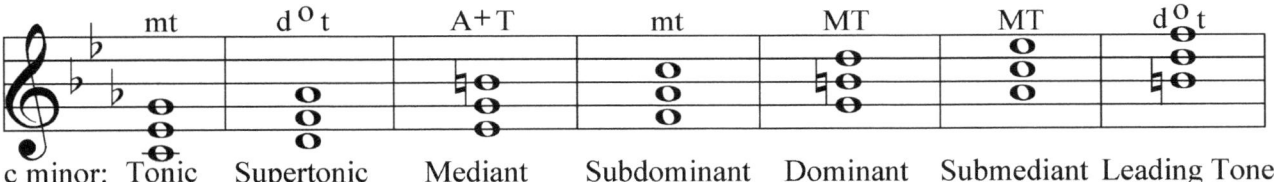

Example 7–21: the seven triads of the natural minor

Example 7–22: the seven triads of the harmonic minor

Roman Numeral Chord Symbols

In Chapter 3, we learned that each note of the scale and mode can be referred to as a scale degree and assigned a number according to its position within the scale in relation to the tonic pitch, with the tonic identified as scale degree 1. Additionally, each scale degree has one of the following names: tonic, supertonic, mediant, subdominant, dominant, submediant, and leading tone. When scale degree 7 is located one whole step below the tonic note, as in the natural minor, we use the term subtonic to distinguish it from the leading tone of the major mode, the harmonic minor, and the ascending form of the melodic minor. The subtonic lacks the compelling drive to move upwards by half step to scale degree 8, the tonic.

Ultimately, the numbers and names that represent the scale degrees of the mode constitute an important means for providing information about music; as such, the numbers and names are referential, serving as symbols for communication between those who create music and those who listen to and/or study it. Another method for providing information about music designates Roman numerals for the chords that can be formed on each scale degree of the mode; in other words, it is possible to represent each chord, or triad, with a Roman numeral according to the scale degree on which its root occurs. A longstanding convention of Roman numeral chord symbols maintains the following two practices:

(1) if the chord, or triad, has a major 3rd between the root and its third, then the Roman numeral is expressed in uppercase (e.g., major and augmented triads);

(2) if the chord, or triad, has a minor 3rd between the root and its third, then the Roman numeral is expressed in lowercase (e.g., minor and diminished triads).

Both practices cited here are related to the use of the uppercase for major and augmented intervals and the lowercase for minor and diminished intervals. The two practices also correspond to the designation of major modes with uppercase letters and minor modes with lowercase letters.

In addition to using uppercase and lowercase Roman numerals to distinguish major and augmented triads from minor and diminished triads, augmented triads are further identified with a plus sign (+), diminished triads with a superscript circle (°). As stated earlier, the plus sign is the traditional designation for showing augmented quality, while the superscript circle is a conventional sign for indicating diminished quality.

Example 7–23 presents the Roman numeral chord symbols for the triads that occur in the major mode. The three major triads are indicated as I, IV, and V, the minor triads as ii, iii, and vi, and the diminished triad as vii°. When triads in the major mode invert, chord symbols and figured bass are combined. It is not necessary to attach figured bass to the chord symbol of a root-position triad. For a triad in $^6_3$ position, the 3 under the 6 is omitted. With the $^6_4$ position, however, the 4 below the 6 cannot be removed because the absence of the 4 would render the figured bass for the first and second inversions indistinguishable. Chord symbols for inverted triads with figured bass include: vii$^{°6}$, V$^6_4$, I^6, vi$^6_4$, iii^6, ii$^6_4$, IV$^6_4$, V^6, I$^6_4$, vi^6, ii^6, iii$^6_4$, IV^6. (For a complete study of triad inversions, see my *Finding The Right Pitch: A Guide To The Study of Music Fundamentals, Or An Introduction To Music Theory*.)

Example 7–23

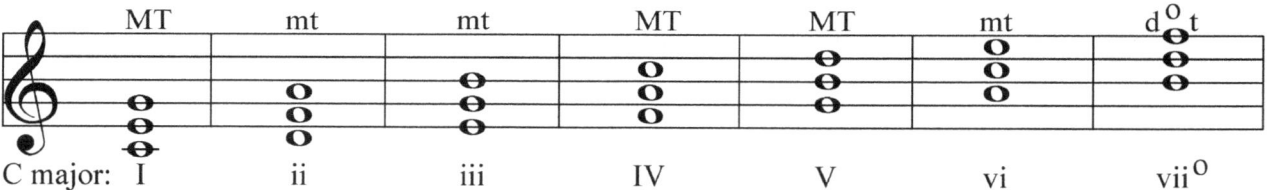

C major: I   ii   iii   IV   V   vi   vii°

Notice that scale degree 3 in C major stands one *major* 3rd above the tonic pitch and that the quality of the mediant triad formed above scale degree 3 is minor (E G B). Conversely, the intervallic relationship between scale degree 3 and the tonic pitch in c minor, as shown in example 7–24 below, is that of a *minor* 3rd. Moreover, the quality of the mediant triad in the minor mode presents two possibilities: major and augmented. Finding the right pitch upon which the mediant triad is formed in the major mode and in the minor mode and distinguishing between the respective qualities of the chord in both modes counts among the most difficult challenges confronting the student of music fundamentals.

Mastering the triadic content of the melodic minor constitutes a formidable challenge indeed, as it has a much richer vocabulary of chords than either the major mode, the natural minor, or the harmonic minor (compare examples 7–20, 21, 22, and 23 above). Example 7–24 revisits the thirteen triads that are formable above each scale degree of the melodic minor. The increased number of triads in the melodic minor is attributed to the presence of variable scale degrees 6 and 7 as either the root, third, or fifth elements of each chord (again, the filled-in note heads designate the variable scale degrees).

Except for the tonic triad, the basic quality for triads in the melodic minor is determined by the presence of a variable scale degree and identified with uppercase and lowercase Roman numerals and the addition of either the plus sign for the augmented triad or the superscript circle for the diminished triad. If the root of the triad is a variable scale degree, then the Roman numeral is preceded by either a flat or a sharp (7–24), just as the individual pitches for the variable scale degrees of the melodic minor are indicated as either ♯6 and ♯7 or ♭6 and ♭7.

As we have said, the use of a sharp or a flat in front of the variable scale degree does not necessarily mean that the pitch carries either a sharp or a flat; rather, the sharp or flat indicates that the pitch is either raised or lowered (see above, pp. 72–74). We apply the same principle to the sharp or flat in front of the Roman numeral. Thus, the major triads of the melodic minor are represented as III, IV, V, ♭VI, and ♭VII, the minor triads as i, ii, iv, and v, the diminished triads as ii°, ♯vi°, and ♯vii°, and the augmented triad as III+. Chord symbols for inverted triads in minor employ the same format as those of the major mode: iv^6, i$^6_4$, III+^{6}, IV$^6_4$, ♯vii°^{6}, ♭VI^6, iv$^6_4$, ii°^{6}, ♭VII$^6_4$, i^6, ♯vi°^{6}, v$^6_4$, V^6, ♭VI$^6_4$, III^6, V$^6_4$, IV^6.

Example 7–24

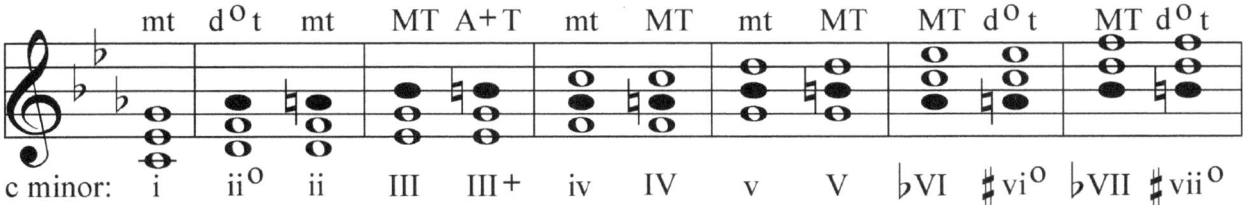

The following list is a guide for verbalizing the Roman numeral chord symbols for the minor mode. As demonstrated in example 7–24, there is more than one chord quality available in every scale degree area of the melodic minor except for the tonic. The quality of the triad is included in the description for the supertonic, mediant, subdominant, and dominant areas. The triads of the ♭VI, the ♯vi°, the ♭VII, and the ♯vii°, however, are all distinguished from one another without including the chord quality in the description. Since there is only one quality for the triad formed on scale degree 1 of the minor mode, we omit the reference to the quality of the chord and describe it simply as "the tonic triad."

Triads with Lowered Variables

ii°	the diminished supertonic triad
III	the major mediant triad
iv	the minor subdominant triad
v	the minor dominant triad
♭VI	the lowered submediant triad
♭VII	the subtonic triad

Triads with Raised Variables

ii	the minor supertonic triad
III+	the augmented mediant triad
IV	the major subdominant triad
V	the major dominant triad
♯vi°	the raised submediant triad
♯vii°	the leading-tone triad

The various chord symbols shown above enable us to determine easily whether the quality of the triad is major (uppercase letters), minor (lowercase letters), diminished (lowercase letters with a superscript circle) or augmented (uppercase letters with a plus sign).

As with the tonic triad of the minor mode, the triads for the major mode can be described more simply because there is only one chord quality for each scale degree area:

I   the tonic triad
ii   the supertonic triad
iii   the mediant triad
IV   the subdominant triad
V   the dominant triad
vi   the submediant triad
vii°   the leading-tone triad

Tonality and the Names of the Scale Degrees

We have discovered that the major mode is not the only mode in music that has a tonal center, that the numbers 1 through 7 can be used to represent each of the scale degrees of the mode, and that each of the scale degrees of the mode has one of the following names: tonic, supertonic, mediant, subdominant, dominant, submediant, and leading tone. When scale degree 7 is located one whole step below the tonic note, the term subtonic is used to distinguish it from the leading tone, as the subtonic lacks the compelling drive of the leading tone to *lead* upwards by half step to the tonic. In this section, we shall see that the names of the scale degrees are derived from their position and function in relation to the tonic, which represents the tonality of the mode.

As stated in Chapter 4, tonality in music is analogous to the gravitational force exerted by the Sun upon any object that comes within its field of attraction. Tonality is a system of pitch organization that establishes its own field of attraction around one central tone. All the other tones of the key and mode seek to revolve around and gravitate toward this central tone in a hierarchical order.

The tonic, as the principal tone of this hierarchy, exerts its gravitational force upon all of the other tones, each of which holds a position of relative strength and stability within the tonic's field of attraction. Since the pitch content of the key and mode provides the material from which chords may be formed on each of the seven scale degrees, the chords also assume a hierarchical position within the tonal framework. Thus, some tones and chords have a stronger relationship to the tonic than others.

Standing at the interval of the perfect 5th above the tonic and serving as the primary definer of a composition's tonality, the dominant scale degree forms the strongest relationship with the tonic. The perfect 5th, which has its origin in a natural phenomenon known as the **harmonic series** (see below, pp. 92–93), constitutes the closest intervallic relationship between two unlike pitches. The field of attraction between the dominant and the tonic is based upon the prominence of the perfect 5th within the harmonic series.

In example 7–25, we have the triad of the dominant addressing the tonic in a falling perfect 5th and rising perfect 4th root and bass relationship. Movement in the bass of either the perfect or tritone 5th and 4th is called **harmonic motion**. The falling perfect 5th (and its inversion, the rising perfect 4th) presents the strongest expression of harmonic motion in tonal music.

When the dominant triad is major, it contains as its chord third the second most important scale degree within the tonal hierarchy, namely, the leading tone. Therefore, as shown in 7–25, the movement between the dominant and tonic chords produces two optimal conditions for affirming the tonality of a musical work: the most effective melodic motion (scale degree 7 to scale degree 8) and the most effective harmonic motion (the falling perfect 5th or rising perfect 4th).

Example 7–25: the harmonic root and bass relationship between the dominant and tonic triads

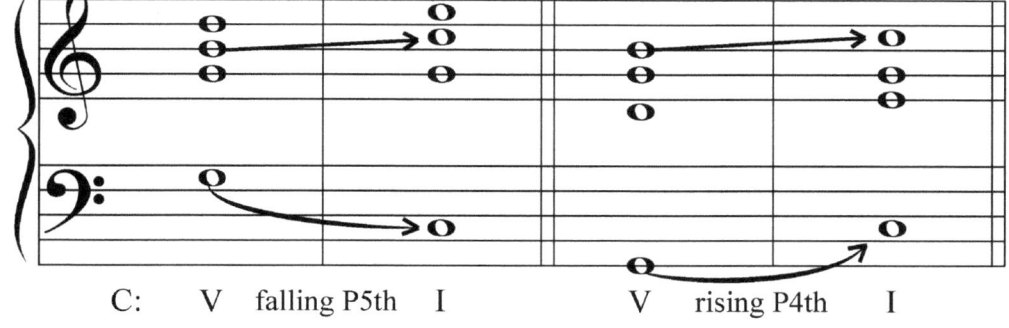

C: V   falling P5th   I   V   rising P4th   I

The next chord within the tonal hierarchy is the triad of the leading tone, which shares two pitches in common with the triad of the dominant. The root and the third of the leading-tone triad are the same pitches as the third and the fifth of the corresponding dominant triad. Example 7–26 demonstrates the common pitch content of the two chords in the key and mode of C major.

For the purpose of comparison in the example, the leading-tone triad is expressed in $^5_3$ position; however, the diminished triad is best limited to $^6_3$ position (first inversion) because of the highly dissonant tritone that would otherwise occur between the bass and one of the upper pitches in the chord's $^5_3$ and $^6_4$ positions. The remaining areas of the supertonic, mediant, subdominant, and submediant assume subordinate status within the key and mode and are so named largely because of their respective locations in relation to the tonic and dominant.

Example 7–26: common pitch content between the leading-tone and dominant triads

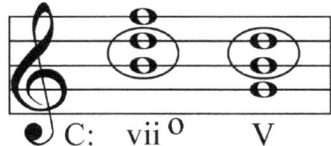

C: vii°   V

Examples 7–27a and 27b display all of the scale degree areas of the key and mode of C major. The areas of the supertonic, the mediant, and the dominant are shown in 7–27a. Scale degree 2 receives the name supertonic because it stands one step above the tonic. Scale degree 5, the dominant, occurs one fifth above the tonic (see the upward arrow).

Scale degree 3 is called the mediant because it falls midway between the tonic and the dominant (see the dotted curved lines). The mediant helps to distinguish the major and minor modes because of its third relationship to the tonic. In the major mode, there is a major 3rd between scale degrees 1 and 3, whereas in the minor mode, the distance between scale degrees 1 and 3 is a minor 3rd.

The areas of the subdominant, the submediant, and leading tone are presented in 7–27b. Scale degree 4, the subdominant, occurs one 5th below the tonic (see the downward arrow) and a 2nd below the dominant. Scale degree 6 is called the submediant because it is located below the tonic and falls midway between the tonic and subdominant (see the dotted curved lines). The leading tone is one half step below the tonic. (Remember that the term subtonic is used in the minor mode to distinguish it from the leading tone, as the subtonic lacks the compelling drive of the leading tone to *lead* upwards by half step to the tonic.)

Example 7–27

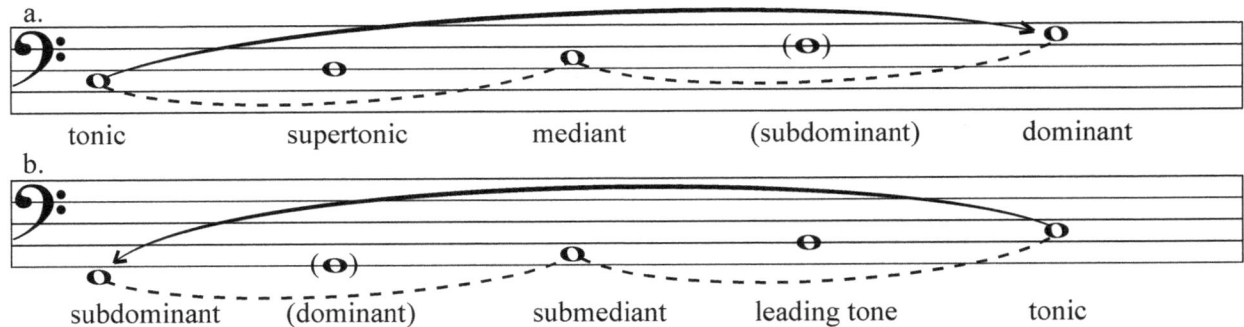

The Harmonic Series

In the foregoing section, we stated that the interval of the perfect 5th is of central importance to the definition of a music composition's tonality. Additionally, it spans the distance from the root to the fifth of the major and minor triad. Both major and minor triads are relatively stable chords, while diminished and augmented triads are relatively unstable. The diminished triad has a diminished 5th from its root to fifth. The augmented triad has a contextual augmented 5th from its root to fifth but not an acoustical 5th; for the sound of the augmented 5th is identical to that of the acoustical minor 6th. As we shall see presently, the major triad is the most stable of all four chord qualities.

The stability of the major triad and the role of the dominant as the chief definer of the tonality is associated with the harmonic series. A portion of the harmonic series with a starting pitch of C is shown below in example 7–28 (the series can begin on any pitch). Before we consider how this series works and how it relates to the strength of the dominant and the stability of the major triad, it would be well to review briefly the nature of musical tones and how they are created.

In Chapter 2, we learned that an object moved by force produces vibrations that are carried through a medium of transmission to the human ear. A sound that generates a regular number of frequencies at a steady rate is perceived as a musical tone. The relative lowness or highness of any pitch corresponds to the rate of the vibrating frequency of the sound-producing object. Slower vibrating frequencies result in lower pitches, while faster vibrating frequencies produce higher pitches. The rate of vibration generating the pitch is called the **fundamental frequency**, also known as the **first partial** or **first harmonic**.

A musical tone is a combination of two components: the fundamental pitch and a spectrum of higher frequencies called **overtones**. Projecting varying degrees of intensity (volume) from within the harmonic series, overtones are usually not loud enough to be heard as pitches in their own right. Rather, the fundamental frequency and its overtones are blended together into a single composite sound. This composite sound is referred to variously as tone quality, tone color, or **timbre** (pronounced *tam*ber).

Although the individual overtones cannot be heard as distinct pitches, they do *color* the fundamental frequency and collectively generate the timbre of a musical instrument—overtones enable us to identify the source of the musical sound. On any given instrument, some overtones are relatively stronger than others. The reason two different instruments sound differently is due to the fact that each makes its own unique selection of overtones from a much larger inventory of weaker overtones. For example, we can distinguish the sound of the clarinet and the violin even when both instruments are playing the exact same pitch because each instrument projects its own unique profile of overtones, its own sonic fingerprint.

The fundamental frequency and its overtones together produce the harmonic series, which is why the harmonic series is also called the **overtone series**. The number of overtones that are generated above the fundamental pitch is potentially infinite; however, in order to maintain a reasonable degree of simplicity, discussions of the harmonic series in publications are usually limited to the first sixteen pitches.

Example 7–28 restricts our view of the harmonic series to the first five pitches, starting with the fundamental on C2. These five pitches reveal two important bits of information:
(1) the first tone that is *not* a duplication of the fundamental is a compound perfect 5th (circled G) and
(2) the first five tones of the harmonic series produce the major triad (measure 2).

Example 7–28: the first five pitches of the harmonic series

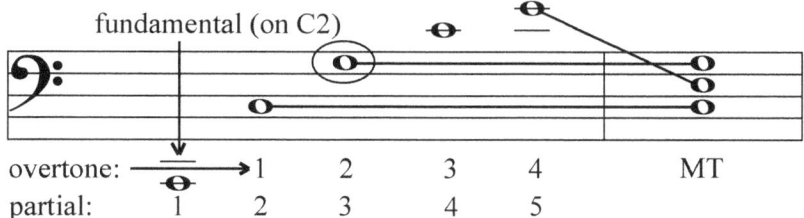

As noted earlier, the fundamental is also called the first partial or first harmonic. When discussing the harmonic series, a distinction should be made between the fundamental and the overtones that occur above it. Although the fundamental is the first partial (or first harmonic), it is *not* the first overtone. Examples 7–28 above and 29 below indicate that the first overtone is actually the second partial (or second harmonic), the second overtone is the third partial (or third harmonic), and so on. Therefore, we never refer to the fundamental frequency as the first overtone.

Example 7–29: the first five pitches of the harmonic series on C2

	Overtone Series		Harmonic Series
C2 :	fundamental		fundamental (first partial or first harmonic)
C3 :	first overtone	=	second partial (second harmonic)
G3 :	second overtone	=	third partial (third harmonic)
C4 :	third overtone	=	fourth partial (fourth harmonic)
E4 :	fourth overtone	=	fifth partial (fifth harmonic)

Chapter 8 The Church Modes

Mode, or modality, is a collection of pitch relationships exhibiting certain characteristic melodic and chordal configurations that confirm and establish the key of a musical work. Our present-day concept of mode is the result of centuries of evolution and practice. Out of this evolution, the major-minor tonal system emerged as the most widely used system of pitch organization in the Western world. But long before the development of this system in the late-seventeenth century, other modes existed.

Known as the **church modes**, or **ecclesiastical modes**, they were used for hundreds of years, through the Middle Ages and the Renaissance. Thereafter, the church modes receded from view for about two hundred years but then recaptured the imagination of composers during the second half of the nineteenth century. Before we consider the modal system in its current state, let us take a brief excursion into the early history of this system.

The church modes were developed during the eighth and ninth centuries of the Common Era as a means for analyzing and classifying the monophonic music of the Roman Catholic Church. **Monophony** is a type of musical texture that consists of a single melodic line. The music of the Roman Church is referred to generally as **plainchant** (*cantus planus*) and more specifically as **Gregorian chant**. The latter reference is an attribution to the charismatic pope St. Gregory I (540?–604), who traditionally receives credit for composing the chant for the services of the Roman Church during his papacy. St. Gregory is a central figure in the history of the Roman Church, one of the four Doctors (teachers) of the Church, along with St. Ambrose (340?–397), St. Augustine (354–430), and St. Jerome (340?–420?).

Although St. Gregory may have helped to bring the chant repertory of the Roman Church together through his extraordinary service as an administrator, it is unlikely that he composed any of the music himself. Still, given the magnitude of St. Gregory's role in establishing both the papacy as a world power and the independence of the Western Church, it is understandable that the surviving corpus of Western chant would bear his name.

The first discussions of the church modes began to appear in the treatises of the ninth century. Based upon certain references to the scale system of the ancient Greeks found in a sixth-century treatise called *De institutione musica* (The Fundamentals of Music), some writers concluded that the modes were of Greek origin. The treatise was written by the Roman statesman Boethius (ca. 480–ca. 524), the most widely read authority on the music theory of antiquity.

Misinterpreting Boethius's account of the Greek scales, medieval theoreticians improperly assigned the Greek names associated with these scales to the modes of the Roman Church. Although the musical scales of ancient Greece had nothing in common with the modal system of the Middle Ages, the church modes as we understand them today retain their Hellenistic names.

The history of the church modes is one in which the usage differs from one era to another, from the Middle Ages through the second half of the nineteenth century. The treatment of the church modes during the last hundred and fifty years or so, however, constitutes a relatively consistent practice. Focusing on the characteristics of the modes as they occur in the music literature of the recent past will deepen our understanding of the concepts that concern beginning music students, especially pitch, key, scale, mode, key signature, interval, and harmony.

Example 8–1 below illustrates the seven church modes with their Greek names, half-step profiles, and tonic triads. All of the modes shown in the example appear as diatonic scales, each with five whole steps and two half steps. The placement of the half steps, however, is different for each of the seven modes. Two modes should be recognized immediately, the Ionian mode and the Aeolian mode. The half-step profile of the Ionian mode is identical to that of the major mode, whereas the half-step profile of the Aeolian mode is identical to that of the natural minor.

96 Chapter 8 The Church Modes

Example 8–1: the seven church modes with their Greek names, tonic triads, and half-step profiles

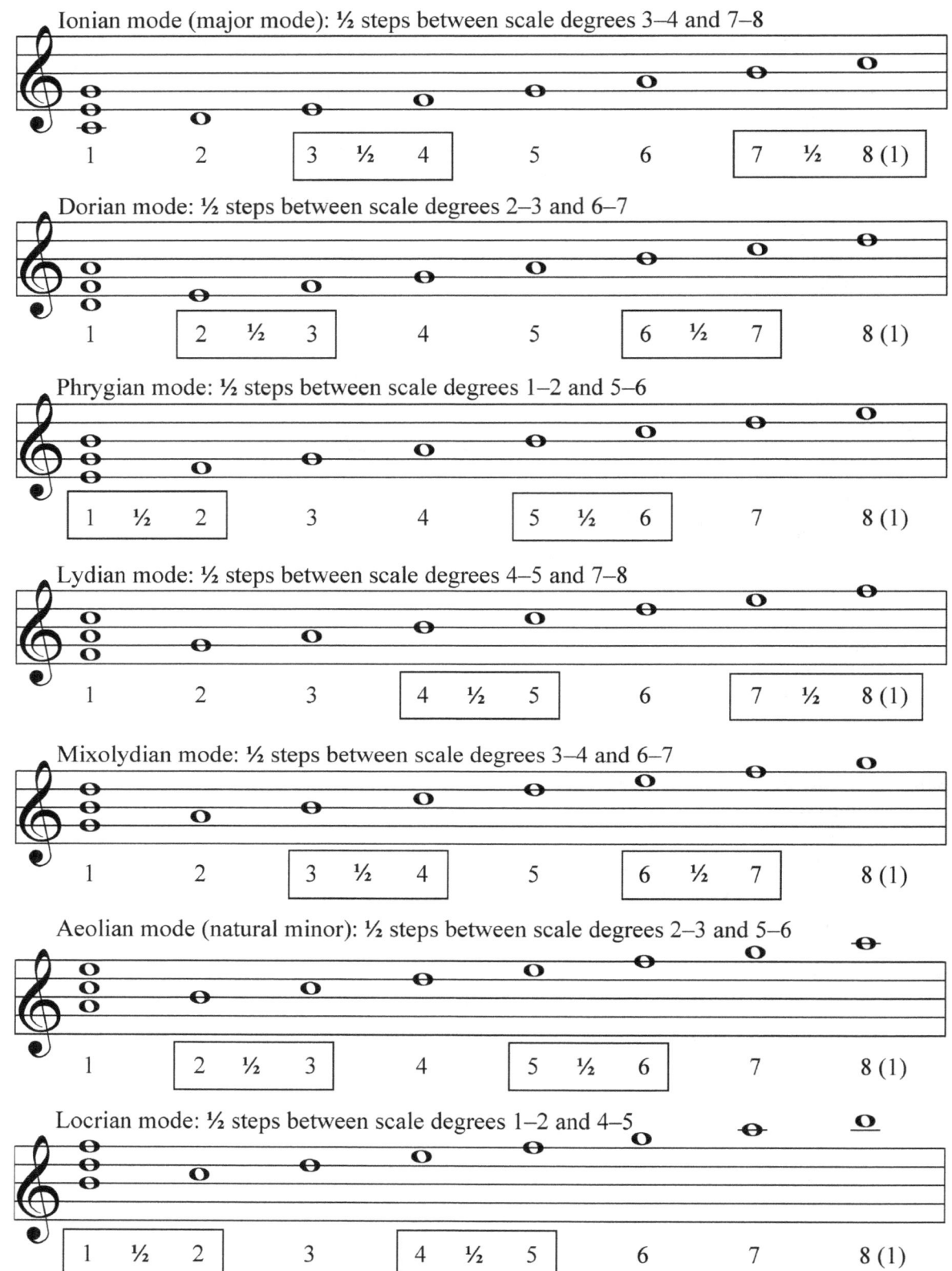

The white keys of the piano keyboard contain all of the pitch content for each of the seven modes in their *untransposed* forms. As displayed in example 8–1 above, the untransposed Ionian mode (or major mode) spans the white keys of the C octave, the Dorian mode the D octave, the Phrygian mode the E octave, the Lydian mode the F octave, the Mixolydian mode the G octave, the Aeolian mode the A octave, and the Locrian mode the B octave. In the next section, we shall place the seven untransposed modes into two separate categories according to the quality of their respective tonic triads and the intervallic relationship between their tonic and mediant scale degrees.

Major and Minor Prototypes

The Lydian and Mixolydian modes are "major prototypes" because they have both a major triad on the tonic and a major 3rd between their tonic and mediant scale degrees (example 8–2).

Compare the untransposed mode of F Lydian to its parallel major, F major. Notice that there are similarities between the two modes, except that F Lydian's scale degree 4 is raised one half step in relation to the F-major scale. F Lydian contains a B natural, F major a B♭ (examples 8–2a and 2b). The untransposed Mixolydian mode on G is similar to its parallel major, G major, except that G Mixolydian's scale degree 7 is lowered one half step in relation to the G-major scale. G Mixolydian contains an F natural, G major an F♯ (examples 8–2c and 2d).

Example 8–2: major prototype modes

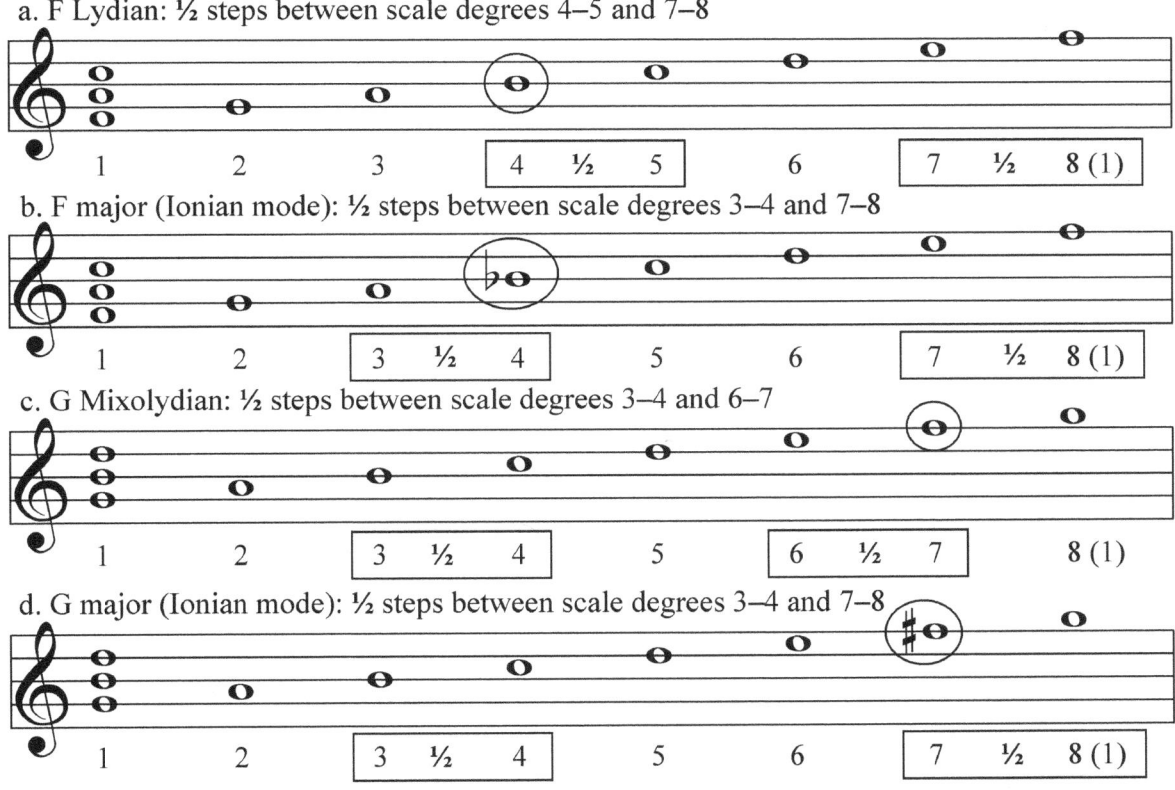

The Dorian and Phrygian modes, on the other hand, are "minor prototypes" because they have both a minor triad on the tonic and a minor 3rd between their tonic and mediant scale degrees (example 8–3). The untransposed Dorian mode on D resembles the parallel natural minor on D, except that D Dorian's scale degree 6 is raised one half step in relation to the d-minor scale. D Dorian contains a B natural, d minor a B♭ (examples 8–3a and 3b). The untransposed Phrygian mode on E is similar to its parallel natural minor, e minor, except that E Phrygian's scale degree 2 is lowered one half step in relation to the e-minor scale. E Phrygian contains an F natural, e minor an F♯ (examples 8–3c and 3d).

Example 8–3: minor prototype modes

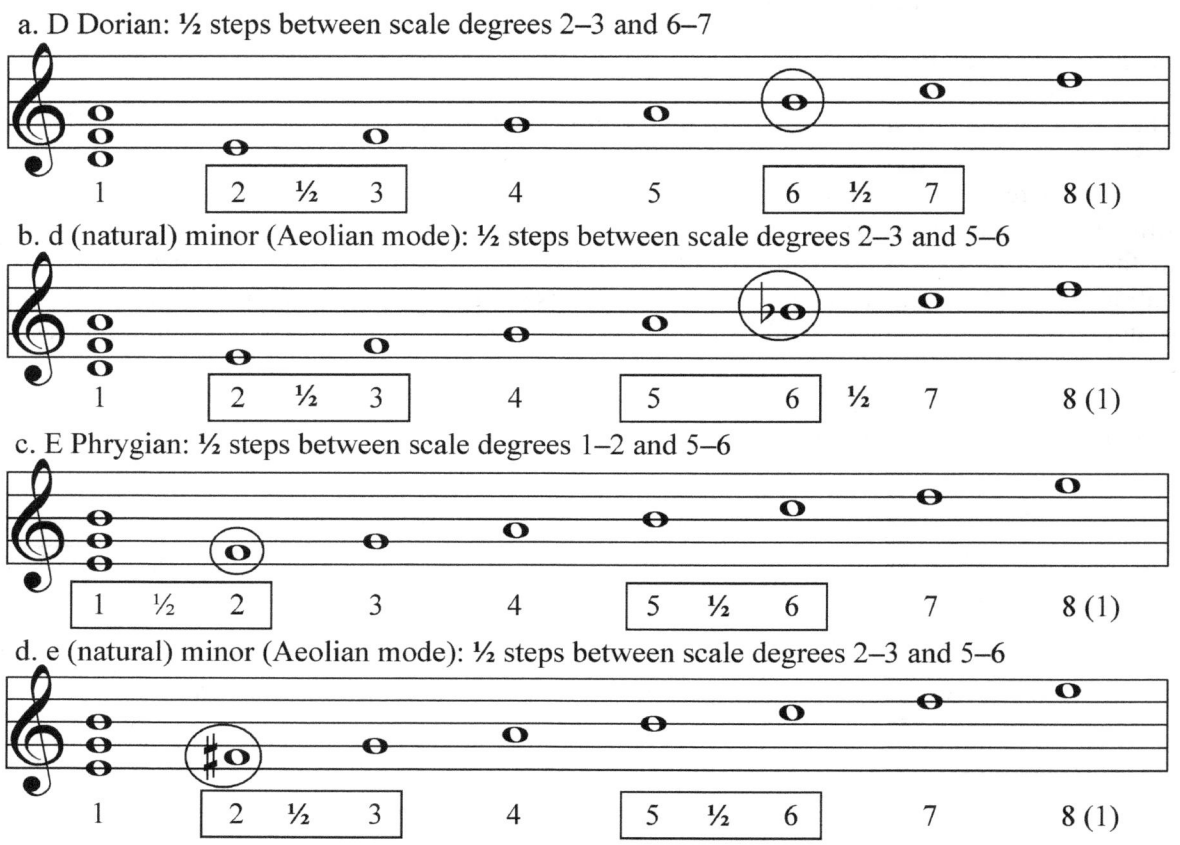

Example 8–4: the exceptional Locrian mode

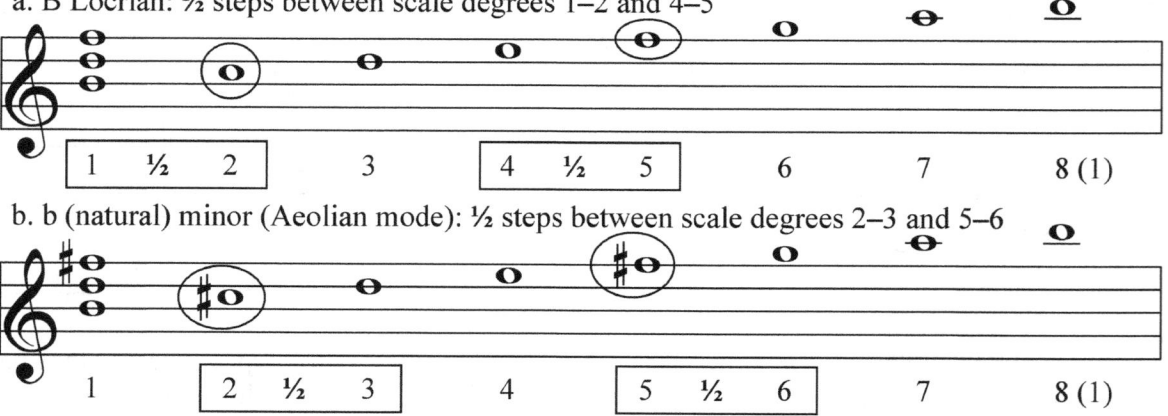

The Locrian mode, as illustrated in 8–4 above, is an exceptional case for two reasons: the mode has two scale degrees that differ from the natural minor and its tonic triad is diminished and therefore inherently unstable. B Locrian's scale degrees 2 and 5 are each lowered one half step in relation to its parallel natural minor, b minor. The untransposed Locrian mode on B contains a C natural and an F natural, whereas b minor has both a C♯ and an F♯. Still, because the Locrian mode has a minor 3rd between its tonic and mediant scale degrees (as does the Dorian and Phrygian modes), we classify Locrian as a minor prototype, albeit an unusual one.

Relating the Church Modes to the Major Mode

Earlier in this chapter, we noted that the white keys of the piano keyboard contain all of the pitch content for the seven modes in their untransposed forms. As demonstrated in example 8–5, the first note of each mode may be placed within the context of the C-major scale. Accordingly, we assign the names of the seven church modes to each of the seven scale degrees of C major, starting with the untransposed Ionian mode.

Thus, the keynote of the Ionian mode begins on C, the keynote of the Dorian mode on D, the keynote of the Phrygian mode on E, the keynote of the Lydian mode on F, the keynote of the Mixolydian mode on G, the keynote of the Aeolian mode on A, and the keynote of the Locrian mode on B.

Example 8–5: the church mode areas within the context of the C-major scale

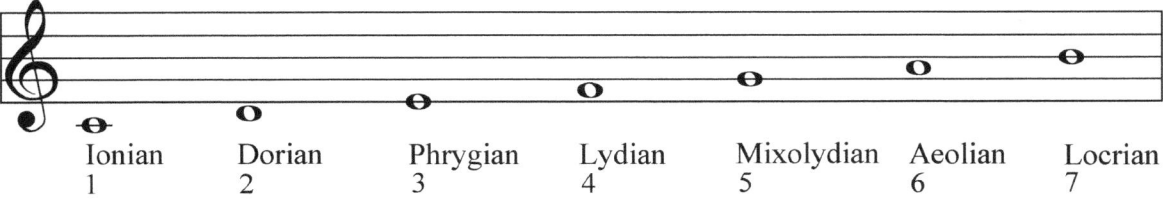

Mode Transposition

Since all seven church modes in their untransposed forms use only the white keys of the piano keyboard and appear within the context of the C-major scale, the respective key signatures and pitch content of D Dorian, E Phrygian, F Lydian, G Mixolydian, A Aeolian, and B Locrian are all *related* to the key signature and pitch content of C major (or C Ionian).

As we observed in Chapter 6, any two modes standing in a relative relationship to one another will share the same key signature and the same pitch content but have different tonics and different octave ranges. For example, any major mode, transposed or untransposed, has a relative minor key area with which it shares the same key signature and pitch content.

Presently, we shall apply the concept of relative relationships between major and minor modes to all of the church modes, designating scale degree 2 of C major as its relative Dorian area, scale degree 3 as its relative Phrygian area, scale degree 4 as its relative Lydian area, scale degree 5 as its relative Mixolydian area, scale degree 6 as its relative Aeolian area, and scale degree 7 as its relative Locrian area (see 8–5 above).

As we explore the characteristics of the church modes, our reference point will be the untransposed key and mode of C major. Let us begin with the relationship between the untransposed mode of C major and its relative Dorian, D Dorian, as shown in example 8–6 below. Notice that both modes share the same pitch content but have different tonics and different ranges.

Example 8–6: the relative Dorian of C major (scale degree 2 of C Major)

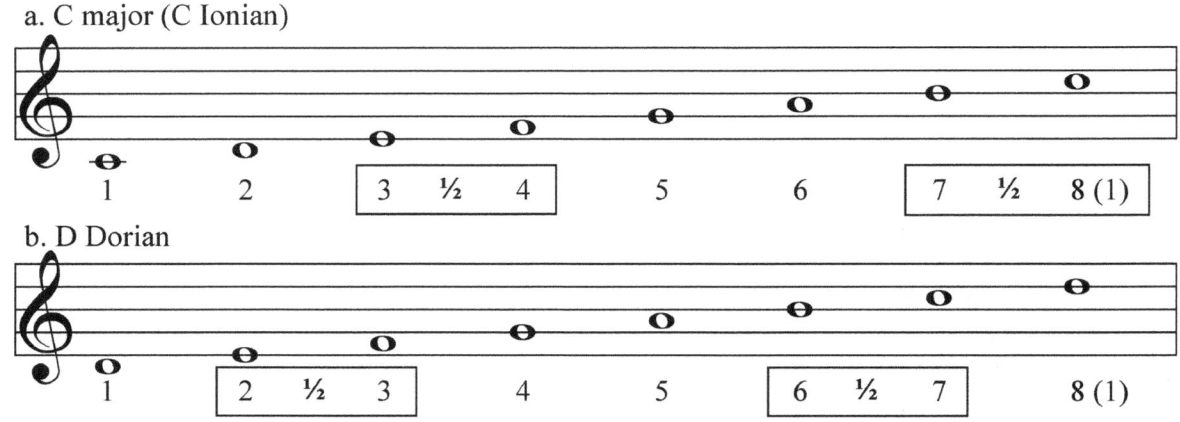

The names of the seven church modes remain unchanged when transposing C major to another key (example 8–7).

Example 8–7: the church mode areas of B♭ major

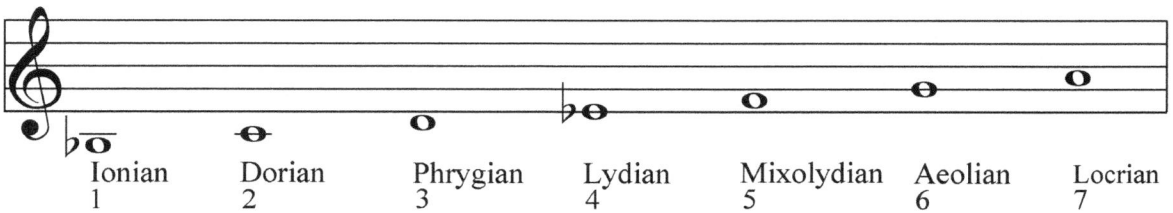

Example 8–8 moves the relationship between C major and D Dorian down one whole step, to B♭ major and C Dorian; both modes share the same pitch content, including a B♭ and an E♭, but have different tonics and different ranges.

Example 8–8: the relative Dorian of B♭ major (scale degree 2 of B♭ major)

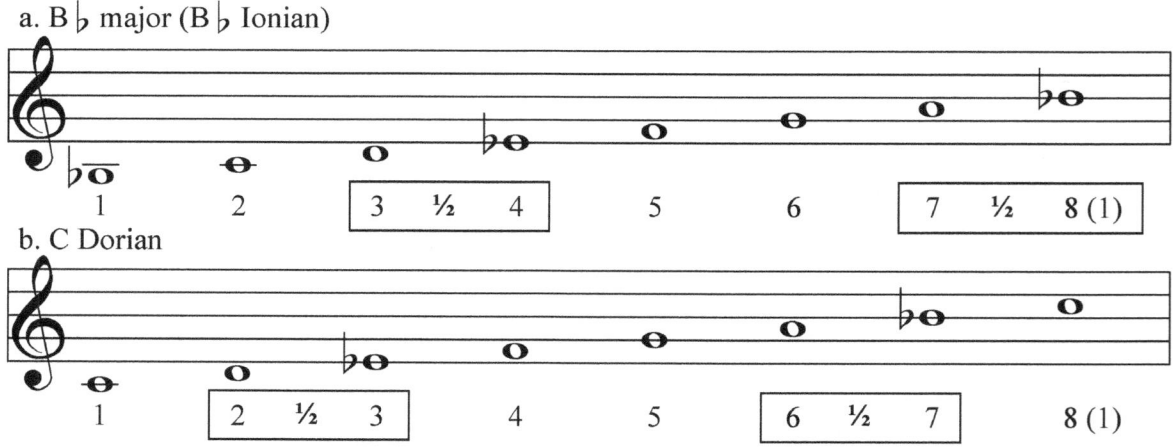

Let us stay with B♭ major for a few more examples. If C Dorian has the same pitch content as B♭ major, then any of the other relative modes of B♭ major will also have seven tones in common. In example 8–9, we have B♭ major and its relative Phrygian, D Phrygian. Both C Dorian (example 8–8b) and D Phrygian (8–9b) have the same key signature as B♭ major: two flats, B♭ and E♭. All three modes (B♭ major, C Dorian, and D Phrygian), however, have different tonics and different ranges.

Example 8–9: the relative Phrygian of B♭ major (scale degree 3 of B♭ major)

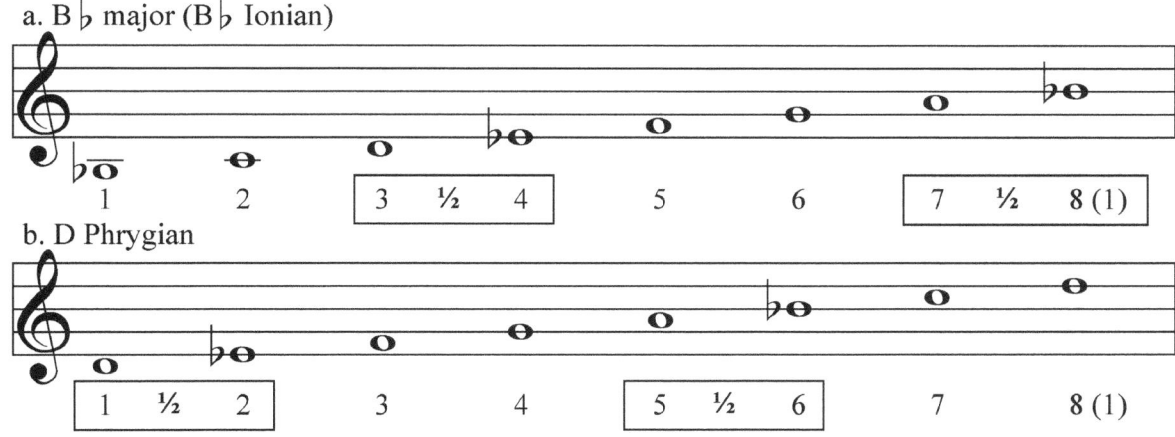

Example 8–10 compares B♭ major to its relative Lydian, E♭ Lydian; again, the pitch content is the same for both modes but their respective tonics and ranges are different.

Example 8–10: the relative Lydian of B♭ major (scale degree 4 of B♭ major)

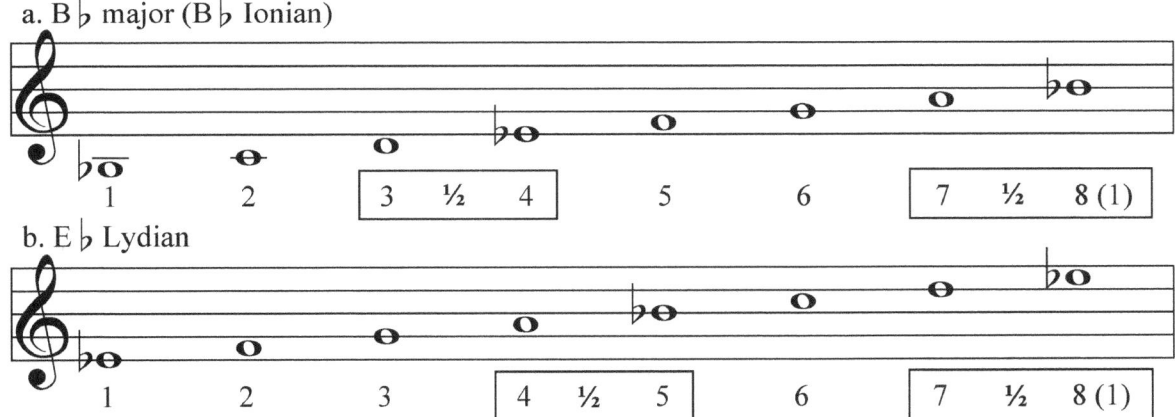

As shown in example 8–11, the relative Mixolydian of B♭ major is F Mixolydian. Both modes have the same pitch content but different tonics and different ranges.

Example 8–11: the relative Mixolydian of B♭ major (scale degree 5 of B♭ major)

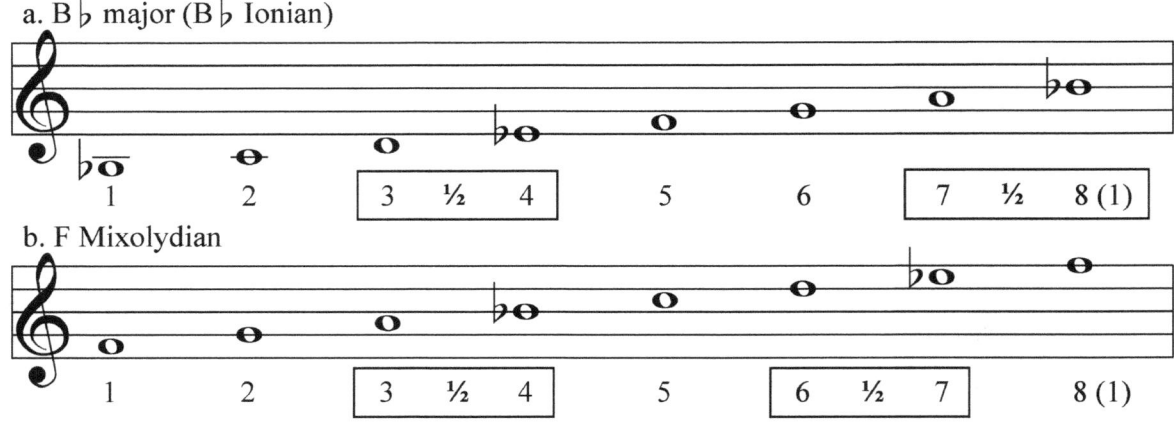

Example 8–12 illustrates the relative Aeolian of B♭ major, G Aeolian. As we have observed, the Aeolian mode is identical to that of the natural minor; therefore, the relationship between the two modes shown below is the same as the relationship between B♭ major and its relative minor.

Example 8–12: the relative Aeolian of B♭ major (scale degree 6 of B♭ major)

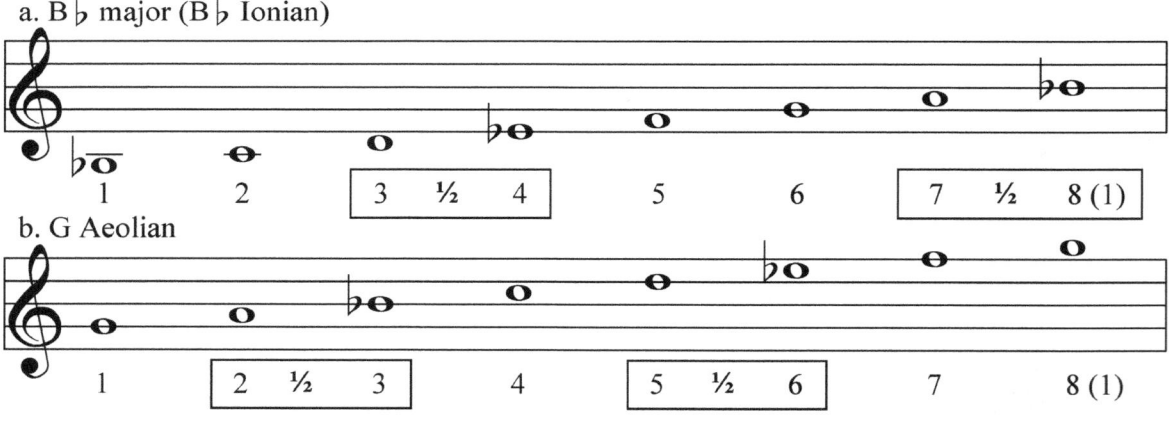

Finally, example 8–13 presents the relative Locrian of B♭ major, A Locrian. We know that the Locrian mode's tonic scale degree projects a diminished triad. The Locrian mode is the only church mode that has a diminished 5th between its scale degrees 1 and 5. The unstable properties of the Locrian mode has tended to discourage its use throughout most periods of music history; indeed, the tritone relationship between its tonic and dominant as well as the lack of a stable tonic triad make it difficult to establish a strong tonal center.

Example 8–13: the relative Locrian of B♭ major (scale degree 7 of B♭ major)

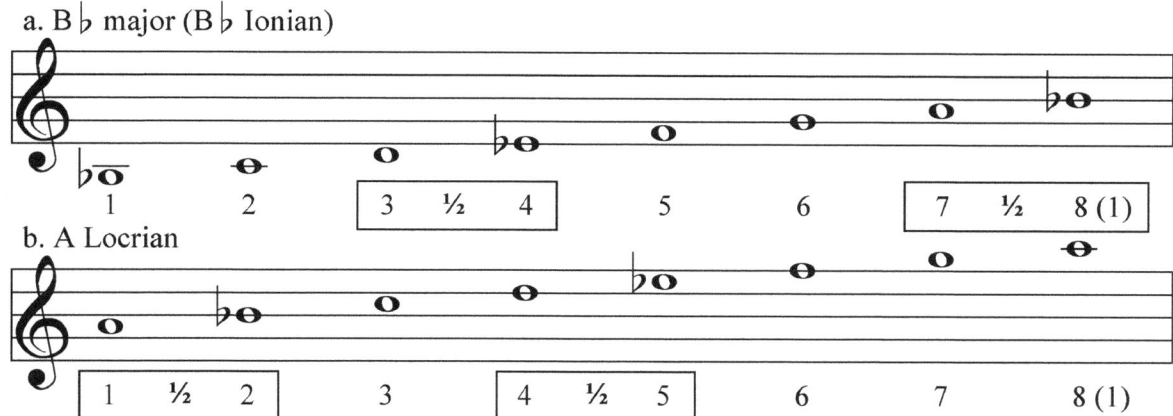

Given the Key and Mode, Find the Right Key Signature

In the previous section, we learned that if the relative modal key areas of C major share the same pitch content and key signature as C major, then the relative modal key areas of B♭ major share the same pitch content and key signature as B♭ major. Finding the relative modal key area of any transposed major mode is one way of understanding the principle of mode transposition. There are, however, other ways to approach this inquiry.

Drawing upon the information gleaned from the modal relationships considered in examples 8–8 through 13, we shall now arrange two pairs of conditions into the following proposition in order to find the relationship between them: *untransposed major is to untransposed mode as transposed major is to transposed mode*.

As presented in example 8–14, the first pair of conditions contains two known values and is therefore complete; the second pair, however, contains one unknown value and is therefore incomplete: C major is to D Dorian as the unknown value (X) is to C Dorian. Finding the correct value will tell us the keynote of the transposed major and provide the answer to the following question:

(1) What is the key signature for the transposed mode of C Dorian (8–14)?
(2) D Dorian is the untransposed mode and scale degree 2 of the untransposed major, C major.
(3) C Dorian occurs on scale degree 2 of what transposed major (X)?
(4) C major is to D Dorian (a major 2nd) as X major is to C Dorian; what is a major 2nd *below* C?
(5) If you cannot find a major 2nd below C, find a minor 7th above C (the inversion of a major 2nd). B♭ is a minor 7th above C and therefore a major 2nd below C.
(6) C major is to D Dorian as B♭ major (X) is to C Dorian.
(7) B♭ major has two flats (B♭ and E♭) and so does C Dorian.

Example 8–14: the key signature of C Dorian

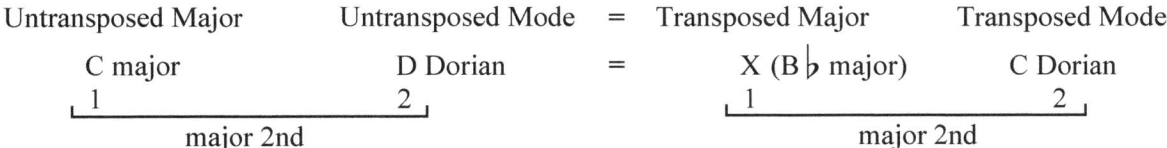

Two skills are absolutely necessary at this point in your study. You must know the major key signatures *and* be able to calculate easily the intervals of the major 2nd, major 3rd, perfect 4th, perfect 5th, major 6th, and major 7th *below* any given tone (if necessary, review the following sections of Chapter 5: The Essential Diatonic Intervals of Major, pp. 50–51, example 5–4, and Interval Inversion, pp. 60–61). In this exercise, the given tone represents the transposed mode; X represents the key signature of that transposed mode.

(1) What is the key signature for the transposed mode of D Phrygian (example 8–15)?
(2) E Phrygian is the untransposed mode and scale degree 3 of the untransposed major, C major.
(3) D Phrygian occurs on scale degree 3 of what transposed major (X)?
(4) C major is to E Phrygian (a major 3rd) as X major is to D Phrygian; what is a major 3rd *below* D?
(5) If you cannot find a major 3rd below D, then find a minor 6th above D (the inversion of a major 3rd). B♭ is a minor 6th above D and therefore a major 3rd below D.
(6) C major is to E Phrygian as B♭ major (X) is to D Phrygian.
(7) B♭ major has two flats (B♭ and E♭) and so does D Phrygian.

Example 8–15: the key signature of D Phrygian

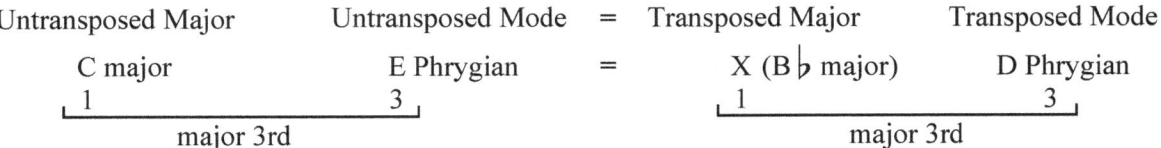

(1) What is the key signature for the transposed mode of E♭ Lydian (example 8–16)?
(2) F Lydian is the untransposed mode and scale degree 4 of the untransposed major, C major.
(3) E♭ Lydian occurs on scale degree 4 of what transposed major (X)?
(4) C major is to F Lydian (a perfect 4th) as X major is to E♭ Lydian; what is a perfect 4th *below* E♭?
(5) If you cannot find a perfect 4th below E♭, then find a perfect 5th above E♭ (the inversion of a perfect 4th). B♭ is a perfect 5th above E♭ and therefore a perfect 4th below E♭.
(6) C major is to F Lydian as B♭ major (X) is to E♭ Lydian.
(7) B♭ major has two flats (B♭ and E♭) and so does E♭ Lydian.

Example 8–16: the key signature of E♭ Lydian

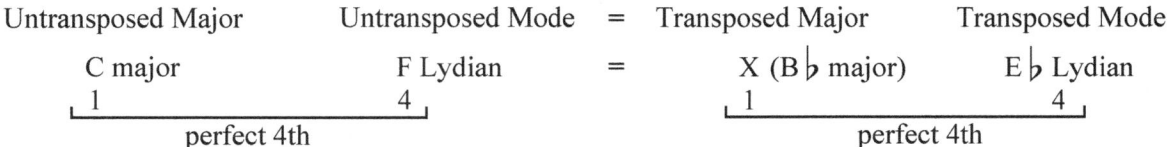

(1) What is the key signature for the transposed mode of F Mixolydian (example 8–17)?
(2) G Mixolydian is the untransposed mode and scale degree 5 of the untransposed major, C major.
(3) F Mixolydian occurs on scale degree 5 of what transposed major (X)?
(4) C major is to G Mixolydian (a perfect 5th) as X major is to F Mixolydian; what is a perfect 5th *below* F?
(5) If you cannot find a perfect 5th below F, then find a perfect 4th above F (the inversion of a perfect 5th). B♭ is a perfect 4th above F and therefore a perfect 5th below F.
(6) C major is to G Mixolydian as B♭ major (X) is to F Mixolydian.
(7) B♭ major has two flats (B♭ and E♭) and so does F Mixolydian.

Example 8–17: the key signature of F Mixolydian

Untransposed Major	Untransposed Mode	=	Transposed Major	Transposed Mode
C major	G Mixolydian	=	X (B♭ major)	F Mixolydian
1	5		1	5
perfect 5th			perfect 5th	

(1) What is the key signature for the transposed mode of G Aeolian (example 8–18)?
(2) A Aeolian is the untransposed mode and scale degree 6 of the untransposed major, C major.
(3) G Aeolian occurs on scale degree 6 of what transposed major (X)?
(4) C major is to A Aeolian (a major 6th) as X major is to G Aeolian; what is a major 6th *below* G?
(5) If you cannot find a major 6th below G, then find a minor 3rd above G (the inversion of a major 6th). B♭ is a minor 3rd above G and therefore a major 6th below G.
(6) C major is to A Aeolian as B♭ major (X) is to G Aeolian.
(7) B♭ major has two flats (B♭ and E♭) and so does G Aeolian.

Example 8–18: the key signature of G Aeolian

Untransposed Major	Untransposed Mode	=	Transposed Major	Transposed Mode
C major	A Aeolian	=	X (B♭ major)	G Aeolian
1	6		1	6
major 6th			major 6th	

(1) What is the key signature for the transposed mode of A Locrian (example 8–19)?
(2) B Locrian is the untransposed mode and scale degree 7 of the untransposed major, C major.
(3) A Locrian occurs on scale degree 7 of what transposed major (X)?
(4) C major is to B Locrian (a major 7th) as X major is to A Locrian; what is a major 7th *below* A?
(5) If you cannot find a major 7th below A, then find a minor 2nd above A (the inversion of a major 7th). B♭ is a minor 2nd above A and therefore a major 7th below A.
(6) C major is to B Locrian as B♭ major (X) is to A Locrian.
(7) B♭ major has two flats (B♭ and E♭) and so does A Locrian.

Example 8–19: the key signature of A Locrian

Untransposed Major	Untransposed Mode	=	Transposed Major	Transposed Mode
C major	B Locrian	=	X (B♭ major)	A Locrian
1	7		1	7
major 7th			major 7th	

Up to this point in our study of mode transposition, we have systematically explored the possibilities of modes with two flats from two different but related perspectives. First, we ascended through the modal key areas of B♭ major one scale degree at a time (pp. 100–103). Second, armed with the knowledge of the first perspective, or approach, we held the key signature of B♭ major in the background as an unknown quantity (X) and then endeavored to find the key signatures for the transposed modes of C Dorian, D Phrygian, E♭ Lydian, F Mixolydian, G Aeolian, and A Locrian (pp. 103–105).

Of course, we already knew that all six transposed modes of examples 8–14 through 19 would have two flats in their respective key signatures, as that fact was determined from our prior consideration of examples 8–8 through 13. For the next several examples, however, let us practice finding the key signatures of transposed modes *without the benefit of knowing from previous exercises* what key would be entered into the unknown quantity of X.

(1) What is the key signature for the transposed mode of F Dorian (example 8–20)?
(2) D Dorian is the untransposed mode and scale degree 2 of the untransposed major, C major.
(3) F Dorian occurs on scale degree 2 of what transposed major (X)?
(4) C major is to D Dorian (a major 2nd) as X major is to F Dorian; what is a major 2nd *below* F?
(5) If you cannot find a major 2nd below F, then find a minor 7th above F (the inversion of a major 2nd). E♭ is a minor 7th above F and therefore a major 2nd below F.
(6) C major is to D Dorian as E♭ major (X) is to F Dorian.
(7) E♭ major has three flats (B♭, E♭, and A♭) and so does F Dorian.

Example 8–20: the key signature of F Dorian

Untransposed Major	Untransposed Mode	=	Transposed Major	Transposed Mode
C major	D Dorian	=	X (E♭ major)	F Dorian
1	2		1	2
major 2nd			major 2nd	

(1) What is the key signature for the transposed mode of C Lydian (example 8–21)?
(2) F Lydian is the untransposed mode and scale degree 4 of the untransposed major, C major.
(3) C Lydian occurs on scale degree 4 of what transposed major (X)?
(4) C major is to F Lydian (a perfect 4th) as X major is to C Lydian; what is a perfect 4th *below* C?
(5) If you cannot find a perfect 4th below C, then find a perfect 5th above C (the inversion of a perfect 4th). G is a perfect 5th above C and therefore a perfect 4th below C.
(6) C major is to F Lydian as G major (X) is to C Lydian.
(7) G major has one sharp (F♯) and so does C Lydian.

Example 8–21: the key signature of C Lydian

Untransposed Major	Untransposed Mode	=	Transposed Major	Transposed Mode
C major	F Lydian	=	X (G major)	C Lydian
1	4		1	4
perfect 4th			perfect 4th	

(1) What is the key signature for the transposed mode of F♯ Aeolian (example 8–22)?
(2) A Aeolian is the untransposed mode and scale degree 6 of the untransposed major, C major.
(3) F♯ Aeolian occurs on scale degree 6 of what transposed major (X)?
(4) C major is to A Aeolian (a major 6th) as X major is to F♯ Aeolian; what is a major 6th *below* F♯?
(5) If you cannot find a major 6th below F♯, then find a minor 3rd above F♯ (the inversion of a major 6th). A is a minor 3rd above F♯ and therefore a major 6th below F♯.
(6) C major is to A Aeolian as A major (X) is to F♯ Aeolian.
(7) A major has three sharps (F♯, C♯, and G♯) and so does F♯ Aeolian.

Example 8–22: the key signature of F♯ Aeolian

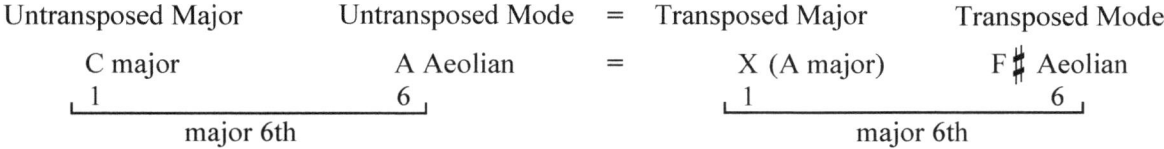

Again, a reminder: with respect to the key signature, the relative Aeolian and the relative minor are equivalent terms. The relative minor of A major is F♯ minor; both modes have three sharps.

(1) What is the key signature for the transposed mode of F Phrygian (example 8–23)?
(2) E Phrygian is the untransposed mode and scale degree 3 of the untransposed major, C major.
(3) F Phrygian occurs on scale degree 3 of what transposed major (X)?
(4) C major is to E Phrygian (a major 3rd) as X major is to F Phrygian; what is a major 3rd *below* F?
(5) If you cannot find a major 3rd below F, then find a minor 6th above F (the inversion of a major 3rd). D♭ is a minor 6th above F and therefore a major 3rd below F.
(6) C major is to E Phrygian as D♭ major (X) is to F Phrygian.
(7) D♭ major has five flats (B♭, E♭, A♭, D♭, and G♭) and so does F Phrygian.

Example 8–23: the key signature of F Phrygian

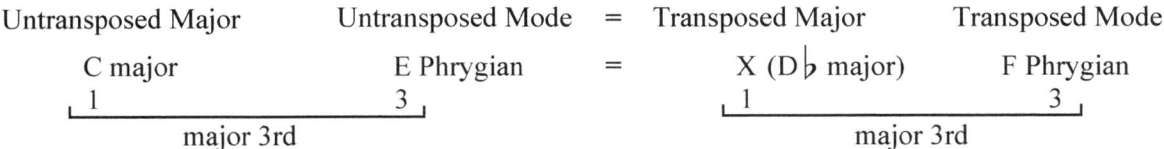

(1) What is the key signature for the transposed mode of D♯ Locrian (example 8–24)?
(2) B Locrian is the untransposed mode and scale degree 7 of the untransposed major, C major.
(3) D♯ Locrian occurs on scale degree 7 of what transposed major (X)?
(4) C major is to B Locrian (a major 7th) as X major is to D♯ Locrian; what is a major 7th *below* D♯?
(5) If you cannot find a major 7th below D♯, then find a minor 2nd above D♯ (the inversion of a major 7th). E is a minor 2nd above D♯ and therefore a major 7th below D♯.
(6) C major is to B Locrian as E major (X) is to D♯ Locrian.
(7) E major has four sharps (F♯, C♯, G♯, and D♯) and so does D♯ Locrian.

Example 8–24: the key signature of D♯ Locrian

Untransposed Major	Untransposed Mode	=	Transposed Major	Transposed Mode
C major	B Locrian	=	X (E major)	D♯ Locrian
1	7		1	7
major 7th			major 7th	

(1) What is the key signature for the transposed mode of D♭ Mixolydian (example 8–25)?
(2) G Mixolydian is the untransposed mode and scale degree 5 of the untransposed major, C major.
(3) D♭ Mixolydian occurs on scale degree 5 of what transposed major (X)?
(4) C major is to G Mixolydian (a perfect 5th) as X major is to D♭ Mixolydian; what is a perfect 5th *below* D♭?
(5) If you cannot find a perfect 5th below D♭, then find a perfect 4th above D♭ (the inversion of a perfect 5th). G♭ is a perfect 4th above D♭ and therefore a perfect 5th below D♭.
(6) C major is to G Mixolydian as G♭ major (X) is to D♭ Mixolydian.
(7) G♭ major has six flats (B♭, E♭, A♭, D♭, G♭ and C♭) and so does D♭ Mixolydian.

Example 8–25: the key signature of D♭ Mixolydian

Untransposed Major	Untransposed Mode	=	Transposed Major	Transposed Mode
C major	G Mixolydian	=	X (G♭ major)	D♭ Mixolydian
1	5		1	5
perfect 5th			perfect 5th	

Chapter 9 Seventh Chords

The seventh chord is a tertian harmony consisting of four chord tones: a root, third, fifth, and seventh. As shown in example 9–1, the seventh chord is produced by adding the interval of the 3rd above the fifth of the triad. The additional 3rd produces a *dissonant* 7th between the root and the seventh of the chord.

Example 9–1: the chord of the seventh

Example 9–2 demonstrates the formation of tertian harmonies with vertical structures containing more than four chord tones: the ninth chord has five tones (9–2a), the eleventh chord six (9–2b), and the thirteenth chord seven (9–2c). Chords of the seventh, ninth, eleventh, and thirteenth exist as extensions of the triad. These extensions do not alter the status or function of the triad within the key and mode in which it occurs.

Example 9–2: chords of the ninth, eleventh, and thirteenth

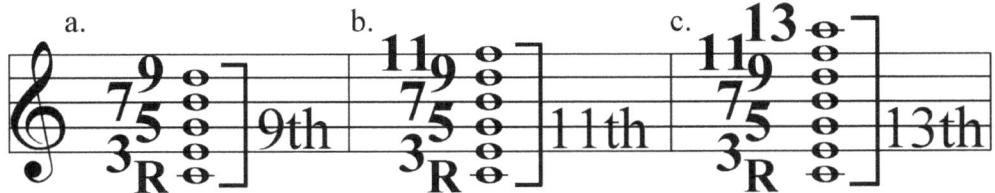

A comprehensive examination of ninth, eleventh, and thirteenth chords would take us into areas of music theory that lie beyond the purview of this text. Indeed, these chords appear within a segment of the musical repertory that rewards study only after mastering the basic concepts of diatonic harmony and voice leading (i.e., the process that regulates the linear succession of tones in each melodic line, optimizing how each line proceeds through time in relation to the rest of the musical texture).

Still, for the student interested in commercial music and jazz who wants to learn more about these chords without examining the theory behind them and without delving into their correct treatment within the framework of tonal music, Chapter 10 provides an introduction.

Adding the Seventh to the Triad

The creation of *root-position* seventh chords involves the addition of either a major or minor 3rd above the fifth of the triad; seventh chords are never produced by adding either augmented or diminished 3rds. Therefore, if we add a 3rd above the fifth of a C-major triad, as in example 9–3 below, the tone is either B♮ (a major 3rd above G) or B♭ (a minor 3rd above G); neither B♯ (an augmented 3rd above G) nor B♭♭ (a diminished 3rd above G) can be used as the seventh of the chord.

Placing a B♯ above the fifth of the C-major triad produces a tone that is enharmonic with the root, resulting in a doubled root (one of which is misspelled as B♯) and no seventh. The addition of a B♭♭ above the fifth creates a chord that contains an enharmonic and acoustical interval of a 6th above the root (C up to A) but no chord seventh. Although it is possible to hear the B♭♭ as the misspelled root (A) of a seventh chord with its third in the bass (C E G A), our concern in this section is with seventh chords in *root position*.

Example 9–3

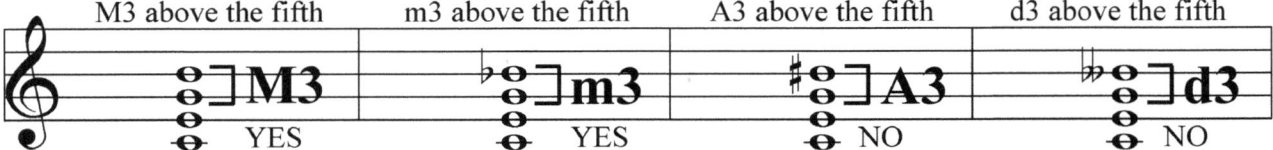

The Origin of the Seventh Chord

The principal origin of the seventh chord is the descending **passing tone**. Either dissonant or consonant with another pitch, the passing tone usually connects two harmonic consonances; it is approached and left by step and may occur on either a strong or weak beat. The passing tone also appears on either a strong or weak portion of a beat.

In example 9–4a, the tone F (P) fills in the interval of a 3rd between G and E. A dissonant passing 7th occurs on beat 3 of the first measure between the bass and the top melodic line (in half notes). The passing 7th connects two harmonic consonances, a perfect octave and a major 3rd (the compound intervals in the example are identified in their simple forms). Despite the limitations of the two-line texture shown in the example, the arrival of the major 3rd (C/E) in the second measure implies a C-major triad. The figure 8—7 indicates the downward movement of the octave to the 7th over a stationary bass (G).

Example 9–4b places the passing 7th (P) more clearly within a chordal framework. On beat 3 of the first measure, we have the tones G B D F, the four elements of the most common type of seventh chord, the dominant seventh. The dominant seventh will be discussed later in this chapter; for now, suffice it to say that the chord has a major triad and a minor 7th from the root to its seventh. As in 9–4a, the passing 7th in 9–3b moves down by step to form a consonant 3rd in the second measure (C/E).

Example 9–4: the passing 7th

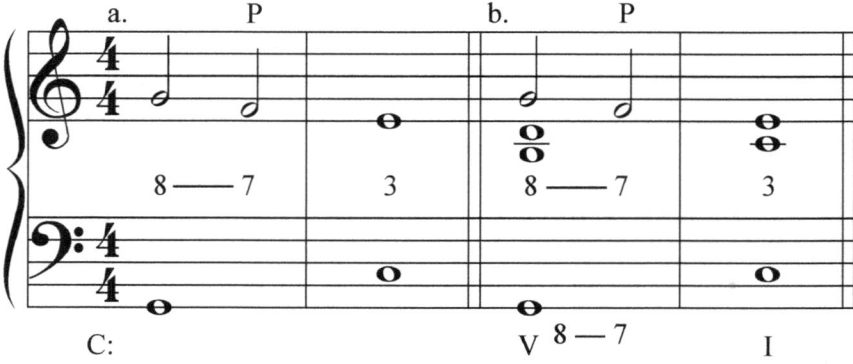

The Real Seventh Chord

In the course of our studies, we shall find that the seventh component of a *real* seventh chord always seeks to move down by step to form a consonance within the next chord—*if there is a tone of resolution available in the next chord*. This downward resolution to a consonance is central to the authenticity of the seventh chord because it replicates the operation of its progenitor, the descending dissonant passing tone.

A second requirement for a real seventh involves the root relationship it shares with the chord of resolution. In the traditional study of harmony, one of the following conditions must be met to have a real seventh chord:

(1) either the seventh chord stands in a rising 2nd root relationship to the chord it addresses; or,

(2) the seventh chord stands in either a rising 4th or falling 5th root relationship to the chord it addresses.

If the conditions cited above are not met, then we are not dealing with a real seventh chord. Some other explanation accounts for the presence of the seventh in the chord. Fortunately, in 9–4b, the meaning of the seventh is clear, as the motion is between two chords that stand in a rising 4th (or falling 5th) root relationship to each other: a G-dominant seventh chord resolves to a C-major triad (with an omitted fifth).

In any case, the authenticity of the seventh chord is a consideration reserved for the study of traditional harmony. In commercial music and jazz, all kinds of harmonies containing sevenths, ninths, and other tones may or may not resolve as we might expect when progressing from one chord to the next.

The Four Principal Types of "White-Key" Seventh Chords

This section focuses primarily on the white keys of the piano keyboard and examines the four types of seventh chords that emerge therefrom. Later, in example 9–18, we shall encounter three other types of seventh chords that can be created from a combination of both the white and black keys of the piano keyboard, seventh chords that arise (though not exclusively) from the properties of the melodic minor.

As stated above, converting a triad into a seventh chord, regardless of the triad's quality, does not alter the status or function of the chord within the key and mode in which it occurs. The seventh element of the chord is simply an extension of the basic triad, just as ninth, eleventh, and thirteenth elements are all extensions of the underlying seventh chord.

All four triad qualities may have a seventh component added to their respective structures. However, remember that the diatonic pitch content of the major mode (as well as that of the church modes) cannot support the formation of the augmented triad. The augmented triad usually shows up in music that involves either the harmonic minor, the melodic minor, or some degree of mixture between the major mode and the minor mode. Modal mixtures are common in music literature; however, the study of this practice is best reserved for those who first develop a thorough understanding of music fundamentals and basic harmony.

Example 9–5 displays the four types of seventh chords formable on the white keys of the piano keyboard, namely, the major seventh (M7), the minor seventh (m7), the dominant seventh (D7), and the half-diminished seventh ($\varnothing$ 7). The major seventh has a major triad and a major 7th from the root to the seventh (MT / M7), the minor seventh has a minor triad and a minor 7th (mt / m7), the dominant seventh has a major triad and a minor 7th (MT / m7), and the half-diminished seventh has a diminished triad and a minor 7th (d°t / m7).

There are three areas in which major triads appear on the white keys of the piano keyboard: C, F, and G. Both the C-major triad and the F-major triad may form major seventh chords (9–5). The major triad on G can have the dominant seventh. There are three areas where minor triads occur: D, E, and A, all of which may have minor seventh chords. Finally, on B, there is the one diminished triad available and therefore one half-diminished seventh chord. (Although 9–5 features the C octave, the four qualities of white-key seventh chords may be constructed on any white key in any octave register.)

Example 9–5

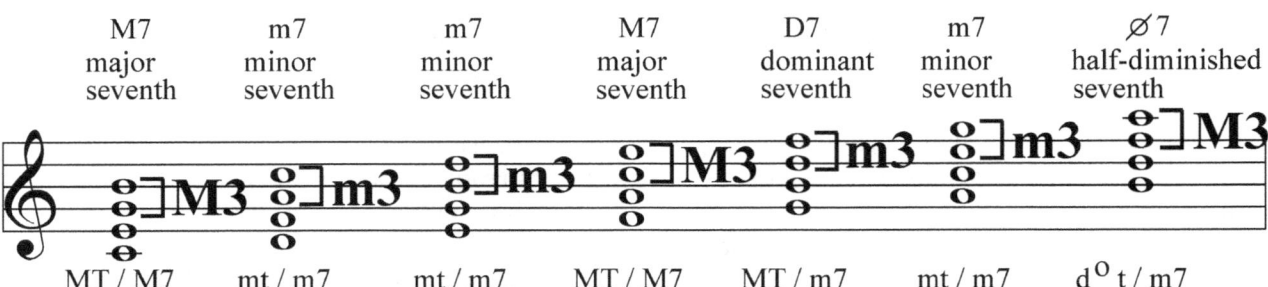

The half-diminished seventh is so named to distinguish it from another seventh chord referred to generally as the diminished seventh and more specifically as the *fully* diminished seventh. The association of the term fully with the chord description underscores the presence of two diminished components: a diminished triad and a diminished 7th from the root to the seventh (d°t / d7).

The fully diminished seventh is one of the three types of seventh chords produced from both white and black keys of the piano keyboard. Having a neutral-sounding profile, its intervallic structure consists entirely of minor 3rds rather than a combination of major and minor 3rds. Example 9–18 below includes a fully diminished seventh on the leading tone consisting of the pitches B D F A♭. In the same example (and in 9–5 above), there is a half-diminished seventh consisting of the tones B D F A♮. Example 9–18 also contains the other two seventh chords created from a mixture of both white and black keys: the minor-major seventh (mt / M7) of the tonic and the augmented-major seventh (A + T / M7) of the mediant.

The Formation of Seventh Chords in the Church Mode System

In example 9–6, we consider the white-key seventh chords from the perspective of the church modes, starting once again with the C octave, but referred to here as the Ionian mode rather than as the major mode. (The major mode has exactly the same seventh chord content as the Ionian mode.)

The circled Roman numerals constitute a generalized type of chord symbol that, without describing the specific chord quality, nonetheless indicates the exact scale degree of the mode upon which a triad or seventh may be formed. Since this generalized type of chord symbol makes no distinction between triad or seventh chord qualities, the Roman numerals are all expressed in uppercase. The Arabic number 7 attached to each Roman numeral indicates the presence of the seventh element for each root-position seventh chord.

Example 9–6: seventh chords in the Ionian mode

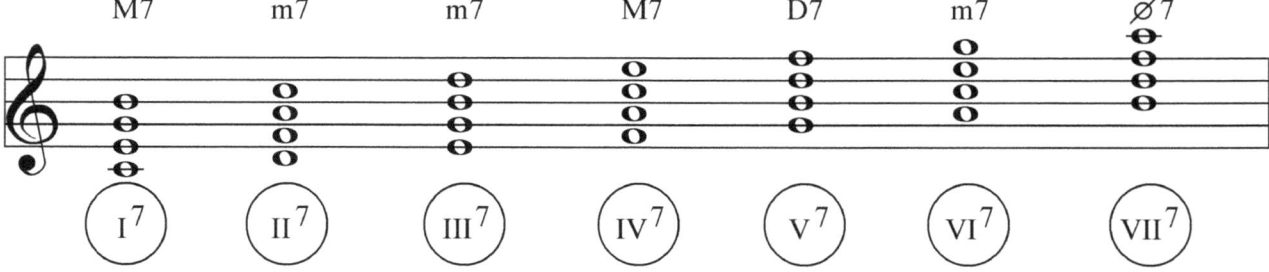

The Ionian mode supports the major seventh on the tonic and subdominant, the minor seventh on the supertonic, mediant, and submediant, the dominant seventh on the dominant, and the half-diminished seventh on the leading tone. In the course of our studies, we shall see that the dominant seventh is the most important seventh chord for the major-minor tonal system. The chord is called the dominant seventh because it is usually associated with the dominant scale degree of the major (and the equivalent Ionian), harmonic, and melodic minor modes.

However, the dominant seventh also occurs in areas other than the dominant scale degree in six of the seven church modes: it appears on the subdominant of the Dorian mode, the mediant of the Phrygian mode, the supertonic of the Lydian mode, the tonic of the Mixolydian mode, the subtonic of the Aeolian mode, and the submediant of the Locrian mode. The dominant seventh also exists on the subdominant, dominant, and subtonic scale degrees of the melodic minor. Thus, the chord can be used on various scale degrees within the context of several different modes, not just those that comprise the major-minor tonal system.

If the dominant seventh exists within a diverse range of modal contexts, then the same degree of applicability holds true for the other white-key seventh chords (the major seventh, half-diminished seventh, and minor seventh). The following examples demonstrate the variety of seventh-chord vocabularies for the Dorian, Phrygian, Lydian, Mixolydian, Aeolian, and Locrian modes. But regardless of the mode, understand that of the four types of white-key seventh chords, there are three minor sevenths, two major sevenths, one dominant seventh, and one half-diminished seventh in each mode.

Example 9–7 displays the seventh chords in the Dorian mode. The tonic, supertonic, and dominant scale degrees support the minor seventh. The Dorian mediant and subtonic take the major seventh. As mentioned above, the dominant seventh occurs on the subdominant while the half-diminished seventh falls on the submediant.

It would behoove us to *memorize* the seventh-chord qualities that occur on the white keys of the piano keyboard and then consider them within the various contexts of the seven church modes. Naming and then spelling a particular seventh chord of any transposed mode becomes a relatively simple task if we know how to use the white-note modes as referential scales. In fact, it is not even necessary to know the key signature of a given transposed mode, if we know the seventh-chord vocabulary of its untransposed counterpart.

Example 9–7: seventh chords in the Dorian mode

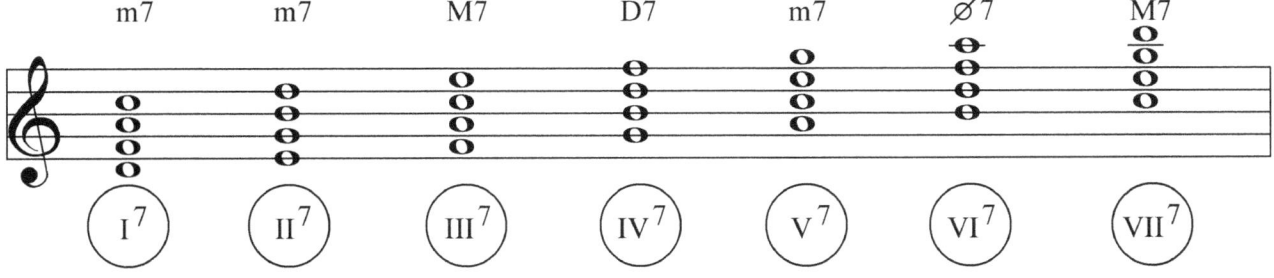

For instance, to build the seventh chord on scale degree 5 of B♭ Dorian, proceed to the untransposed D Dorian. Recall that scale degree 5 of D Dorian is a perfect 5th above the tonic and that the pitch content of the mode supports a minor seventh chord. A perfect 5th above B♭ is F; a minor seventh chord on F is spelled F A♭ C E♭. It is that easy (or that difficult). To be sure, we can always find the key signature first (which would be four flats: B♭, E♭, A♭, D♭); however, at this point in our study of music fundamentals, we should be able to draw easily upon the seventh-chord content (as well as the triadic content) of the untransposed modes.

The seventh-chord content of the Phrygian mode is shown in example 9–8. As with the Dorian, Mixolydian, Aeolian and Locrian modes, the Phrygian mode has a subtonic scale degree and therefore a whole-step approach to its tonic. The subtonic lacks the compelling drive of the leading tone to *lead* upwards by half step to the tonic. Accordingly, the key center is less clear in those modes that have subtonics than in those employing leading tones.

The Phrygian mode has a half step between its supertonic and tonic scale degrees. The half-step relationship between the Phrygian mode's supertonic and tonic scale degrees is sometimes referred to as the "upper leading tone." (The Locrian mode also has a half step between its supertonic and tonic scale degrees.) Apart from the upper leading tone, the Phrygian mode's most notable characteristic is the diminished triad and half-diminished seventh chord that stand on its dominant scale degree. The inherent instability of both the half-diminished seventh and its underlying triad weakens the *harmonic root relationship* between the Phrygian's dominant and tonic chords (see above, pp. 90–91).

The dominant seventh of the Phrygian mode occurs on its mediant. The tonic, subdominant, and subtonic scale degrees project the minor seventh chord. The supertonic and submediant support the major seventh.

Example 9–8: seventh chords in the Phrygian mode

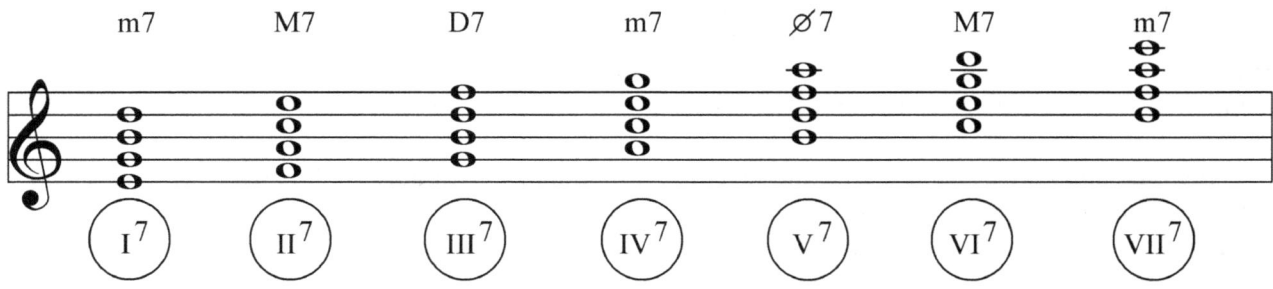

The properties of the Lydian mode are similar to those of the Ionian mode. Both modes have a leading tone; however, there are some differences. The Lydian mode has an augmented 4th between its tonic and subdominant scale degrees. Conversely, the distance between the tonic and subdominant scale degrees of the remaining six church modes, including the Ionian, is a perfect 4th. Other differences between the Ionian and Lydian modes are found in the projection of seventh chords above their respective scale degrees.

Example 9–9 presents the vocabulary of seventh chords for the Lydian mode. Both the Lydian tonic and dominant have the major seventh. The supertonic supports the dominant seventh. The mediant, submediant, and leading-tone scale degrees of the Lydian mode all project the minor seventh. The Lydian subdominant is the half-diminished seventh.

Example 9–9: seventh chords in the Lydian mode

In example 9–10, we have an arrangement of the four white-key seventh chords within the Mixolydian mode. The tonic seventh of the Mixolydian mode is the dominant seventh. The supertonic, dominant, and submediant scale degrees project the minor seventh, while the subdominant and subtonic carry the major seventh. The mediant supports the half-diminished seventh. (The range of the Mixoydian mode in 9–10 begins one octave register lower in relation to the range of the Lydian mode in example 9–9 above.)

Example 9–10: seventh chords in the Mixolydian mode

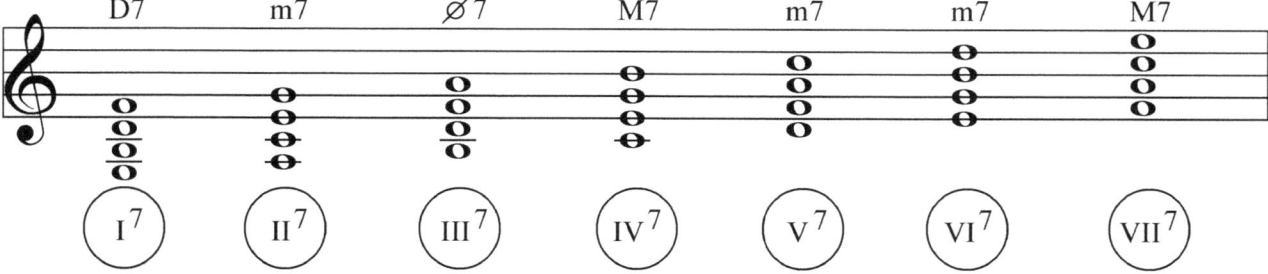

Example 9–11 illustrates the formation of seventh chords for the Aeolian mode, which may be more familiar to us as the natural minor. As with the Dorian and Phrygian modes, the tonic seventh of the Aeolian mode is the minor seventh; the remaining two minor sevenths are on the mode's subdominant and dominant. Both the Aeolian mediant and submediant scale degrees support the major seventh. The Aeolian mode has a half-diminished supertonic and a dominant-seventh subtonic.

Example 9–11: seventh chords in the Aeolian mode

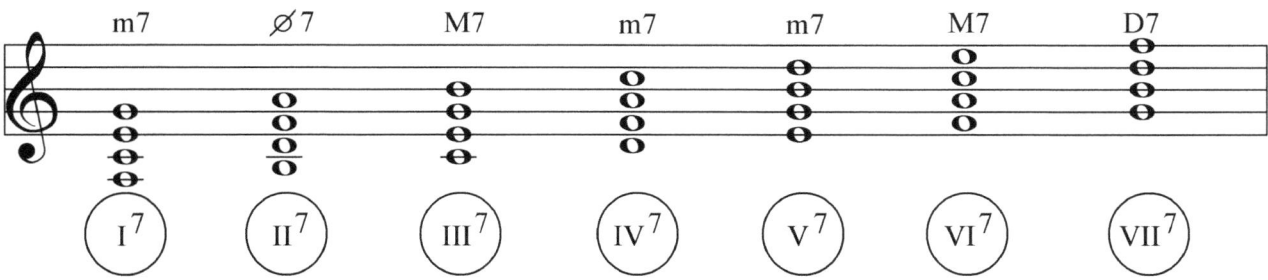

The addition of chord sevenths to the triads of the Locrian mode is shown in example 9–12. The Locrian mediant, subdominant, and subtonic all carry the minor seventh, while the submediant projects the dominant seventh. Both the supertonic and the dominant take major sevenths. These additions present no difficulties for those who would use the Locrian mode in music composition. However, as we observed in Chapter 8, there are certain problems associated with the Locrian mode (see above, pp. 99, 102), despite the fact that the sevenths do enrich the mode's chordal vocabulary.

The unstable diminished triad of the tonic becomes, with the addition of the seventh, an unstable half-diminished seventh chord. Further, the root relationship between the tonic and dominant chords of the Locrian mode is weak; for the distance between the scale degrees upon which they stand remains a diminished 5th (B to F) rather than a perfect 5th (B to F♯).

Example 9–12: seventh chords in the Locrian mode

⌀7	M7	m7	m7	M7	D7	m7
I⁷	II⁷	III⁷	IV⁷	V⁷	VI⁷	VII⁷

The Formation of Seventh Chords in the Major Mode

Let us review the formation of the four types of white-key seventh chords and describe them within the context of the major mode. As with the diatonic church modes, the seventh chord content for major has two major sevenths, three minor sevenths, one dominant seventh, and one half-diminished seventh (example 9–13). Attaching the Arabic number 7 to the Roman numeral chord symbol accounts for the presence of the seventh in root-position seventh chords.

The method for describing the location of the roots and qualities of the sevenths that occur in the major mode is identical to the approach implemented for the signification of triads. If the basic triad has a major 3rd between the root and its third, then the Roman numeral of the seventh chord is expressed in uppercase. If the basic triad has a minor 3rd between the root and its third, then the Roman numeral of the seventh chord is expressed in lowercase.

Both the half-diminished seventh and the fully diminished seventh (in minor) take a superscript circle because the underlying triad is diminished. A superscript circle without a slash (O 7) represents the fully diminished seventh (example 9–18); a circle with a diagonal slash (⌀ 7) represents the half-diminished seventh (9–13).

Example 9–13: the seventh-chord content for the major mode

M7	m7	m7	M7	D7	m7	⌀7
MT / M7	mt / m7	mt / m7	MT / M7	MT / m7	mt / m7	d°t / m7

C: I⁷   ii⁷   iii⁷   IV⁷   V⁷   vi⁷   vii⌀⁷

Inversions of the Seventh Chord

Since the seventh chord consists of four tones, it has four chord positions: root position, first inversion, second inversion, and third inversion. In first inversion, the third is the bass pitch, in second inversion the fifth, and in third inversion the seventh.

The previous examples of seventh chords shown in this chapter are all in root position. Example 9–14 shows all four positions of the dominant seventh in C major. If the seventh chord is in root position, then *the bottom note of the interval of the 7th indicates the location of the root* (see the bracketed arrow).

The *complete* figured-bass description for the intervals above the lowest tone of the seventh chord in root position is signified with the Arabic numbers $^7_5{}_3$. The numbers designate the intervals of the 3rd, 5th, and 7th above the root of the chord. When either an alphabet letter or a Roman numeral precedes the figured bass of the seventh chord in root position, we omit the Arabic numbers 5 and 3 and retain the 7 (see 9–14a).

The first inversion of the seventh chord (9–14b) has the third in the bass. Upon inversion, the interval of the 7th above the root (G/F) becomes the interval of the 2nd (F/G). If the bottom note of the 7th indicates the location of the root, then *the upper note of the 2nd identifies the root of the seventh chord in all three of its inverted positions* (see the bracketed arrows in examples 9–14b, 14c, and 14d).

The *complete* figured-bass description for the intervals above the third of the seventh chord in first inversion is signified with the Arabic numbers $^6_5{}_3$. The numbers indicate the intervals of the 3rd, 5th, and 6th above the third of the chord (B D F G). When either an alphabet letter or a Roman numeral precedes the figured bass of the seventh chord in first inversion, we omit the Arabic number 3 and retain the 6 and the 5 (9–14b).

Example 9–14: the seventh chord in root position, first inversion, second inversion, and third inversion

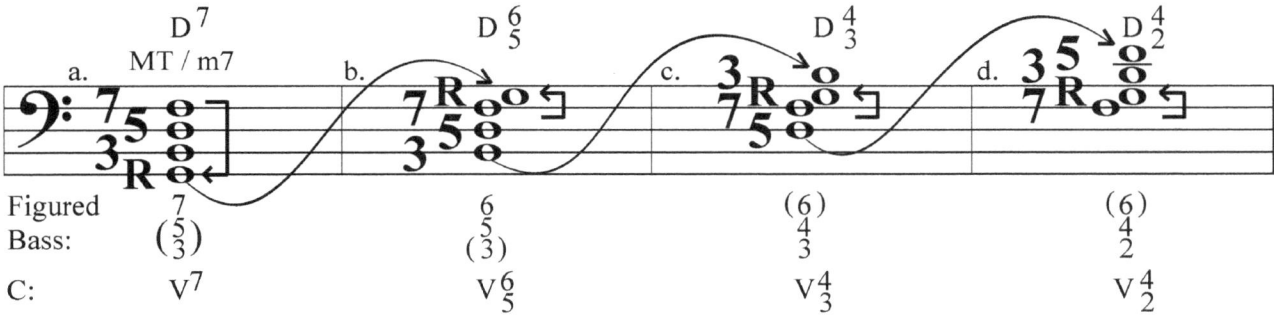

The second inversion of the seventh chord (9–14c) has the fifth in the bass. Again, upon inversion, the upper note of the 2nd identifies the root of the seventh chord. The *complete* figured-bass description for the intervals above the fifth of the seventh chord in second inversion is signified with the Arabic numbers $^6_4{}_3$. The numbers represent the intervals of the 3rd, 4th, and 6th above the fifth of the chord (D F G B). When either an alphabet letter or a Roman numeral precedes the figured bass of the seventh chord in second inversion, we omit the Arabic number 6 and retain the 4 and the 3 (9–14c).

The third inversion of the seventh chord (9–14d) has the seventh in the bass. As in examples 9–14b and 14c, the upper note of the 2nd identifies the root of the seventh chord. The *complete* figured-bass description for the intervals above the seventh of the seventh chord in third inversion is signified with the Arabic numbers $\begin{smallmatrix}6\\4\\2\end{smallmatrix}$. The numbers denote the intervals of the 2nd, 4th, and 6th above the seventh of the chord (F G B D). When either an alphabet letter or a Roman numeral precedes the figured bass of the seventh chord in third inversion, we omit the Arabic number 6 and retain the 4 and the 2 (9–14d). In sum, the four positions of the seventh chord are abbreviated as: 7, $\begin{smallmatrix}6\\5\end{smallmatrix}$, $\begin{smallmatrix}4\\3\end{smallmatrix}$, and $\begin{smallmatrix}4\\2\end{smallmatrix}$.

The Treatment of the Dissonant Seventh

This section examines the treatment of the chord seventh within the context of a four-chord succession consisting of the tonic, subdominant, dominant, and tonic. Musicians usually refer to any succession of harmonies as a "chord progression." Moreover, commercial and jazz musicians may use the term "changes" to describe the process by which one chord proceeds to another, producing a succession (or progression) of harmonies.

The addition of the seventh element to the triad may potentially constitute a powerful connective agent between chords. For when a seventh chord stands in either a rising 2nd or rising 4th or falling 5th root relationship to another chord, the resolution of the 7th dissonance intensifies the motion between the two chords.

In 9–15, a seventh chord of the subdominant leads to a seventh chord of the dominant. Two different operations involving the treatment of the dissonant 7th are taking place within this chord progression, each of which demonstrates an important principle for the resolution of real seventh chords:

(1) If a seventh chord stands in a rising 2nd root relationship to another chord, then the seventh of the first chord will move down by step to become the fifth of the second chord.
(2) If a seventh chord stands in a rising 4th or falling 5th root relationship to another chord, then the seventh of the first chord will move down by step to become the third of the second chord.

Example 9–15: treatment of the seventh in the IV^7 and the V^7

In measure 2, the seventh of the IV ^{7} is the result of a suspension from the previous tonic chord. The IV ^{7} stands in a rising 2nd root relationship to the V ^{7}; thus, the seventh of the IV ^{7} moves down by step to become the fifth of the V ^{7} (E to D). In measures 3–4, there is a rising 4th root relationship between the V ^{7} chord and the final tonic chord. The seventh of the dominant, which is approached by leap but could have been prepared as a suspension, moves down by step to become the third of the tonic chord (F to E).

The Seventh Chord of the Leading Tone

We know that the leading-tone triad and the major triad of the dominant share two tones in common; that is to say, the root and the third of the leading-tone triad are the same pitches as the third and the fifth of the corresponding dominant triad (see Chapter 7, p. 91).

As example 9–16 demonstrates, adding a chord seventh (F) to the major triad of the dominant (G B D) brings the relationship between the two chords even closer together; for the resulting dominant seventh of C major contains all of the components of the leading-tone triad, its root, third, and fifth (B D F).

Sharing three of the dominant seventh's four chord tones, the leading-tone triad is sometimes considered to be a dominant chord with a missing root (that is, B D F minus the G). Because of its key-defining function and common pitch content with the dominant, the leading-tone triad serves in most cases as a dominant. As such, all of the chords built on the leading tone belong to the "dominant family" of chords. To be sure, there are circumstances in which the chord of the leading tone may not be functioning as a dominant but rather serving some other purpose within a particular musical context. However, most of the time, the leading-tone triad is appropriately recognized as a chord of the dominant family.

Example 9–16: common tones between the leading-tone triad and the dominant seventh chord

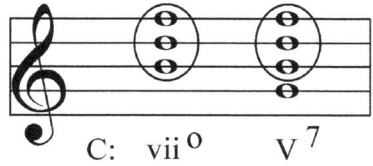

The half-diminished seventh chord of the leading tone, which stands in a rising 2nd root relationship to the tonic and occurs in *all chord positions* (including root position), is often used as a dominant chord. Notice that the seventh of the leading-tone seventh chord (B D F A) in example 9–17 moves down by step to become the fifth of the tonic chord (A to G). (In the minor mode, the fully diminished seventh rather than the half-diminished seventh addresses the tonic chord.)

Example 9–17: voice leading the tonal melodic dominant in the major mode

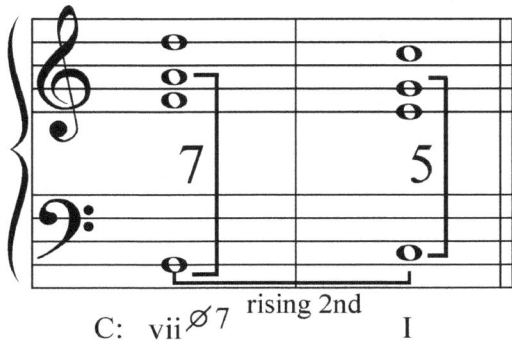

The Formation of Seventh Chords in the Minor Mode

As we have seen, the pitch content of the major mode yields a formation of seven seventh chords, one for each of its diatonic scale degrees. This section focuses on the richest form of minor in terms of pitch content, the melodic minor; for here, we have a greater number of potential seventh chords than those found in any of the seven-tone diatonic scales, including the harmonic minor and the natural minor.

In Chapter 6 (p. 73), we learned that a sharp in front of a number designating a variable scale degree does not necessarily mean that the pitch itself carries a sharp, nor does a flat in front of a number necessarily mean that the pitch itself carries a flat. Rather, the accidental merely indicates that there are two pitches with the same letter name and that one pitch is either raised or lowered in relation to the other one. For example, if c minor has both an A♮ and an A♭, then A♮ is raised in relation to A♭ and A♭ is lowered in relation to A♮. Thus, A♮ is raised 6 (♯6) and A♭ is lowered 6 (♭6).

Similarly, in Chapter 7 (p. 89), we said that if the root of a triad in the melodic minor is a variable scale degree, then the Roman numeral chord symbol is preceded by either a flat or a sharp, just as individual pitches for the variable scale degrees are indicated as either ♯6 and ♯7 or ♭6 and ♭7. The principles cited here and in the foregoing chapters are applicable to the formation of seventh chords in the melodic minor.

The pitch content of the melodic minor produces a vocabulary of thirteen triads, more chords than either the major mode, the natural minor, or the harmonic minor. The addition of the chord seventh to the triads of the melodic minor increases the number of chords to sixteen. In actual practice, however, the melodic minor's capacity for seventh chords falls somewhat short of its potential. Still, how does a mode with nine pitches give rise to sixteen potential seventh chords?

Example 9–18 demonstrates how the addition of the chord seventh increases the number of chords on three scale degrees: the tonic, subtonic, and leading tone (the filled-in note heads designate the variable scale degrees). Variables ♭7 and ♯7 become seventh components of two chords on the tonic, while variables ♭6 and ♯6 form sevenths for two chords on the subtonic and for two chords on the leading tone—six chords.

In 9–18, we find that ♯7 (B) produces the augmented-major seventh of the mediant (E♭ G B D) and the minor-major seventh of the tonic (C E♭ G B). Despite their existence within the melodic minor, both chords are rare occurrences in music literature. The use of ♯6 (A) as the seventh of the subtonic major seventh (B♭ D F A) and as the seventh of the leading-tone half-diminished seventh (B D F A) renders both chords impractical; for the linear demands of ♯6 to move upwards to ♯7 conflicts with the harmonic tendency of the dissonant 7th to resolve downwards.

Although it is possible to assign chord symbols to all of the seventh chords of the melodic minor, just as we did in Chapter 7 with the triads of the melodic minor, accounting for the addition of the chord seventh to all sixteen chords presents certain complications that are beyond the scope of this text, a text intended primarily for the beginning commercial musician (as explained in the preface). We shall soon discover that the most important form of chord notation for our purposes is the lead-sheet terminology introduced in Chapter 10.

In any case, for almost all of the seventh chords of the melodic minor, attaching the Arabic number 7 to the Roman numeral is sufficient to indicate the presence of the seventh element. For the seventh element of the two leading-tone seventh chords, no additional descriptive terminology is needed beyond the inclusion of the superscript circle mentioned earlier: the circle without the slash represents the fully diminished seventh (o 7); the circle with the diagonal slash (ø 7) represents the half-diminished seventh.

Study the chord formations in 9–18 until you understand how sixteen seventh chords are theoretically possible in the melodic minor. For the commercial musician, expressing the chords with Roman numerals and various other symbols is far less important than understanding the pitch content of the melodic minor and the potential richness of its seventh-chord vocabulary. (The chord symbols for the seventh chords of the melodic minor are discussed in *Finding The Right Pitch II: A Guide To The Study Of Basic Harmony*.)

Example 9–18: the seventh-chord content of the melodic minor

c:	m7	m-M7	ø7	m7	M7	A-M7	m7	D7
	mt / m7	mt / M7	d°t / m7	mt / m7	MT / M7	A+T / M7	mt / m7	MT / m7

c:	m7	D7	M7	ø7	D7	M7	°7	ø7
	mt / m7	MT / m7	MT / M7	d°t / m7	MT / m7	MT / M7	d°t / d7	d°t / m7

The Added 6th

Every seventh chord in root position has two components: the basic triad (root, third, and fifth) and the interval of the 7th above the root, forming the seventh element. We refer to the basic triad of the seventh chord as the "root triad." The first inversion of the seventh chord, however, projects the sound of a "false triad" upwards from its bass, consisting of the seventh chord's third, fifth, and seventh elements.

Although you hear what sounds like the root, third, and fifth of a triad, the "root" is actually the third, the "third" is actually the fifth, and the "fifth" is actually the seventh. This false triad has a different quality than the actual root triad for each seventh chord (except for the fully diminished seventh, which contains a neutral-sounding profile consisting of three acoustical minor 3rds, regardless of its written position).

Thus, in the first-inversion seventh chords of example 9–19, the major seventh projects a false minor triad (19a), the dominant seventh a false diminished triad (19b), the minor-major seventh a false augmented triad (19c), the augmented-major seventh a false major triad (19d), the minor seventh a false major triad (19e), and the half-diminished seventh a false minor triad (19f).

Example 9–19: the false triads of first-inversion seventh chords

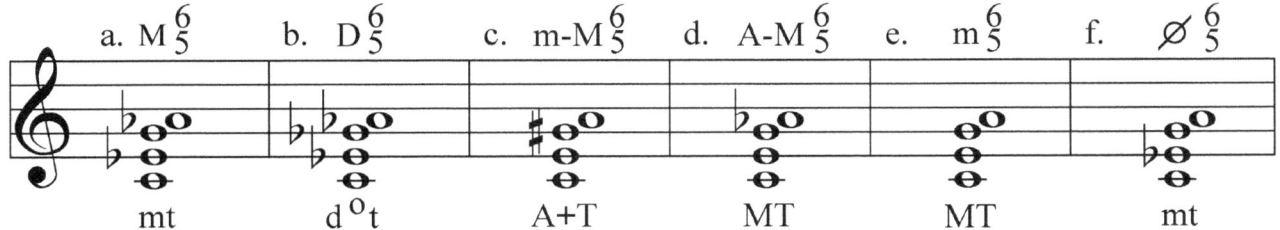

The two most important false triads for our purposes are shown in examples 9–19e and 19f above and in 9–20 below (note the key signatures). In 9–20a, the first inversion of the minor seventh chord (C E G A) displays a false major triad ("C E G"). In 9–20b, the first inversion of the half-diminished seventh chord (C E♭ G A) shows a false minor triad ("C E♭ G").

Both false triads have a major 6th above their respective false roots ("C" up to A). In each chord, the 6th also constitutes a major 2nd above the false fifth ("G" up to A). In certain circumstances, the major 2nd above the chord fifth is viewed by musicians as an addition to the basic triad, an "added 6th." It is possible to add tones to the triad, tones positioned most frequently at the intervals of the 4th, 6th, and 9th above the root. In this section, our concern is with the addition of the 6th to the false triads contained within the first inversion of the minor seventh and the half-diminished seventh.

Example 9–20: added-6th chord or seventh chord in first inversion?

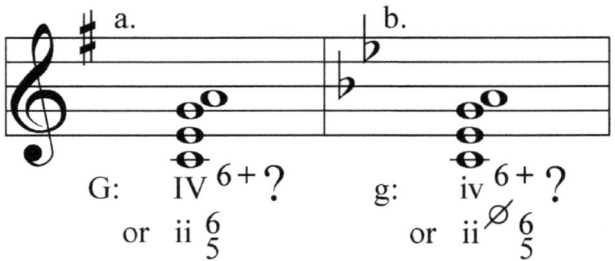

Students of traditional harmony might be inclined to interpret both chords as first-inversion sevenths; however, could the presence of the 6th be considered an addition to the basic triad? Although the limits of space prevent a complete answer to this question, suffice it to say that a real seventh chord should have its seventh component function as a dissonance in relation to the root of the chord. A real seventh component should resolve down by step into the next chord, if there is a tone of resolution available in that chord. If the two chords share a rising 4th or falling 5th or rising 2nd root relationship, then we probably have a chord of the seventh in first inversion.

Still, in some cases, the tone may not be a seventh but rather an addition to the triad, the added 6th. If the triad has an added 6th, then our chord symbol would be a plus sign attached to the *right* of the number 6. The plus sign positioned to the *left* of the figured bass designates an augmented triad. In 9–20a, there is not enough musical context to determine if the chord is either a IV $^{6+}$ or a ii $^6_5$ in the key and mode of G major.

In commercial music and jazz, the default interpretation always favors the added 6th; from this perspective, there is no indication that the tone in question (the added 6th) is the root of either the minor seventh chord or the half-diminished seventh chord. In 9–20b, the chord is either a iv $^{6+}$ or a ii$^{\varnothing}$ $^6_5$ in the key and mode of g minor; however, for commercial musicians, it is the former, an added-6th chord.

Finally, before we examine the notation for commercial music and jazz in Chapter 10, let us conclude with two stipulations: the added 6th should not involve
(1) a minor 6th above the root of the basic major or minor triad,
(2) nor should an added 6th appear above the root of the diminished triad or the augmented triad.
These stipulations eliminate the first inversion of the major seventh, dominant seventh, minor-major seventh, and augmented-major seventh as added-6th chords.

Chapter 10 Lead-Sheet Terminology

The use of Roman numerals in conjunction with figured bass, introduced in Chapter 7, constitutes not just a form of chord description but also an application of music analysis. The Roman numeral and figured-bass symbols tell us the location of the root within the key and what element of the chord is the lowest note of the musical texture. Figured bass also indicates any additional tones contained within the basic triad (such as the added 6th). The case of the Roman numeral along with such symbols as the plus sign and the superscript circle with or without a diagonal slash drawn through it help to distinguish the qualities of the chords. These descriptive components enhance our understanding of the music by giving us information about the chords and placing them within the functional context of the major-minor tonal system.

As informative as these chord symbols are, however, it is not necessary for the musician to enjoy such analytical insights during a music performance, particularly if he or she plays commercial music or jazz. In this chapter, we will undertake a brief survey of the basic types of chord symbols commonly used by commercial and jazz musicians who read from a musical score known as the **lead sheet**, a notational device that provides limited information about a music composition, primarily, the root of the chord, its quality, and when it is to be performed in relation to the melody.

The term "changes" as it pertains to commercial music and jazz refers to the successions (or progressions) of chords in a music composition that are notated in the lead sheet and thus made available to the musician as a performance guide. The lead sheet consists of a time signature, a key signature, a melody notated in the treble clef on a single staff, and chord symbols placed above the staff. Usually, the musician reading the lead sheet is either a guitarist or a keyboard player who uses the chord symbols to create an accompaniment for the melody. Additionally, the lead sheet often includes guitar tablature, which consists of diagrams located above the staff showing the musician where to place his or her fingers on the fingerboard to play the chords.

Despite the laudable attempts of commercial and jazz musicians to standardize the chord symbols that appear in lead sheets, several alternative notations may exist for any single chord. As a consequence, we shall present those chord symbols most frequently referenced in surveys of this type.

Triads

An uppercase letter with no other symbol attached denotes a major triad in root position (example 10–1a). If the triad appears in an inverted position, then the bass pitch is given and preceded by a forward slash. Such dispositions are commonly referred to as "slash chords." Thus, C / E designates a C-major triad in first inversion (10–1b); C / G signifies a C-major triad in second inversion (10–1c). A letter to the right of a slash may also indicate a tone in the bass that does not belong to the chord. In any event, lead-sheet symbols do not always show chord inversions.

Example 10–1: lead-sheet symbols for the major triad in all positions

The preferred indication for the minor triad is an uppercase letter representing the chord in root position. In order to identify the triad quality as minor, the uppercase symbol MI immediately follows the triad designation at about half the size of the chord name (example 10–2a). Inversions are shown with the forward slash and pitch name of the bass tone (examples 10–2b and 2c).

Alternative expressions for the minor triad follow the initial chord symbol with either the letter m in lowercase or a minus sign. A word of caution when using the minus sign: sometimes it causes interpretative problems because the minus can also serve the same function as the flat, which is used to lower a chord tone, such as the fifth or the ninth.

Example 10–2: lead-sheet symbols for the minor triad in all positions

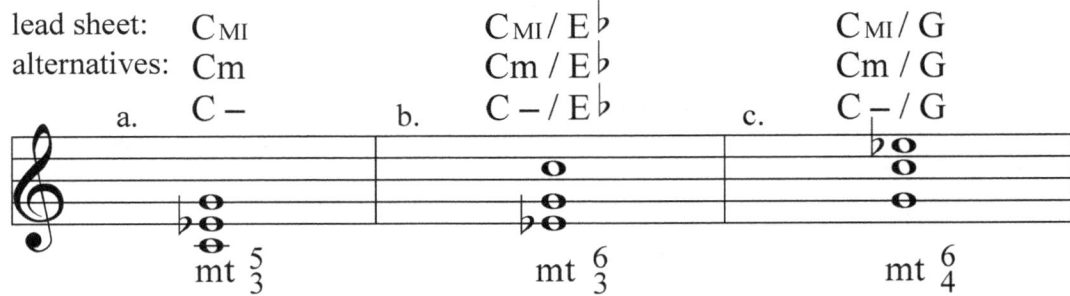

Lead sheets represent the diminished triad as a minor triad with a lowered fifth (example 10–3). The notation for the chord consists of the chord name followed in parentheses by a flat attached to the number 5 ($\flat 5$). Musicians refer to the lowered fifth variously as the "flat fifth," "flatted fifth," or "flat five." This method for describing the diminished triad is unambiguous and presents no interpretative problems.

However, when the diminished triad is expressed with either the abbreviation "DIM" or the superscript circle instead of the lowered fifth in parentheses, musicians often assume that the chord has a seventh and play a fully diminished seventh, a chord that projects a neutral-sounding profile of acoustical minor 3rds.

We therefore reserve the superscript circle for the fully diminished seventh and describe the diminished triad instead as a minor triad with a lowered fifth. Inversions of the diminished triad are shown with the forward slash and pitch name of the bass tone (examples 10–3b and 3c). We also include the forward slash to indicate the inversions for the alternative descriptions of the diminished triad with the understanding that musicians may play a fully diminished seventh instead of a triad.

Example 10–3: lead-sheet symbols for the diminished triad in all positions

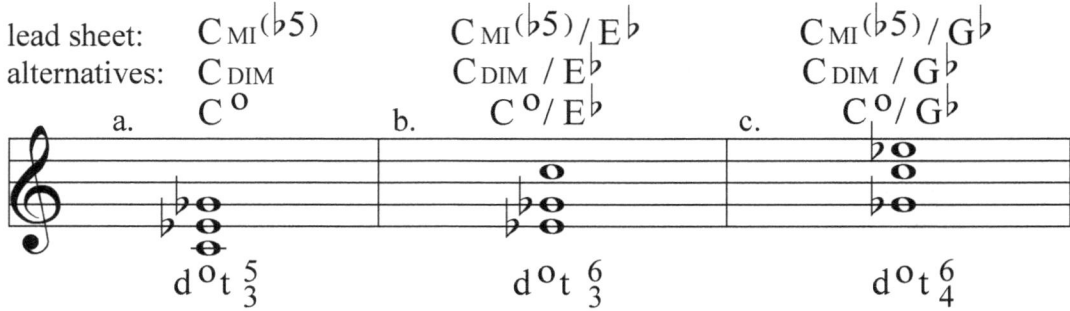

Another chord with a neutral-sounding profile is the augmented triad, which projects two acoustical major 3rds, regardless of its written position (see above, pp. 84–85). It is unlikely that a musician reading a lead sheet will find the augmented triad in any voicing other than root position. In any case, chords with neutral-sounding profiles are often misspelled because their performance is not dependent on an accurate expression of chord position.

The preferred symbol for the augmented triad is the plus sign, placed to the right of the chord name (in uppercase). Occasionally, however, lead-sheet terminology uses the abbreviation "AUG" for the augmented triad or notates the chord as a major triad with a raised fifth ($\sharp5$).

Example 10–4: lead-sheet symbols for the augmented triad, always interpreted in root position

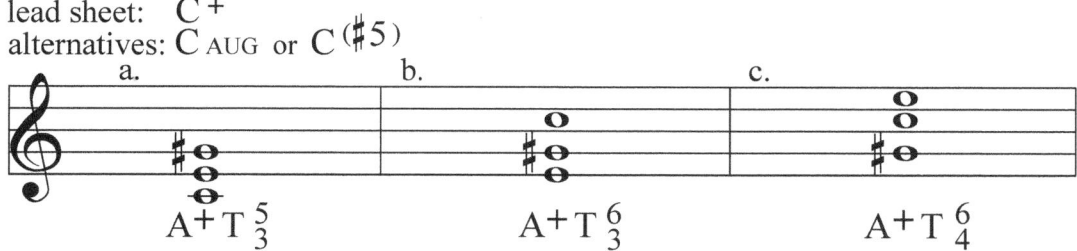

The Major Seventh, Dominant Seventh, Minor Seventh, and Half-Diminished Seventh

Seventh chords are distinguished from triads by including the number 7 in their chord names. For the major seventh chord in root position (10–5a), the chord name consists of an uppercase letter representing the root and (major) triad quality followed by the uppercase symbol MA at about half the size of the chord name.

The MA symbol indicates that the interval of the major 7th occurs above the root (C up to B). A less common symbol for representing the major 7th attaches a triangle (the fourth letter of the Greek alphabet, Delta) to the chord name. But regardless of which notational figure is employed, we interpret the major 7th above the root of the chord as an *alteration* of the minor 7th.

For the dominant seventh in root position (10–5b), the chord name consists of an uppercase letter denoting the root and (major) triad quality followed by the number 7. The absence of MA indicates an unaltered minor 7th above the root of the chord (C up to B$\flat$).

The symbols for the minor seventh chord in root position (10–5c) resemble those used for the minor triad; the preference in this text is for placing MI between the chord name and the number 7 to signify the minor triad. Common alternatives to MI are m or min in lowercase.

The half-diminished seventh (10–5d) is indicated as a minor triad with a lowered fifth enclosed in parentheses ($\flat5$) to the right of the number 7 (a minor 7th above the root). Alternatively, you might encounter the superscript circle with a diagonal slash drawn through it.

Example 10–5: the major seventh, dominant seventh, minor seventh, and half-diminished seventh

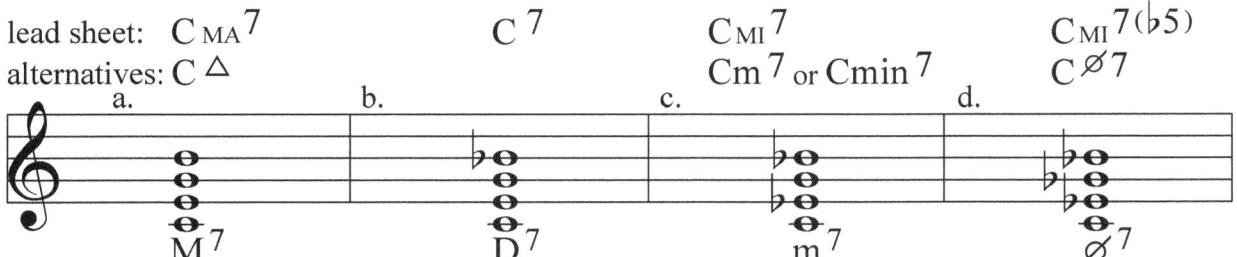

Inversions of the Major Seventh, Dominant Seventh, Minor Seventh, and Half-Diminished Seventh

Inversions of sevenths are indicated with a forward slash between the number 7 and the bass pitch (examples 10–6, 7, and 8). The third inversion of any seventh chord can *omit* the number 7, express the chord name as a triad, and position the pitch name of the seventh component to the right of the slash (examples 10–6d, 7d, and 8d). The inclusion of the number 7 is unnecessary because setting the pitch name of the seventh element directly to the right of the forward slash automatically creates the seventh chord in third inversion.

Lead sheets observe one additional exception to both the slash and the number 7: the first inversions of the minor seventh and the half-diminished seventh are written as triads with added 6ths (examples 10–9b and 9d).

Example 10–6 illustrates the major seventh in all four chord positions. *The only circumstance in which the MA symbol should appear immediately after the chord name is when the interval of the 7th above the root is major.* Again, the absence of MA implies that the interval of the minor 7th stands unaltered above the root. As mentioned above, the third inversion of the chord omits the number 7, expresses the chord name as a triad, and places the pitch name of the seventh component to the right of the slash.

Example 10–6: the major seventh in all four positions

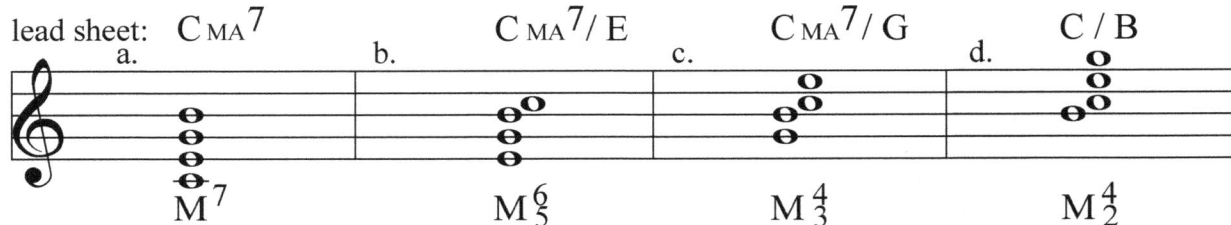

The lead sheet for the dominant seventh, shown in example 10–7, resembles the description for the major seventh except that it lacks the MA symbol. We understand that a minor 7th spans the distance between the root and the seventh.

Example 10–7: the dominant seventh in all four positions

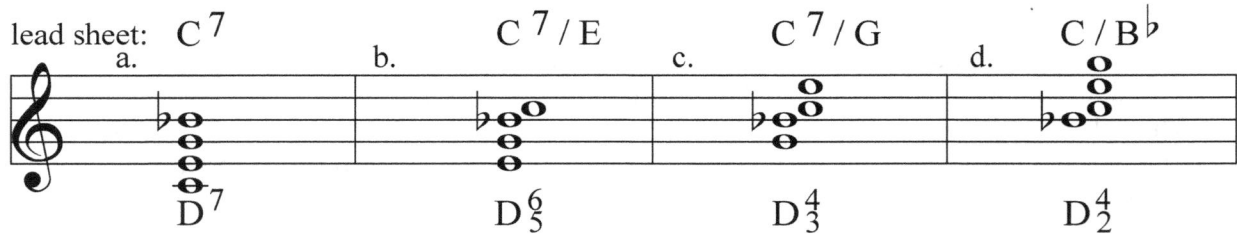

Example 10–8 exhibits the second and third inversions for the minor seventh and the half-diminished seventh. The lead sheet for the second and third inversions of the minor seventh includes the MI symbol and the name of the bass pitch to the right of the forward slash (examples 10–8a and 8b).

As shown in example 10–5d above, we indicate the half-diminished seventh in root position as a minor triad with a lowered fifth enclosed in parentheses to the right of the number 7. For second and third inversions of the chord, the symbol for the lowered fifth precedes the forward slash and the name of the bass pitch (examples 10–8c and 8d).

Example 10–8: second and third inversions of the minor seventh and the half-diminished seventh

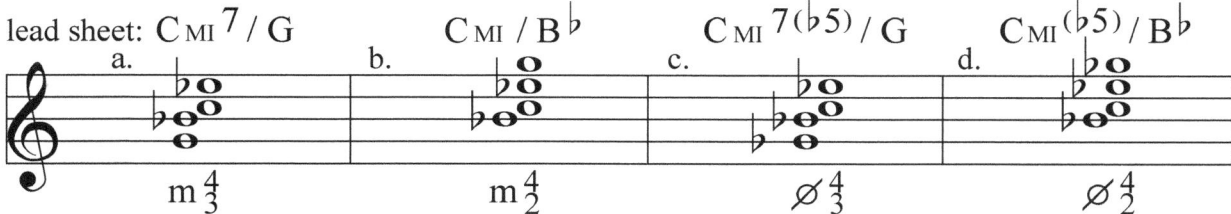

The Added 6th and Added 9th

Examples 10–9a and 9c display the minor seventh and half-diminished seventh in root position. Examples 10–9b and 9d present what could be interpreted as the first inversion of each chord. We know that the third, fifth, and seventh elements of the minor seventh and the half-diminished seventh in first inversion constitute false major and minor triads (see Chapter 9, pp. 121–122). Commercial musicians interpret the three lowest pitches of these first-inversion chords as triads with a 6th added above their respective "roots."

In 10–9b, we have an E♭-major triad (E♭ G B♭) with an added 6th (C), and in 10–9d, an E♭-minor triad (E♭ G♭ B♭) with an added 6th (C). The lead sheet for the triad with the added 6th is the number 6 positioned to the right of the chord name. The minor triad (10–9d) also takes the MI symbol to distinguish it from the major triad (10–9b).

Example 10–9: the minor seventh and half-diminished seventh as added-6th chords

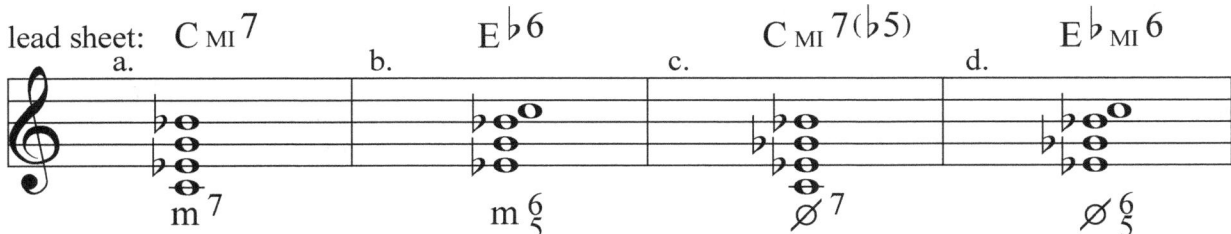

If the added-6th chord appears within the context of a key signature, such as the minor mode, the 6th will have to be adjusted to maintain the interval of the major 6th above the root. As demonstrated in example 10–10, which expresses the key and mode of e♭ minor, the added 6th is raised to C♮. Studying the intervallic structure of the chords that commonly occur in lead sheets will help you to make the necessary adjustments more easily whenever confronted with a key signature.

Example 10–10: maintaining the major 6th of the added-6th chord when there is a key signature

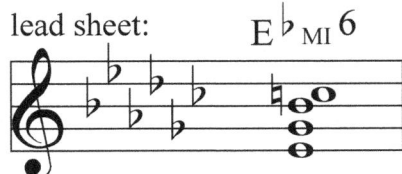

Example 10–11 shows how to notate the added 6th with a seventh chord in root position by placing "ADD6" in parentheses to the right of the number 7.

Example 10–11: adding the 6th to a seventh chord

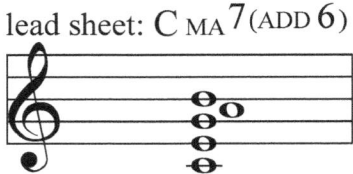

In Chapters 7 and 9, we learned that a tertian harmony consisting of four superimposed 3rds is a chord of the ninth. If, however, the seventh component is not present in a triad that nonetheless has the interval of the 9th above the root, then we refer to the resulting harmony as an added-9th chord rather than as an actual ninth chord. The "ADD9" indication is enclosed in parentheses and attached to the chord name (examples 10–12a and 12b). If adding both the 6th and the 9th to the triad, place the numbers 6 and 9 after the chord name to the left and right of the forward slash as follows: 6 / 9 (examples 10–12c and 12d).

Example 10–12: adding the 9th or both the 6th and 9th to the major and minor triads

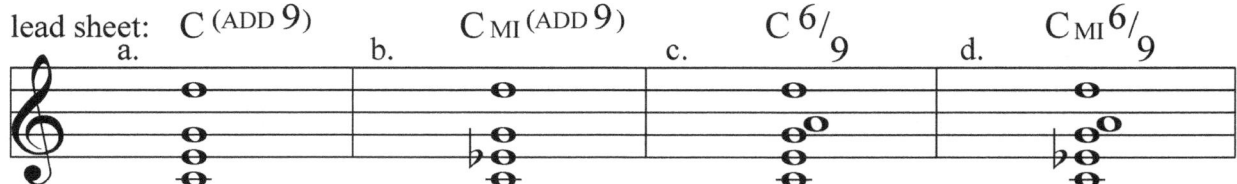

Finally, it should be understood that a marking such as "ADD2" means that you place an additional tone in the chord at the interval of a major 2nd above the root, not at the interval of a major 9th. An alternative notation simply includes the number 2 after the chord name (for example: C2 means a major triad with an added 2nd, C D E G). Usually, the third of the chord is retained; however, one way to specify the omission of the third is to write "SUS2" after the chord name. The SUS2 sign directs the musician to suspend a 2nd above the root of the chord and omit the third (for example: C SUS2 indicates C D G).

Chords of the Ninth

As stated above, an actual ninth chord should also contain the chord seventh; otherwise, the ninth is simply an added component of the underlying triad. Example 10–13 exhibits four chords of the ninth; here, the seventh is included in the chord structure and the uppermost extension of the ninth remains *unaltered*. That is to say, the interval from the root up to the ninth is a major 9th, an unaltered ninth. However, if the top note of the ninth is either raised or lowered from its original major quality, then we have an alteration of the highest component of the chord.

The chord in 10–13a is called a *dominant ninth* because its underlying seventh-chord quality is that of a dominant seventh, with a minor 7th from the root to the seventh. The chord in 10–13b is termed a *major ninth* because it contains a major 7th (the MA refers to the seventh) from the root to the seventh. Technically, the major 7th above the root of the major ninth chord is an altered component; therefore, strictly speaking, a ninth chord with an altered seventh is an altered chord. We refer to the chord in 10–13c as a *minor ninth* because the basic triad is minor, with the MI symbol attached to the chord name designating its quality. The 7th is minor as well (C up to B♭).

Although we have yet to present the lead sheet for the underlying seventh chord in 10–13d, the minor-major seventh, the MI indicates the quality of the triad as minor while the MA7 in parentheses identifies the 7th as major (an altered 7th). The chord may be referred to as the "minor-major ninth." Using the number 9 in the lead-sheet symbol implies a complete chord with both the ninth *and* seventh elements.

Example 10–13: chords of the ninth

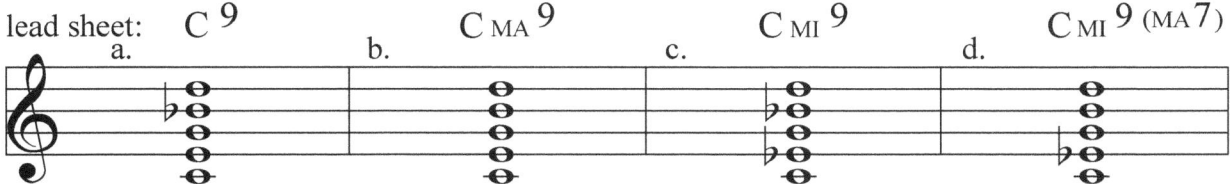

The Fully Diminished Seventh, Minor-Major Seventh, and Augmented-Major Seventh

Examples 10–14, 15, and 16 display the structures and chord symbols for the three remaining seventh-chord types, starting with the fully diminished seventh. As recommended earlier, we avoid using the superscript circle to indicate the diminished *triad* because musicians usually add an unspecified seventh to the chord. It is less ambiguous to describe the diminished triad as a minor triad with a lowered fifth, reserving the superscript circle for the fully diminished seventh (10–14a). A common variant finds the superscript circle positioned between the chord name and the number 7.

Since the fully diminished seventh projects a neutral-sounding profile of acoustical minor 3rds, regardless of how it is written, the lead-sheet description assumes that the chord name is the root. Therefore, musicians execute the lead-sheet symbol for the fully diminished seventh by superimposing three minor 3rds above the chord name without concern for its functional identity as either the root, third, fifth, or seventh of the chord. Attempting to show the actual chord position using the forward slash and name of the bass pitch would only complicate the musician's task.

The other two chords in 10–14, the minor-major seventh and the augmented-major seventh, do include the slash in their respective chord symbols. Our recommendation for the minor-major seventh (10–14b) is to follow the chord name with the MI symbol, which tells us that the triad is minor. Secondly, place the major 7th symbol in parentheses to the right of MI. One common alternative for the minor-major seventh combines the chord name with the minus sign and then designates the quality of the seventh as MAJ7.

We identify the augmented-major seventh with a plus sign after the chord name followed by MA7 in parentheses (10–14c). Another way to represent this chord would be to indicate an E-major triad with a C bass; in this instance, the third, fifth, and seventh of the augmented-major seventh project a false major triad (E G♯ B). It is also possible to place MA7 after the chord name and follow both symbols with the raised fifth sign in parentheses (♯5).

Example 10–14: the fully diminished seventh, the minor-major seventh, and the augmented-major seventh

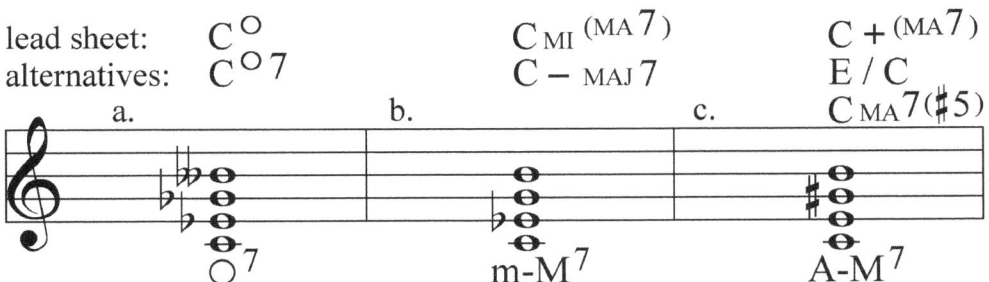

Inversions of the Minor-Major Seventh and Augmented-Major Seventh

Example 10–15 has the minor-major seventh in all four positions. Notice that in first inversion (10–15b), the minor-major seventh produces a false augmented triad (E♭ G B) from the actual third, fifth, and seventh of the chord. As previously mentioned, the third inversion does not require the number 7 because the pitch name following the forward slash *is* the seventh of the chord.

Example 10–15: the minor-major seventh in all four positions

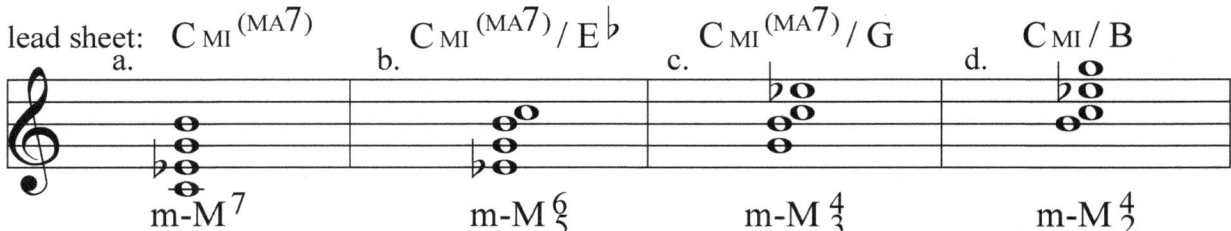

Example 10–16 demonstrates the lead sheet for the augmented-major seventh in all four positions. In first inversion (10–16b), we have a false major triad (E G♯ B) consisting of the actual third, fifth, and seventh of the chord.

Example 10–16: the augmented-major seventh in all four positions

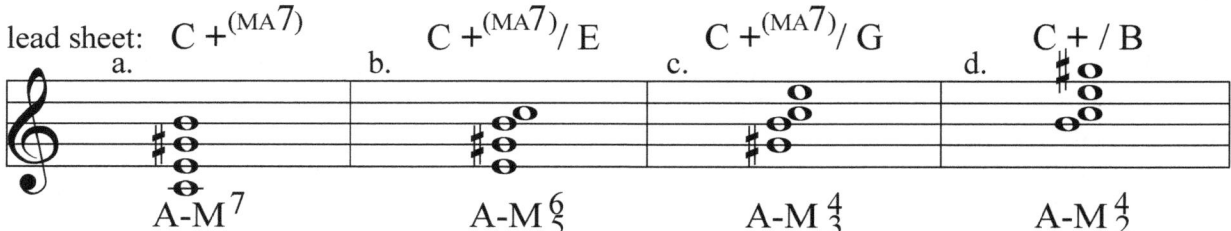

The Suspension

In commercial music and jazz, the traditional techniques of dissonance resolution may not be applied as outlined in Chapters 5 and 9 of this text. Dissonant tones may or may not move down by step to consonant tones. The dissonant suspension in commercial music and jazz is not necessarily prepared from the preceding chord nor must it resolve to a consonance. To be sure, dissonances can be treated as we might expect; but there is no theoretical doctrine mandating such operations.

The dissonant suspension in both commercial music and jazz is not unlike adding a tone to a chord, or substituting one tone for another; for as stated above, preparation and resolution of the dissonance does not have to occur. From this perspective, any tone can be "suspended"; however, the most common suspension involves the interval of the 4th above the root of the chord. Typically, the 4th takes the place of the third.

As shown in example 10–17, the word sus positioned to the right of the chord name or to the right of a number such as 7 or 9 implies the addition of the 4th above the root of the chord. One alternative, often found in older lead sheets, such as those from the 1970s, removes the implication by adding the number 4 to the symbol: sus4. Today, musicians understand that "SUS" without a number denotes the 4th.

Example 10–17: "suspending" the 4th

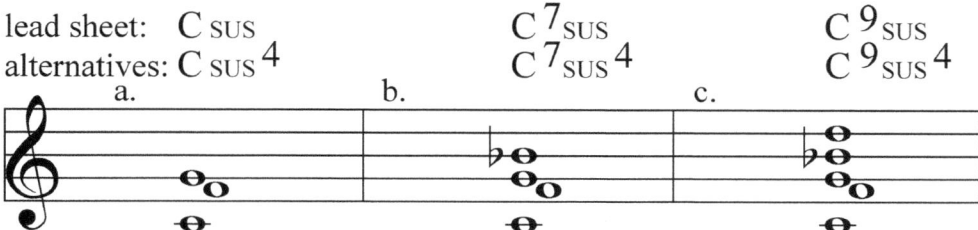

The Altered Fifth and Altered Ninth

In lead-sheet terminology, a flat or sharp appearing in conjunction with numbers such as 5, 9, 11, or 13 indicates an alteration of a chord in which one or more of elements of the chord is either raised or lowered (the eleventh occurs only at the interval of a perfect or augmented 11th above the root of the chord; it cannot be lowered). We prefer enclosing both the accidental and the number in parentheses to represent the alteration.

In examples 10–3, 5, 8, and 9, we encountered the lowered-fifth sign ($\flat 5$), which was used to express the diminished triad (a minor triad with a lowered fifth) as well as the half-diminished seventh (a minor triad with a lowered fifth and a minor 7th between its root and seventh). Example 10–18 displays the lead sheet for the diminished triad, the half-diminished seventh, and what is termed either the half-diminished ninth or the minor ninth with the flat fifth. Again, the inclusion of the number 9 implies the presence of the seventh element of the chord.

Example 10–18: the lowered-fifth sign with the diminished triad, seventh, and ninth

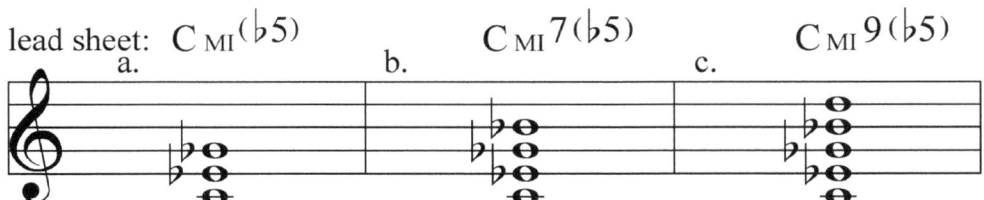

As we have said, the lowered fifth is referred to variously as the flat fifth, flatted fifth, or flat five. The raised fifth is usually associated with the augmented triad and called the "augmented fifth," "sharp fifth," or "sharp five." The flat fifth is shown below with the major triad (example 10–19a), the dominant seventh (10–19b), and dominant ninth (10–19c). Although it is possible to have altered fifths in chords of the eleventh and thirteenth, *unaltered* fifths are often omitted from the texture in chords above the ninth.

Example 10–19: the major triad, dominant seventh, and dominant ninth (flat fifth)

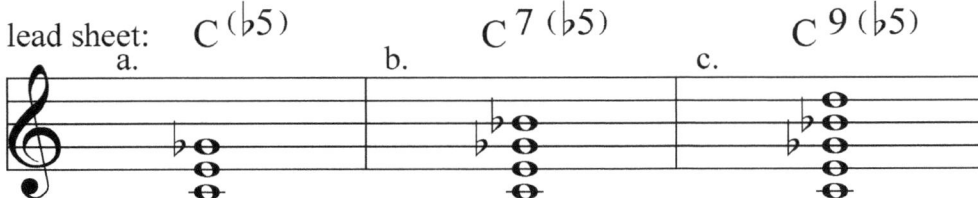

The major triad with the flat fifth (example 10–20a) may also carry a major 7th (10–20b) and a major 9th (10–20c) above its root.

Example 10–20: the major triad, major seventh, and major ninth (flat fifth)

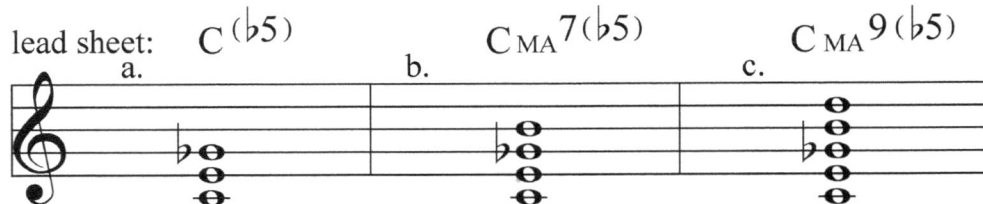

We know that when the fifth of the major triad is raised one half step, the chord becomes an augmented triad. The augmented triad takes a plus sign after the chord name (example 10–21a), the augmented-major seventh adds MA7 in parentheses to its lead-sheet description (10–21b), and the augmented-major ninth places the number 9 between the plus sign and the symbol for the major 7th (10–21c).

As observed earlier, the augmented-major seventh C E G♯ B can be described as an E-major triad with a C bass. Musicians often recognize the augmented-major ninth C E G♯ B D as an E-dominant seventh with a C bass (10–21c).

Example 10–21: the augmented triad, augmented-major seventh, and the augmented-major ninth

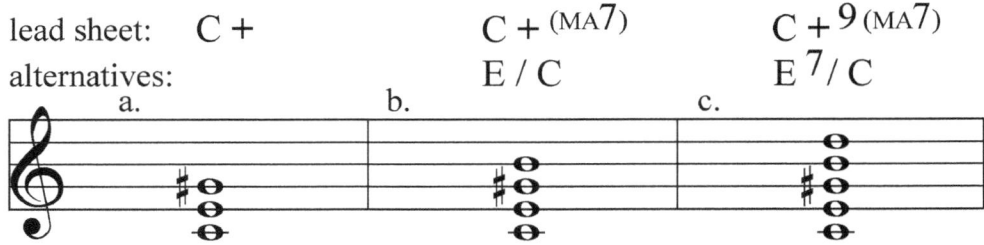

The unaltered ninth stands at the interval of a major 9th above the root of the chord. To alter the ninth, convert the major 9th into either a minor or augmented interval by lowering or raising its pitch one half step. As demonstrated in example 10–22, the chord symbol for altering the ninth involves placing either a flat or a sharp before the number 9 and enclosing both figures in parentheses.

When the ninth is altered, we must show the presence of the seventh element by including the number 7 directly to the right of the chord name. Remember that the MI symbol between the chord name and the number 7 refers to the minor quality of the basic triad (10–22b).

Example 10–22: the dominant ninth (flat ninth), minor ninth (flat ninth), and dominant ninth (sharp ninth)

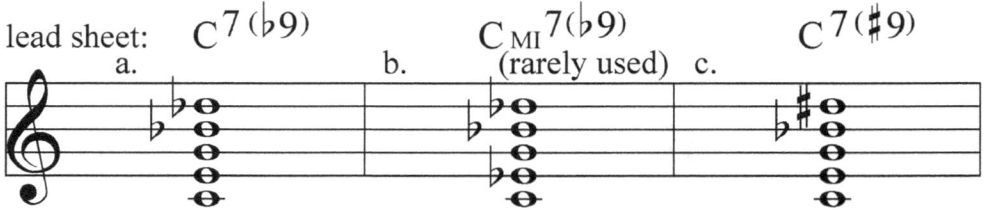

As with the major seventh chord, the altered ninth incorporates the MA symbol into the chord name if the interval between the seventh and the root is a major 7th. Example 10–23 shows the major ninth chord with the sharp ninth, a chord with a relatively high level of dissonance because of the major 7ths between the root and the seventh (C up to B) and between the third and the ninth (E up to D♯).

Example 10–23: the major ninth (sharp ninth)

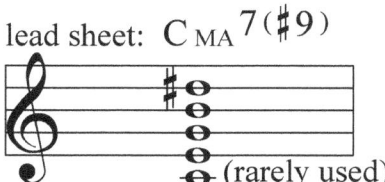

The Altered Fifth and Altered Ninth Together

The raised fifth is often used together with the flat ninth or sharp ninth as altered components of the dominant chord (example 10–24). Since raising the fifth of the major triad produces the augmented triad, it is unnecessary to combine the symbol for the sharp fifth with either of the altered ninth symbols, as the plus sign between the chord name and the number seven accounts for the altered fifth. Still, despite the advantage of having the plus sign available, you will probably encounter some lead sheets that exhibit a preference for the sharp fifth sign (♯5).

Example 10–24: the dominant ninth (sharp fifth, flat ninth or sharp ninth)

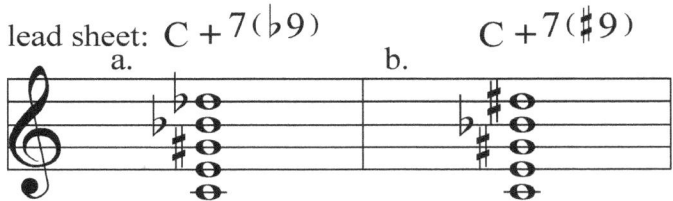

However, if the basic triad of the ninth chord does not have a raised fifth, then the symbols for the altered components are stacked vertically and usually enclosed in a single set of parentheses. As illustrated in example 10–25, place the lowest altered element(s) of the chord below the highest. The first two ninth chords shown below have lowered components, producing the dominant ninth with the flat fifth and flat ninth (10–25a) and the minor ninth with the flat fifth and flat ninth (10–25b). The third ninth chord is a dominant ninth with the flat fifth and sharp ninth (10–25c).

Notice that the underlying seventh chord of the second ninth (10–25b) is actually the half-diminished seventh. Both commercial and jazz musicians would recognize the half-diminished seventh with its chord ninth but nonetheless read the lead-sheet symbol as the minor seventh with the flat fifth (and flat ninth).

Example 10–25: the dominant ninth and minor ninth (flat fifth, flat ninth or sharp ninth)

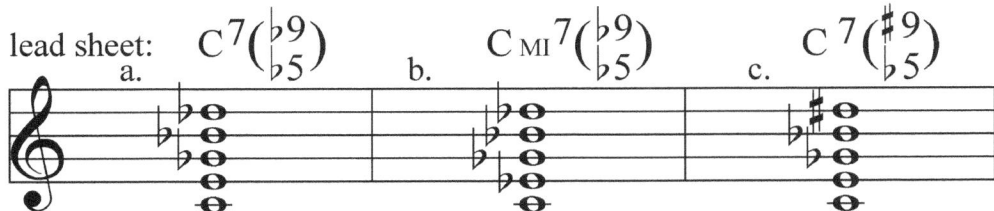

Chords of the Eleventh and Thirteenth

Chords of the eleventh and thirteenth often omit one or more elements of their respective chord structures. This section will show when these omissions are advisable. We shall also encounter some of the most common chromatic alterations to these "higher powered" chords.

The uppermost component of the eleventh chord occurs at the interval of a perfect or augmented 11th above the root. As demonstrated in example 10–26a, the eleventh chord frequently *omits its third* when
(1) the distance from the root to the eleventh is a perfect 11th (that is, an unaltered eleventh), and,
(2) the distance from the root to the third is a major 3rd. This formation produces a minor 9th between the third and the eleventh of the chord, a very dissonant interval (E up to F). The most likely chord to omit the third is the dominant eleventh. In 10–26a: C (E) G B♭ D F (the omitted chord tone is represented as a filled-in note head in parentheses).

On the other hand, 10–26b confirms a different set of options for the minor eleventh chord. Since the major 9th between the third and the eleventh (E♭ up to F) is less dissonant than the minor 9th, the third is usually retained. However, the chord might omit its fifth if that tone is unaltered, in other words, if the distance between the root and the fifth constitutes a perfect 5th, rather than a diminished 5th or augmented 5th: C E♭ (G) B♭ D F.

Example 10–26: the chords of the dominant eleventh and minor eleventh

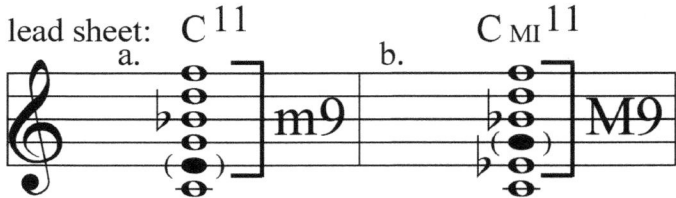

In all instances of the thirteenth chord (example 10–27), we interpret its major 13th as an *unaltered* interval; therefore, a minor 13th or augmented 13th would be considered an altered element of the chord. Moreover, just as the sixth component of the added-6th chord may require an adjustment to maintain the interval of the major 6th above the root within the context of the key signature, it may be necessary to adjust the uppermost element of the thirteenth chord in order to preserve the interval of the major 13th (see example 10–10 above).

Example 10–27a indicates that if the thirteenth chord has a major 3rd between its root and third and a perfect 11th between its root and eleventh (an unaltered eleventh), then once again, a dissonant minor 9th results between the third and the eleventh (E up to F). In this case, the chord is likely to be a dominant thirteenth. Usually, the dominant thirteenth *omits the eleventh* rather than the third. Since the chord retains the third, we can also omit the fifth, if unaltered: C E (G) B♭ D (F) A. The minor thirteenth, shown in 10–27b, is usually expressed with all chord tones present; however, an unaltered fifth would be the most expendable tone should you want an incomplete disposition of the chord: C E♭ (G) B♭ D F A.

Example 10–27: the chords of the dominant thirteenth and minor thirteenth

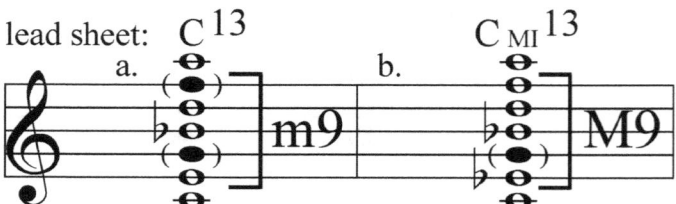

Altered Eleventh and Thirteenth Chords

There are myriad forms of altered chords in the music literature. Some are exceedingly rare, even impractical, while others appear in virtually every popular music or jazz composition. In this section, we draw upon those lead-sheet symbols that most clearly represent the altered chords typically notated and read by those who use this terminology. Let us begin with some alterations of the dominant chord with the eleventh as its uppermost extension.

In example 10–28a, the dominant eleventh contains a flat ninth (♭9). Since the eleventh element itself is not altered, the number 11 immediately follows the chord name. With the exception of using the plus sign for representing the augmented fifth of a triad, the most acceptable practice places the altered symbol in parentheses. Thus, we enclose the flat ninth symbol in parentheses and situate it to the right of the number 11. In this disposition of the chord, *the third is omitted* and the unaltered eleventh retained.

Examples 10–28b and 28c call for a slightly different approach. In 10–28b, we have a dominant eleventh with an unaltered ninth and a raised eleventh (an augmented 11th above the root of the chord). The number 9 represents the unaltered ninth and is placed after the chord name but before the parentheses, which enclose the altered eleventh. Since the distance from the chord third to the eleventh is a major 9th (E up to F♯), we retain both elements and have the option of leaving out the fifth (G), the most expendable tone.

Example 10–28c combines the alterations of 28a and 28b. The ninth is flatted, the eleventh sharped. Both alterations are expressed in parentheses. The seventh, which is unaltered, appears between the chord name and the alterations. Again, the fifth is expendable; its omission will not upset the balance or identity of the chord.

It is notable, however, that without the fifth (G), many musicians will re-interpret the F♯ and E of the chord as G♭ and F♭ respectively and recognize a G♭-dominant seventh over a C bass: G♭ B♭ D♭ F♭ over C. (Musicians could also re-interpret the B♭ and D♭ of the chord as A♯ and C♯ respectively and recognize an F♯-dominant seventh over a C bass: F♯ A♯ C♯ E over C). If we retain the fifth, a very convincing case can be made for a G♭-major triad over a C-major triad. Example 10–28d illustrates the common practice of indicating a "chord over a chord" with one chord name standing directly above the other, both marked and separated by a straight horizontal line.

Example 10–28: altered dominant eleventh

(1) 10–28a: C-dominant eleventh, flat ninth
(2) 10–28b: C-dominant ninth, sharp eleventh
(3) 10–28c: C-dominant seventh, sharp eleventh, flat ninth
(4) 10–28d: G♭-major triad over C-major triad

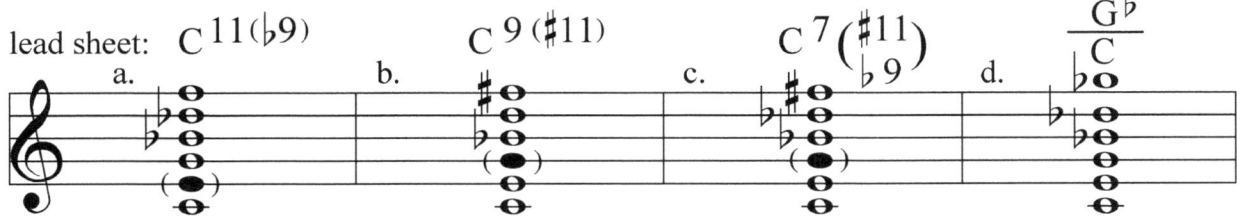

There are two different ways to indicate the dominant eleventh in example 10–29. Since the two uppermost extensions are altered and appear in parentheses (the ninth and the eleventh), we attach the number 7 to the chord name, instead of 9 or 11. The plus sign represents the raised fifth, which produces an augmented triad. Using the chord over a chord method of notation introduced in example 10–28d, we can re-interpret the F♯ of the chord enharmonically and describe the chord as a G♭-major triad over a C-augmented triad.

Example 10–29: altered dominant eleventh

(1) 10–29a: C-dominant seventh, sharp eleventh, flat ninth, sharp fifth
(2) 10–29b: G♭-major triad over C-augmented triad

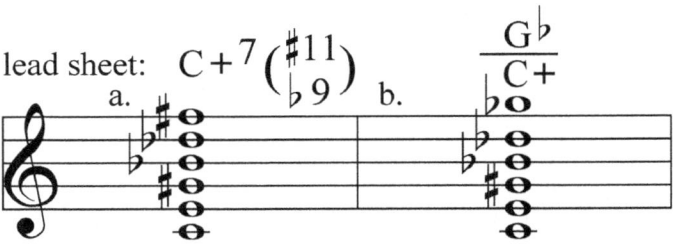

Example 10–30 lists some of the possibilities for the chord of the eleventh with the minor triad as the basic tertian unit. In two instances, the fifth of the minor triad is lowered one half step (examples 10–30a and 30b); in the other two, the fifth remains unaltered and therefore constitutes the most expendable chord tone (examples 10–30c and 30d).

The only altered tone in 10–30a is the lowered fifth; 10–30b adds a lowered ninth to the chord. Examples 10–30c and 30d both contain raised elevenths in their respective chords. The ninth in 10–30c is unaltered, whereas 10–30d shows a lowered ninth.

Example 10–30: altered minor eleventh

(1) 10–30a: C-minor eleventh, flat fifth
(2) 10–30b: C-minor eleventh, flat ninth, flat fifth
(3) 10–30c: C-minor ninth, sharp eleventh
(4) 10–30d: C-minor seventh, sharp eleventh, flat ninth

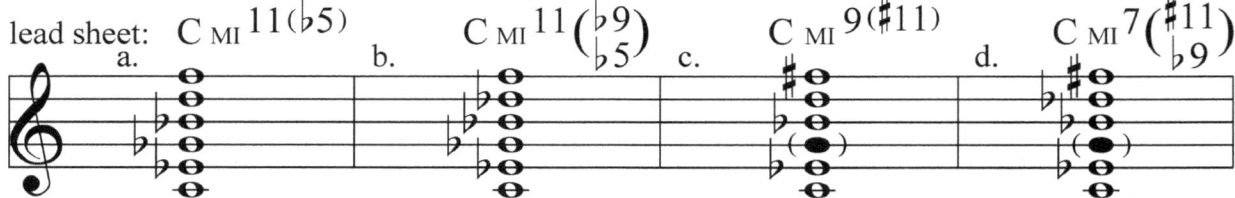

As we have observed, the interval of the major 7th between the root and the seventh of the chord is an alteration of the minor 7th. Accordingly, we refer to the tertian harmony displayed in example 10–31a as an altered eleventh chord because C up to B is a major 7th. Omitting the third of the chord avoids the dissonant minor 9th between the third and the eleventh (E up to F).

In both examples 10–31b and 31c, the unaltered fifth is the most expendable tone while the raised eleventh (an augmented 11th above the root) of the chord in each example allows us to retain the third. Additionally, 10–31c raises the ninth. If we chose not to omit the fifth of 10–31c, then using the chord over a chord notation in 10–31d enables us to put forward a simple lead-sheet description that also stipulates a complete disposition of the chord.

Example 10–31: altered major eleventh

(1) 10–31a: C-major eleventh
(2) 10–31b: C-major ninth, sharp eleventh
(3) 10–31c: C-major seventh, sharp eleventh, sharp ninth
(4) 10–31d: B major triad over C-major triad

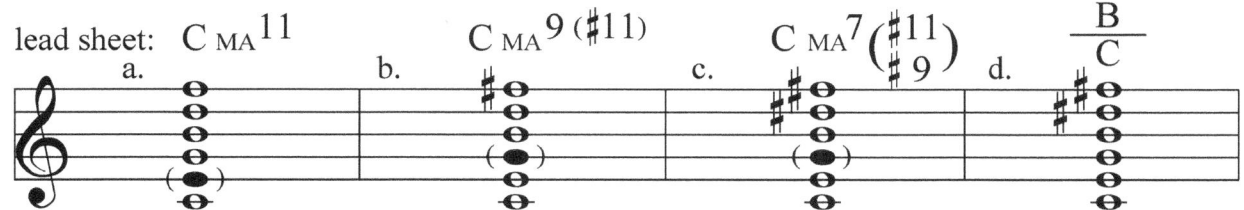

The dominant thirteenth in example 10–32a, which has a lowered ninth, may omit its unaltered fifth and eleventh. However, the dominant thirteenth in 10–32b has an altered (raised) eleventh which is therefore retained in the chord's disposition. We must assume the presence of an unaltered ninth (a major 9th) because there is no indication of an altered ninth in the chord symbol. Example 10–32c combines the lowered ninth and raised eleventh in its chord description, leaving only the fifth as an option for omission. Accounting for all of the elements in each respective version of the altered dominant thirteenth in 10–32 yields the following descriptions:

Example 10–32: altered dominant thirteenth

(1) 10–32a: C-dominant thirteenth, flat ninth
(2) 10–32b: C-dominant thirteenth, sharp eleventh
(3) 10–32c: C-dominant thirteenth, sharp eleventh, flat ninth

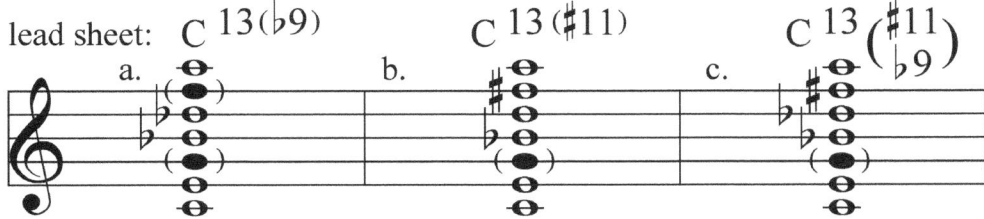

138 Chapter 10 Lead-Sheet Terminology

Example 10–33 presents some additional alterations of the dominant thirteenth with the same options for omission as example 10–32. Notice that alterations to the ninth and thirteenth (10–33a) require the chord name to take the number 7. Similarly, alterations to the thirteenth and eleventh (10–33b) require the number 9, while alterations to the eleventh and ninth (10–33c) require the number 13. Regardless of the number attached to the chord name, however, each tertian harmony in the example constitutes a different altered version of the dominant thirteenth.

Example 10–33: altered dominant thirteenth

(1) 10–33a: C-dominant thirteenth, flat thirteenth, flat ninth
(2) 10–33b: C-dominant thirteenth, flat thirteenth, sharp eleventh
(3) 10–33c: C-dominant thirteenth, sharp eleventh, sharp ninth

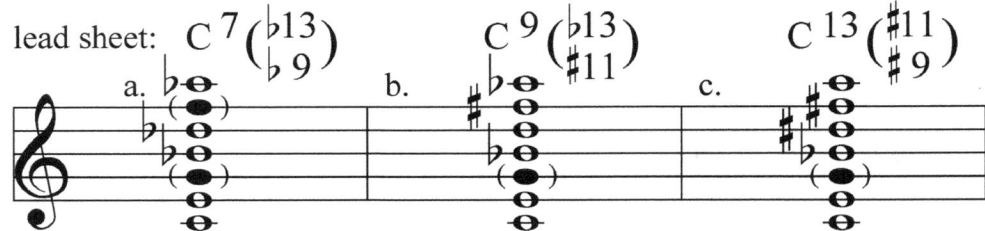

The three major thirteenth chords in example 10–34 all have one or more altered components in their respective dispositions. The fifth in each chord is unaltered and therefore expendable. Example 10–34a has a major 7th from its root to seventh. The thirteenth chord in 10–34b cannot omit its eleventh because it is raised. In 10–34c, the three uppermost extensions are raised; hence, the chord name takes the number 7.

Example 10–34: altered major thirteenth

(1) 10–34a: C-major thirteenth
(2) 10–34b: C-major thirteenth, sharp eleventh
(3) 10–34c: C-major seventh, sharp thirteenth, sharp eleventh, sharp ninth

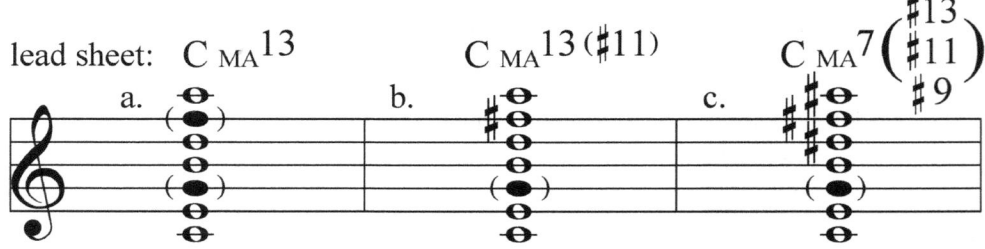

Simplifying the Notation

Most of the chords that appear in lead sheets can be expressed in a variety of ways; some of these expressions are simpler to read and interpret than others. A few of the examples presented in the foregoing pages offer notations that are easier to interpret than those the beginning student might encounter; to be sure, those who prepare lead sheets attempt to make them as accessible to the reader as possible.

Example 10–35 revisits five of the chords discussed previously and demonstrates two different ways to notate each tertian harmony. Above the chords and staff, we have the conventional chord symbols, whereas simplified descriptions appear below the chords and staff.

Example 10–35a illustrates the common practice of writing the third inversion of the seventh chord with a 7 between the chord name and the forward slash. However, as we have said, identifying the pitch name of the seventh element with the forward slash automatically creates the seventh chord in third inversion. In this instance, then, both the MA symbol and the number 7 are unnecessary additions to the lead-sheet description of the chord—though you may find them in the literature.

Example 10–35: alternative notations

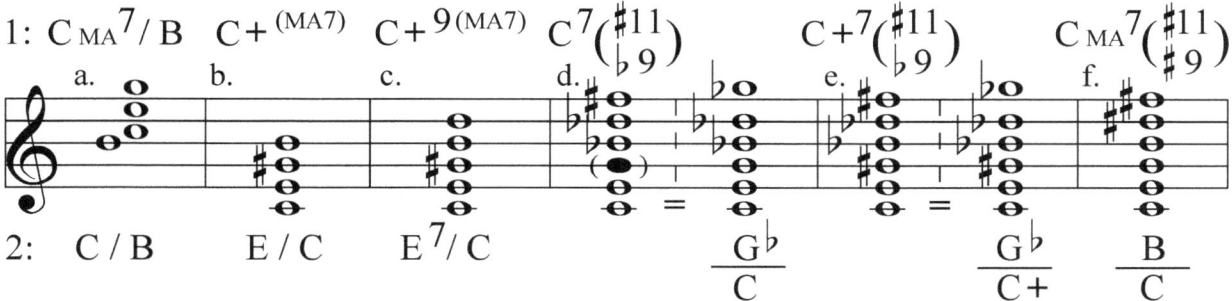

Examples 10–35b and 35c show how the slash method indicates what at first glance appears to be a tone in the bass that does not belong to the chord: an E triad over a C bass and an E-dominant seventh over a C bass. In both instances, the respective components above the root of these two chords (C) happen to form tertian harmonies that can be named individually as a triad and a seventh chord—simpler alternatives to the conventional chord symbols.

Example 10–35d displays a C-dominant seventh, sharp eleventh, flat ninth, with a potential omission of its unaltered fifth. However, re-interpreting the F♯ of the chord as G♭ and then describing the eleventh chord as a G♭-major triad over a C major triad facilitates reading. Moreover, playing a triad over a triad prevents the fifth (G) from being omitted and thus ensures a complete disposition of the chord with all six tones present. Using the chord over a chord method with tertian harmonies of higher extensions is a good way to prevent or discourage the omission of chord tones.

Example 10–35e employs the chord over a chord method to represent a G♭-major triad over a C-augmented triad. The chord would otherwise be called a C-dominant seventh, sharp eleventh, flat ninth, sharp fifth. Finally, in 10–35f, a B-major triad over a C-major triad expresses more clearly a C-major seventh, sharp eleventh, sharp ninth.

Other Abbreviations and Symbols

In our survey of chords with higher extensions, particularly chords of the eleventh and thirteenth, we have seen various options for the omissions of chord tones. If the composer wants a complete disposition of the chord, using the chord over a chord notation helps to avoid leaving out one or more tones. Still, there are times when the composer may specify an omission in the chord symbol.

The OMIT indication illustrated in example 10–36, usually enclosed in parentheses, directs the player to leave out either the third or fifth by attaching the number 3 or 5 to the chord symbol. Alternatively, some lead sheets use the word NO enclosed in parentheses followed by the number, such as NO 3rd or NO 5th.

Example 10–36: omitting chord tones

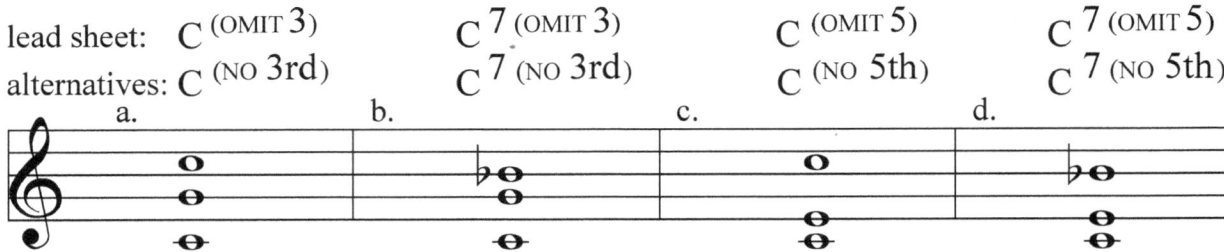

Example 10–37a shows the ALT symbol, a somewhat vague directive that indicates an altered chord. Frequently, the chord is a dominant seventh, sharp ninth, sharp eleventh, sharp fifth. However, since there is no clear specification of which chord tones should be altered and how, we find the ALT sign to be one of the weakest of all lead-sheet symbols. It would be better to simply represent the chord in 10–37a as an E♭-minor triad over a C-augmented triad (10–37b).

Example 10–37: the ALT symbol

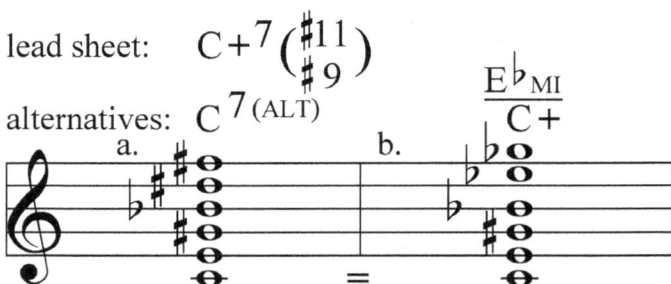

One type of symbol that appears frequently in lead sheets for rock music and/or guitar music is C5 and C5/2. As demonstrated in example 10–38a, the number follows the chord name and indicates an open 5th structure. Example 10–38b represents an open 5th with an added 2nd. In all probability, a guitarist would play what is commonly known as a "power chord," usually a two-note combination of tones involving either 5ths or 4ths played at high volume with a substantial amount of distortion and an attendant capability for sustaining notes.

Depending on the level of distortion and volume, the power chord may produce secondary sounds, that is to say, overtones and pitches sounding above and below the written tones. Explaining the mechanics of this phenomenon are beyond the purview of this text; however, suffice it to say that the C5 indication in a lead sheet could result in much more sound than what is actually notated.

Sometimes the composer does not want any chord played at a certain point in the song. In this instance, he or she writes in N.C. or NC, which means no chord is be played in the corresponding passage (10–38c).

Example 10–38: C5, C5/2, and N.C.

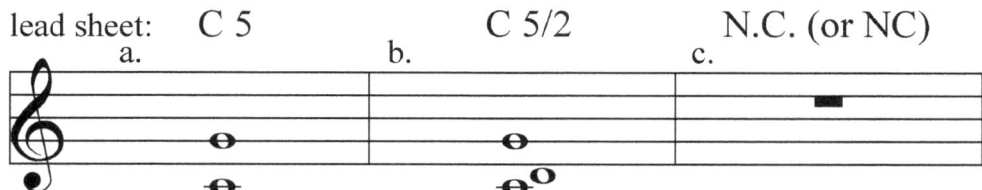

Glossary

accidental   A sign preceding a note that either raises or lowers both its pitch name and sound.

acoustic interval   An interval whose quality and numerical distance has only one aural interpretation regardless of how it is written. For example, even if a minor 6th is notated as an augmented 5th, the interval always sounds like the former rather than the latter.

active tones   Certain scale degrees of a mode are relatively stable while other scale degrees are relatively unstable. The relatively unstable scale degrees seek to move to other scale degrees that have less of a tendency to move. The scale degrees that seek to move are called active tones; they include scale degrees 2, 4, 6, and 7.

arpeggiated chord   The successive presentation of a chord's pitches. Also known as **broken chord** and **arpeggio**.

arpeggio   The successive presentation of a chord's pitches. Also known as **broken chord** and **arpeggiated chord**.

asymmetrical meter   A meter with an odd number of beats per measure, a meter that is not divisible by either 2 or 3. Also known as **odd meter**.

atonality   Atonal music is based upon a system of pitches, either strictly or loosely organized, in which no one tone is more important than any other—there is no key center toward which other tones seek to move, no tonal hierarchy.

augmented triad   A triad with a major 3rd from root to third, a major 3rd from third to fifth, and an augmented 5th from root to fifth.

bar   A unit of musical space created by the distance between two primary accents and enclosed by vertical lines called measure lines or bar lines. Also known as a **measure**.

bar line   Vertical line that marks off a unit of measured musical space called a measure or bar.

bass   The lowest range for the male voice and/or the lowest part of the musical texture.

bass clef   A sign that fixes the pitch F on the fourth line from the bottom of the five-line staff. Also known as the **F clef**.

beam   A thick horizontal line that joins two or more notes that would otherwise take flags.

block chord   A chord given a simultaneous performance of its pitches.

broken chord   The successive presentation of a chord's pitches. Also known as **arpeggio** and **arpeggiated chord**.

chord   A combination of three or more different pitches containing at least two intervals sounding either simultaneously or in succession.

chromatic half step   Two pitches a half step apart with the same letter name. For example: C and C♯.

chromaticism   Pitches that occur in a music composition that are neither native to the mode nor reflected in the key signature.

chromatic scale   A scale that divides the octave into twelve half steps.

church modes   Modes that were developed during the eighth and ninth centuries of the Common Era as a means for analyzing and classifying the monophonic music of the Roman Catholic Church. Also known as the **ecclesiastical modes**.

circle of 5ths   Two individual but related patterns of major and minor keys in which each key is one perfect 5th away from the next key and set in a circular clock-like arrangement. The face of each circle shows twelve keys, each of which adds one sharp or flat to its key signature when proceeding clockwise and counter-clockwise from "twelve o'clock" (which represents C major or a minor).

clef   A sign that identifies one pitch on the staff, usually F or G. Once the pitch has been located, it is possible to find the other pitches because they are ordered alphabetically from A to G.

compound intervals   Intervals exceeding the span of the octave.

compound meters   A meter in which each beat is divided into three equal parts or multiples of three.

conjunct motion   Movement between adjacent pitches separated by either a half step or a whole step. Also known as **melodic motion**.

consonance   A consonance is a combination of intervals that conveys a sense of rest and stability. There are two classes of consonant intervals, perfect consonances and imperfect consonances. The perfect consonances are the unison, the perfect octave, the perfect 5th, and sometimes the perfect 4th. The imperfect consonances consist of both major and minor 3rds and 6ths.

contextual interval   An interval that exists only within a written context, such as the diminished 4th, which always sounds like a major 3rd. The augmented 5th (the inversion of the diminished 4th) is also a contextual interval because the *sound* of the augmented 5th is identical to that of another interval, the minor 6th.

cross accent   Disrupting the normal rhythmic flow at the level of the beat rather than the division of the beat. Also known as a **displaced accent**.

diatonic half step   Two pitches a half step apart with two different letter names. For example: C and D♭.

diatonicism   The principle of diatonicism maintains that every mode has certain tones representing its unique profile of half steps and whole steps, tones reflected in the mode's key signature. The tones specific and appropriate to the pitch content of any given mode are called diatonic tones. Conversely, pitches that are neither native to the mode nor reflected in the key signature are chromatic tones.

diatonic scale   A scale having only one letter name for each of its seven pitches, spanning a single octave, and comprising five whole steps and two half steps.

diminished triad   A triad with a minor 3rd from root to third, a minor 3rd from third to fifth, and a diminished 5th from root to fifth.

disjunct motion   Movement between adjacent pitches separated by an interval greater than a whole step.

displaced accent   Disrupting the normal rhythmic flow at the level of the beat rather than the division of the beat. Also known as a **cross accent**.

dissonance   A dissonance is a combination of intervals that conveys a sense of tension and instability. Dissonant intervals usually seek to form connections to consonant intervals in a process known as resolution. Traditionally, dissonances resolve to consonances. When a dissonant interval is resolved to a consonance, a feeling of relaxation is produced. Resolutions of dissonance endow most of the tonal music of the Western tradition with a sense of forward motion, as the alternation between tension and relaxation propels the music ever forward.

dominant   The name for scale degree 5 of any diatonic mode.

dots   The addition of a dot extends the duration of a note or rest by one half its original value. Adding a second dot extends the duration of a note or rest by one half the value of the first dot.

double bar lines   Two parallel lines running vertically through the staff or staves. If the double bar has one narrow bar line and one thicker bar line, then it marks the end of a composition. However, if two dots precede the double bar, then it functions as a repeat sign. Another type of double bar, consisting of two narrow bar lines of the same thickness, is used to close off a section of music before the end of the composition.

duplet   A simple (two-part) division of the beat occurring in a compound meter.

dynamic accent   A sign (>) that instructs the performer to play certain notes louder than others.

dynamics   A term that refers to marks in the musical score that instruct the performer to play within a wide range of volume levels, from barely audible to extremely loud.

ecclesiastical modes   Modes that were developed during the eighth and ninth centuries of the Common Era as a means for analyzing and classifying the monophonic music of the Roman Catholic Church. Also known as the **church modes**.

enharmonic equivalents   The application of more than one letter name to the same pitch. Every pitch can have at least three different letter names except for G♯ and A♭. For example, F♭, E, and D𝄪 all represent the same tone.

enharmonic keys   Two keys that sound the same but with different spellings for their respective pitch content. In the circle of 5ths for the major mode, the three pairs of keys located on the lower portion of the circle, namely, D♭ and C♯, G♭ and F♯, and C♭ and B are enharmonic keys, keys that close the circle of 5ths by bringing the sharp and flat sides of major together. In the circle of 5ths for the minor mode, there are three pairs of enharmonic keys, namely, b♭ and a♯, e♭ and d♯, and a♭ and g♯.

F clef   A sign that fixes the pitch F on the fourth line from the bottom of the five-line staff. Also known as the **bass clef**.

fermata   Suspends the counting of the beat and extends the length of the note or rest beyond its original value. There is no precise duration for the extension of the note or rest that carries the fermata, but usually, the suspension of time will be longer in a slow tempo than in a fast tempo.

figured bass   Arabic numbers and other symbols that indicate the placement of certain intervals and pitches above the lowest note of the musical texture, the bass note.

first harmonic   The basic rate of vibration generating the pitch. Also known as the **fundamental frequency** and the **first partial**.

first inversion   Disposition of a tertian chord (usually a triad or a seventh) in which the third of the chord is the lowest tone of the musical texture.

first partial   The basic rate of vibration generating the pitch. Also known as the **fundamental frequency** and the **first harmonic**.

flag   A curved notational structure attached to the right side of any stemmed note that has a filled-in note head. In effect, the flag has the opposite function of a dot: the flag shortens the duration of the note value by one half its original value. Thus, one flag transforms a quarter note into an eighth, two flags turns an eighth into a sixteenth, three flags convert a sixteenth into a thirty-second, etcetera.

frequency   The number of sound vibrations completed in one second of time when an object is moved by force.

fundamental frequency   The basic rate of vibration generating the pitch. Also known as the **first harmonic** and the **first partial**.

G clef   A sign that fixes the pitch G on the second line from the bottom of the five-line staff. Also known as the **treble clef**.

grand staff   Two staves joined together by a brace in the left margin. The G clef and F clef occupy the top and bottom staves respectively. An additional line called a ledger line between the two staves designates a pitch called "middle C." Also known as the **great staff** and the **piano staff**.

great staff   An equivalent term for the **grand staff** and the **piano staff**.

Gregorian chant   A type of monophonic music for the Roman Catholic Church originally sung in Latin without instrumental accompaniment. The music is named after St. Gregory I (540?–604). Also known as **plainchant**.

half step   The half step is the smallest possible interval on the piano keyboard and in our Western tradition of music. There are twelve half steps within any single octave. Also known as the **semitone** or the **minor 2nd**.

harmonic interval   A type of interval that results from the simultaneous occurrence of two pitches.

harmonic motion   Movement in the bass between pitches of either a 4th or a 5th.

harmonic series   A spectrum of sounds consisting of both the fundamental frequency and its overtones. Also known as the **overtone series**.

harmony   A composite sound resulting from the simultaneous occurrence of two or more pitches.

hemiola   A process by which a composer may displace the accents in such a way that it transforms either a duple meter into what sounds like a triple meter or a triple meter into what sounds like a duple meter. It may occur within the measure or across measures.

inflection   Refers to a note that has been altered by the addition of an accidental.

interval   The distance between two pitches.

key   The principal note of a mode and the pitch to which all other pitches within that mode are related and toward which they ultimately move. Also known as the **keynote, tonic,** or **tonal center**.

keynote   The principal note of a mode and the pitch to which all other pitches within that mode are related and toward which they ultimately move. Also known as the **key, tonic,** or **tonal center**.

key signature   A type of shorthand notation in which the sharps or flats of any mode appear. The key signature identifies the specific notes that are appropriate to the mode of a musical work.

leading tone   The seventh degree of the scale that is one half step below the tonic.

lead sheet   A notational device that provides limited information about a music composition, primarily, the root of the chord, its quality, and when it is to be performed in relation to the melody. The lead sheet often includes guitar tablature, which consists of diagrams located above the staff showing the musician where to place his or her fingers on the fingerboard to play the chords.

ledger line   Horizontal line(s) located above and below the staff on which notes that lie beyond the staff are placed. Ledger lines retain within a single clef pitches that exceed the limits of any single staff.

lower tetrachord   One of two four-note segments comprising scale degrees 1 through 4 of a diatonic scale.

major-minor tonal system A system of pitch organization that emerged in the late-seventeenth century in Western Europe. The major-minor tonal system developed over time in the course the "common practice period," a span of art music composition that extended from about 1600 to 1900 C. E.

major scale A seven-tone diatonic scale with half steps between scale degrees 3 and 4 and scale degrees 7 and 8.

major 2nd Two consecutive half steps. Also known as the **whole step** (sometimes called a "step").

major triad A triad with a major 3rd from root to third, a minor 3rd from third to fifth, and a perfect 5th from root to fifth.

measure A unit of musical space created by the distance between two primary accents and enclosed by vertical lines called measure lines or bar lines. Also known as a **bar**.

mediant The name for the third scale degree of a diatonic mode.

melodic interval Two pitches occurring in succession rather than simultaneously.

melodic motion Movement between adjacent pitches separated by either a half step or a whole step. Also known as **conjunct motion**.

meter A succession of pulses of relative strength and weakness that together produce what is known as meter. The pulses in this text are called primary and secondary accents. The distance between primary accents determines the meter, a distance measured by the number of intervening secondary accents that both precede and follow the primary accents.

meter signature A sign or symbol that indicates the value of the beat and how many beats are distributed across each measure. The meter signature usually consists of two Arabic numbers, one located directly above the other. There are two principal exceptions, each of which involves a symbol that looks somewhat like the letter C. The first symbol (C), known as "common time," is the same as $\frac{4}{4}$ time. The second symbol (¢), referred to as either "cut time" or *alla breve*, is the equivalent of $\frac{2}{2}$ time. Meter signature is also known as **time signature**.

metronome A device that produces a steady and repeated click that helps the musician know exactly how fast or slow to play a composition.

minor 2nd The smallest numerical distance between two pitches on the piano keyboard and in our Western tradition of music. Also known as the **half step** and the **semitone**.

minor triad A triad with a minor 3rd from root to third, a major 3rd from third to fifth, and a perfect 5th from root to fifth.

mode A collection of pitches which demonstrates certain characteristic patterns and configurations, both melodic and chordal, seeking to confirm and establish the key of a musical work.

monophony A type of musical texture that consists of a single melodic line.

note head   The principal written component representing a musical pitch and/or durational value. The note head appears as either a hollowed-out or filled-in oval structure to which a stem is usually attached. Exceptions are the whole note which has no stem and the double whole note which is sometimes written as a hollowed-out rectangular box with a vertical line on each side of the note box.

octave   Any two pitches of the same letter name that have a frequency ratio of 2:1. An intervallic distance of either 6 whole steps or 12 half steps.

odd meter   A meter having an odd number of beats per measure that is not divisible by either 2 or 3. Also known as **asymmetrical meter**.

overtones   A spectrum of frequencies of varying degrees of intensity (volume) projected above the fundamental pitch from within the harmonic series. Overtones are usually not loud enough to be heard as pitches in their own right. Rather, the fundamental frequency and its overtones are blended together into a single composite sound. This composite sound is referred to variously as tone quality, tone color, or timbre (pronounced *tam*ber). The first overtone, which sounds one octave above the fundamental, is also called the second partial or second harmonic. The overtone series is also known as the **harmonic series**.

overtone series   A spectrum of sounds consisting of both the fundamental frequency and its overtones. Also known as the **harmonic series**.

parallel major   A major mode that shares both the same tonic and range with another mode; however, the pitch content between the two modes is different.

parallel minor   A minor mode that shares both the same tonic and range with another mode; however, the pitch content between the two modes is different.

passing tone   Usually connects two harmonic consonances, is either dissonant or consonant with another voice, may occur on either a strong or weak beat, and also appears on either a strong or weak portion of a beat. The passing tone is approached and left by step. Although more than one passing tone may be used in direct succession, a single passing tone typically fills in the melodic interval of a 3rd.

perfect 4th   An intervallic distance consisting of either 2½ whole steps or 5 half steps.

perfect 5th   An intervallic distance consisting of either 3½ whole steps or 7 half steps.

piano staff   Two staves joined together by a brace in the left margin. The G clef and F clef occupy the top and bottom staves respectively. An additional line called a ledger line between the two staves designates a pitch called "middle C." Also known as the **grand staff** and the **great staff**.

pitch   When sound vibrations are produced at a steady rate in one second of time, the human ear perceives them as pitch. These sound vibrations are called frequencies. The relative lowness or highness of any pitch corresponds to the rate of the vibrating frequency. Slower vibrating frequencies result in lower pitches, while faster vibrating frequencies produce higher pitches. On the standard 88-key piano, from the lowest to the highest pitch, the frequencies range from 27.5 to 4186 hertz (vibrating cycles per second).

plainchant A type of monophonic music for the Roman Catholic Church originally sung in Latin without instrumental accompaniment. Also known as **Gregorian chant**.

primary accents The stronger beats, or stressed beats, in the meter of a music composition. Primary accents are the first accents we perceive when hearing a stream of accents unfold in time as a piece of music is being performed.

quartal harmony A combination of 4th intervals.

relative major Any two modes standing in a relative relationship to one another will share the same key signature and the same pitch content but have different tonics and different octave ranges. Every minor mode has a relative major. To find the relative major, locate scale degree 3 of the minor mode by counting up a minor 3rd from the minor tonic, scale degree 1 (or down a major 6th from the tonic). For example, c minor's relative major is E♭ major; the key signature for both modes is three flats.

relative minor Any two modes standing in a relative relationship to one another will share the same key signature and the same pitch content but have different tonics and different octave ranges. Every major mode has a relative minor. To find the relative minor, locate scale degree 6 of the major by counting up a major 6th from the major tonic, scale degree 1 (or down a minor 3rd from the tonic). For example, D major's relative minor is b minor; the key signature for both modes is two sharps.

repeat sign A sign that instructs the performer to play a segment of music again. The most common repeat sign consists of a double bar preceded by two dots on the second and third spaces of the staff, which tells the performer to return to the beginning of the composition or some designated point in the score and repeat that section of music.

rest tones Certain scale degrees of a mode are relatively stable, while other scale degrees are relatively unstable. The relatively unstable scale degrees, called active tones, seek to move to other scale degrees that have less of a tendency to move. The stable tones are called rest tones; they include scale degrees 1, 3, 5, and 8.

rhythm The measurement of both the primary and secondary accents within the meter. Rhythm involves how the accents are organized, or configured. Rhythm is that particular arrangement of notes and rests within each measure that ultimately helps to inform the individuality of a musical composition.

root position Disposition of a tertian chord (usually a triad or a seventh) in which the root of the chord is the lowest tone of the musical texture.

scale The term scale derives from the Italian word *scala*, which means ladder. A scale is a ladder of tones: a representation of stepwise pitches, each of which is usually identified by one of seven successive alphabet names that proceed upwards or downwards.

secondary accents The weaker beats, or unstressed beats, in the meter of a music composition. Secondary accents occur after and before the primary accents.

second inversion Disposition of a tertian chord (usually a triad or a seventh) in which the fifth of the chord is the lowest tone of the musical texture.

secundal harmony A combination of major and/or minor 2nds, which may also contain 3rd intervals.

semitone The half step is the smallest possible interval on the piano keyboard and in our Western tradition of music. There are twelve half steps within any single octave. Also known as the **half step** or the **minor 2nd**.

simple intervals Intervals that do not exceed the span of the octave.

simple meters Meters in which the beat is divided into two equal parts or multiples of two.

staff A five-line four-space structure used in music notation.

stem A vertical line attached to all note heads shorter in duration than the whole note. The direction of the stem may be either up or down, depending on the relationship of the note to other notes and its position on the staff.

subdominant The name for the fourth scale degree of a diatonic mode.

submediant The name for the sixth scale degree of a diatonic mode.

subtonic The version of scale degree 7 that is a whole step below the tonic pitch, scale degree 8. The subtonic does not share the compelling drive of the leading tone to move upwards by half step to scale degree 8.

supertonic The name for the second scale degree of a diatonic mode.

suspension A special use of consonance, dissonance, and syncopation consisting of three basic parts:
(1) the suspension is prepared usually as a consonance (but sometimes as a dissonance);
(2) the preparation is held, or *suspended*, as the opposing line (usually the bass) moves to form a dissonance with the suspension (a consonant suspension is also possible); and finally
(3) the suspended voice moves down by step to *resolve* to a consonance.
It is important that the actual suspension (part 2) be metrically stronger than the resolution (part 3). The initial preparation (part 1), however, can be made from either a strong or weak position.

symmetrical meters Duple, triple, and quadruple meters in which the top number of the meter signature is divisible by either 2 or 3.

syncopation Disrupting the regular distribution of note values by emphasizing the divisions of beats and/or leaving the strongest part of the primary accent unarticulated or weakened in some way. Syncopation makes strong that which is otherwise weak.

tempo The rate of speed at which the beat in a music composition is performed.

tertian harmony A combination of 3rd intervals.

tetrachords Two four-note segments of a diatonic scale, comprising scale degrees 1 through 4 and 5 through 7 respectively.

third inversion Disposition of a seventh chord in which the seventh of the chord is the lowest tone of the musical texture.

ties A curved line that connects two or more notes together; however, only the first note of any tied pair or group of notes is articulated. The second note of the tied pair (or group of notes) is sustained for the duration of the note values presented. Tied notes are particularly useful for extending the duration of a note across the bar line.

timbre A composite sound consisting of the fundamental frequency and its overtones, referred to variously as tone quality, tone color, or timbre (pronounced *tam*ber). Although the individual overtones cannot be heard as distinct pitches, they do *color* the fundamental frequency and collectively generate the timbre of a musical instrument, making it possible to identify the source of the musical sound. On any given instrument, some overtones are relatively stronger than others. The reason two different instruments sound differently is due to the fact that each makes its own unique selection of overtones from a much larger inventory of weaker overtones. For example, the sound of the clarinet and the violin are distinguishable even when both instruments are playing the exact same pitch because each instrument projects its own unique profile of overtones, its own sonic fingerprint.

time signature A sign or symbol that indicates the value of the beat and how many beats are distributed across each measure. The time signature usually consists of two Arabic numbers, one located directly above the other. There are two principal exceptions, each of which involves a symbol that looks somewhat like the letter C. The first symbol ($\mathbf{C}$), known as "common time," is the same as $\frac{4}{4}$ time. The second symbol ($\mathbf{\mathlarger{\mathlarger{\mathlarger{\mathcal{C}}}}}$), referred to as either "cut time" or *alla breve*, is the equivalent of $\frac{2}{2}$ time. Time signature is also known as **meter signature**.

tonal center The principal note of a mode and the pitch to which all other pitches within that mode are related and toward which they ultimately move. Also known as the **key**, **tonic**, or **keynote**.

tonality Tonality is a system of pitch organization confirmed and established by certain characteristic designs of the mode. Analogous to the gravitational force exerted by the Sun upon any object that comes within its field of attraction, the tonality of a music composition establishes its own field of attraction around one central tone. All of the other tones of the mode seek to revolve around and gravitate toward this central tone in a hierarchical order. The tonic, as the principal tone of this hierarchy, exerts its gravitational force upon all of the other tones of the mode, each of which assumes a position of relative strength and stability within the tonic's field of attraction. Inherent in the system is the principal of consonant or dissonant relationships between different tones.

tonic The name for the first scale degree of a diatonic mode.

treble clef A sign that fixes the pitch G on the second line from the bottom of the five-line staff. Also known as the **G clef**.

triplet A compound (three-part) division of the beat occurring in a simple meter.

tritone An intervallic distance consisting of either 3 whole steps or 6 half steps.

upper tetrachord One of two four-note segments comprising scale degrees 5 through 8 of a diatonic scale.

INDEX

A

accelerando, 16
accidentals, 26, 143
   double flats, 26–27
   double sharps, 26–27
   flat, 26
   natural sign, 26
   sharp, 26
acoustic interval, 85, 92, 124, 129, 143
active tones, 65, 143, 150
ADD6, 128
ADD9, 128
Aeolian mode, 65, 95–97, 98–100, 102, 105, 107, 113–115
alla breve, 7
all'ottava, 33
ALT, 140
Ambrose, Saint, 95
anacrusis, 15
arpeggiated chord, 77, 143
arpeggio, 77, 143
asymmetrical meter, 23–24, 143, 149
atonality, 47–48, 143
AUG, 125
augmented fifth, 84–85
augmented intervals, 50–58, 61–62
augmented-major seventh chord, 112, 120–121, 129–130, 132
augmented triad, 79, 81, 84–89, 112, 120–121, 124–125, 129–130, 132–133, 136, 139–140, 143
Augustine, Saint, 95

B

bar, 4, 143, 148
bar line, 3–4, 12–13, 143, 152
bass, 61–63, 82, 123–124, 143
bass clef, 29, 44, 46, 143, 146
beams, 1, 3, 18–20, 143
beat, 4–9, 17–24
block chord, 77, 143
Boethius, Anicius Manlius Severinus, 95
broken chord, 77, 143

C

chord, 77–78, 143
   eleventh, 109, 134–138
   ninth, 77, 109, 128–129, 131–133, 135–139
   power chord, 140
   quartal harmony, 77, 150
   secundal harmony, 77, 151
   seventh, 77, 109–122, 125–139
   tertian harmony, 77–78, 109, 128, 136–139, 146, 150, 151
   thirteenth, 109, 134–139
   triad, 77–81, 121–122, 123–125, 127–128, 131–132, 135–137, 139, 140
chromatic half step, 28, 31, 47, 144
chromatic scale, 35, 47, 144
chromaticism, 47–48, 144
church modes, 95–108, 144, 145
   Aeolian mode, 65, 95–97, 98–100, 102, 105 107, 113–115
   Dorian mode, 96–99, 100–101, 103, 106, 113–115
   Ionian mode, 95–97, 99–103, 112–114
   Locrian mode, 96–97, 98–99, 100, 102–103, 105, 106, 108, 113–116
   Lydian mode, 96–97, 99, 100–101, 104, 106, 113–115
   Mixolydian mode, 96–97, 99, 100, 102, 105, 106, 108, 113–115
   Phrygian mode, 96–97, 98, 99, 101, 104, 106, 107, 113–115
circle of 5ths, 43, 45, 69–70, 144
clef, 29–30, 144
   bass clef, 29, 44, 46, 143
   F clef, 29–31, 33, 44, 146
   G clef, 29–31, 33, 44, 146
   treble clef, 29, 44, 46, 152
common time, 7

compound intervals, 49, 59, 144
compound meters, 5–6, 8, 17–18, 22, 24, 144
conjunct motion, 49–50, 62, 144, 148
consonance, 61–63, 110–111, 144
consonant 4th, 61–62
contextual interval, 85, 92, 144
crescendo, 17, 144
cross accent, 10–11, 144, 145
cut time, 7

D

Da Capo al Coda, 14–15
Da Capo al Fine, 14
Dal Segno al Coda, 14–15
Dal Segno al Fine, 14
D.C. (*Da Capo*), 14–15
decrescendo, 17, 144
diatonic half steps, 28–29, 31, 47, 144
diatonicism, 47–48, 144
diatonic scale, 35–36, 47, 145
DIM, 124
diminished intervals, 50–54, 56, 61, 62, 79
diminished triad, 79–80, 84, 86–87, 88–89, 91, 99, 111–112, 121–122, 124, 125, 129, 131
disjunct motion, 49–50, 145
displaced accent, 10–11, 144, 145
dissonance, 61–63, 110–111, 118–119, 145
dissonant 4th, 61–63
dominant, 36, 65–66, 78–79, 81, 86–87, 90–92, 113–115, 145
dominant seventh chord, 111–119, 121, 122, 125–126, 128, 131, 135–136, 139, 140
Dorian mode, 96–99, 100–101, 103, 106, 113–115
dots, 3, 145
dotted notes, 3, 5–6, 8, 18, 22, 24
dotted rests, 3
double bar lines, 12–14, 145
double dot, 3
double flats, 26–27
double sharps, 26–27
doubly augmented intervals, 50–53
doubly diminished intervals, 50–53
downbeat, 15
D.S. (*Dal Segno*), 14–15
duple meter, 4–9, 11, 22–23
duplet, 17, 22–23, 145
dynamic accent, 17, 145
dynamic marks, 17
dynamics, 17

E

ecclesiastical modes, 95–108, 144, 145
    See also church modes
eighth note, 1–3, 5–10, 18–20
eighth rest, 1, 3, 10
enharmonic equivalents, 27–29, 31, 39, 58, 145
enharmonic keys, 45, 69, 146
essential diatonic intervals, 50–51, 54–56

F

F clef, 29–31, 33, 44, 146
false triad, 121–122, 127, 129–130
fermata, 14–15, 146
fifth, 78–85
figured bass, 82–85, 117–118, 122, 146
Fine, 14
    See also repeat signs
first ending, 13
    See also repeat signs
first harmonic, 92–93, 146
first inversion, 82–85, 91, 116–117, 121–123, 126–127, 130, 146
    six-five chord ($^6_5$ position), 117–118, 121–122, 126–127
    six-three chord ($^6_3$ position), 82–85, 91, 123–125
first partial, 92–93, 146
first principle of intervals, 51–52, 57
five-three chord ($^5_3$ position or root position), 82–85, 123–125
flags, 1, 3, 146
flat fifth, 124, 131–133, 136
flat five, 124, 131
flat, 26–27, 35, 39–41
flatted fifth, 124, 131
four-three chord ($^4_3$ position), 117–118, 126–127, 130

four-two chord ($^4_2$ position), 117–118, 126–127, 130
frequency, 25, 55, 92–93, 146
fully diminished seventh chord, 112, 116, 120–121, 124, 129
fundamental frequency, 92–93, 146, 149, 152

G

G clef, 29–31, 33, 44, 146, 152
grand staff, 29, 146, 149
great staff, 29, 31, 146, 149
Gregorian chant, 95, 147, 150
Gregory I, Saint (pope), 95

H

hairpins, 17
half note, 1–3, 7, 21, 63
half rest, 1
half step, 25–29, 147, 148, 151
half-diminished seventh chord, 111–116, 119–122, 125–127, 131, 133
harmonic interval, 49, 77, 147
harmonic minor, 65, 71–76, 85, 87–88, 111, 120
harmonic motion, 90, 147
harmonic series, 90, 92–93, 147, 149
   fundamental frequency, 92–93, 146
   overtones, 92–93, 140, 149
   overtone series, 93, 149
harmony, 50, 77–78, 95, 109, 111, 122, 128, 137–139, 147
hemiola, 11, 22, 147

I

inflection, 55, 57–58, 147
interval inversion, 60, 82–83, 103–108, 147
intervals, 25, 49–63, 147
Ionian mode, 95–97, 99–103, 112–114

J

Jerome, Saint, 95

K

key, 36, 44–48, 50, 54, 60, 66–75, 78–79, 85, 90–91, 95, 99–101, 103–108, 109, 111, 114, 119, 122, 123, 127, 147, 152
keynote, 36, 47, 99, 103, 147, 152
key signature, 43–48, 50, 52, 54–58, 66–68, 70–75, 95, 99, 101, 103–108, 113, 122, 123, 127, 134, 147
   parallel major, 67–68, 71, 74, 97, 149
   parallel minor, 67–68, 149
   relative major, 68, 70, 150
   relative minor, 66–68, 70, 99, 102, 107, 150

L

large triplet, 19–21
leading tone, 36, 38–39, 66, 71, 73, 75, 78–79, 81, 86–92, 113–114, 119, 120, 147
ledger line, 29, 31, 33, 44, 146, 147, 149
like inflection, 58
Locrian mode, 96–97, 98–99, 100, 102–103, 105, 106, 108, 113–116
lower tetrachord, 37, 39–41, 66, 147
Lydian mode, 96–97, 99–101, 104, 106, 113–115

M

MA, 125–126, 128–129, 132–133, 138–139
Maelzel, Johann, 16
major intervals, 53, 59–60
major-minor tonal system, 65, 95, 113, 123
major scale, 35–41, 43, 47–48, 51, 54, 55, 65, 78–79, 97, 99–100, 148
major 2nd, 26, 50, 59, 103, 104, 122, 128, 148
major seventh chord, 111, 113–116, 121–122, 125–126, 132–133, 137–139
major triad, 79–84, 86, 88–90, 92–93, 109–111, 119, 121–122, 123, 125, 127–132, 133, 135–137, 139, 148
melodic motion, 50, 71, 73, 90, 144, 148
measure, 4–15, 19, 22–24, 143, 148
mediant, 36, 65–66, 78–79, 81, 86–91, 113–115, 148
melodic intervals, 50, 148
melodic minor, 65, 71–76, 85–89, 111, 113, 120–121

meter, 4–11, 17–24, 148
    asymmetrical meter, 23–24, 143
    compound meters, 5–6, 8, 17–18, 22, 24, 144
    duple meter, 4–9, 11, 18, 22–23
    quadruple meter, 4–7, 11, 23
    simple meters, 5–8, 17–18, 22, 151
    symmetrical meters, 4, 23, 151
    triple meter, 4–6, 10, 11, 22–23
meter exchange, 17
    duplet, 17, 22–23, 145
    large triplet, 19–21
    micro triplet, 19–21
    small triplet, 18–21
    triplet, 17–21, 152
meter signature, 6, 148, 152
metronome, 16, 148
micro triplet, 19–21
minor intervals, 50–51, 56, 59–61, 66
minor-major seventh chord, 112, 121–122, 129–130
minor mode, 65–76
    Aeolian mode, 65, 95–97, 98–100, 102, 105 107, 113–115
    harmonic minor, 65, 71–76, 85, 87–88, 111, 120
    melodic minor, 65, 71–76, 85–89, 111, 113, 120–121
    natural minor, 65–66, 68, 71–76, 85, 87–88, 95, 98–99, 102, 115, 120
minor 2nd, 25, 71, 77, 105, 108, 147, 148, 151
minor seventh chord, 111–116, 121–122, 125–127, 133, 136
minor triad, 79–81, 83–84, 86, 88–89, 92, 111, 121–122, 124–125, 127–129, 131, 136, 140, 148
Mixolydian mode, 96–97, 99, 100, 102, 105, 106, 108, 113–115
mode, 36–37, 43, 47–48, 65, 95–108, 148
mode transposition, 99–108
monophony, 95, 148

N

N.C./NC, 141

NO, 140
note head, 1, 17, 54, 86, 88, 120, 134, 149
natural minor, 65–66, 68, 71–76, 85, 87–88, 95, 98–99, 102, 115, 120
natural sign, 26
ninth, 77, 109, 111, 128–129, 131–133, 135–140

O

octave, 25–26, 28–29, 31, 33, 35–37, 39–40, 43, 47, 49–50, 55, 59–61, 65–66, 68, 82, 93, 97, 99, 110, 112, 115, 149
octave registers, 31
octave signs, 33
    all'ottava, 33
odd meter, 23, 143, 149
OMIT, 140
overtones, 92–93, 140, 149
overtone series, 93, 147, 149

P

parallel major, 67–68, 71, 74, 97, 149
parallel duple meter, 18, 22
parallel minor, 67–68, 149
passing tone, 110–111, 149
perfect 4th, 40, 43, 54, 57–59, 61–62, 83, 90, 104, 106, 108, 114, 149
perfect 5th, 37, 40, 43, 45, 59, 61, 69–70, 80–81, 83–84, 90, 92–93, 104, 106, 108, 113, 115, 134, 149
perfect intervals, 50, 59–60
performance marks, 16–17
Phrygian mode, 96–97, 98, 99, 101, 104, 106, 107, 113–115
piano staff, 29, 146, 149
pick up, 15
pitch, 1, 16, 25–33, 149
plainchant, 95, 147, 150
primary accents, 4–5, 9, 143, 148, 150, 151

Q

quadruple meter, 4–7, 11, 23
quartal harmony, 77, 150

quarter note, 1–9, 11, 16, 18, 20–21
quarter rest, 1–3, 5

R

real seventh chord, 111, 118, 122
relative major, 68, 70, 150
relative minor, 66–68, 70, 99, 102, 107, 150
repeat signs, 12–15, 150
   bis, 13
   Da Capo al Coda, 14–15
   Da Capo al Fine, 14
   Dal Segno al Coda, 14–15
   Dal Segno al Fine, 14
   D.C. (Da Capo), 14–15
   D.S. (Dal Segno), 14–15
   first ending, 13
   second ending, 13
   two-measure repeat, 13
re-sizing principle, 51–52, 57–58
rest tones, 65, 72, 150
rhythm, 9–10, 18–20, 22, 24, 150
rhythmic counting, 7–9
rhythmic syllables, 7–10
ritardando, 16
Roman numeral chord symbols, 87–89, 112, 116–118, 120, 123
root, 78–86, 88–92, 109–112, 114–122, 123–135, 137–139
root position, 78–85, 109–112, 116–117, 119, 121, 123–125, 127–128, 150

S

scale, 35–41, 43–45, 47–48, 50, 150
scale degrees, 36
secondary accents, 4–5, 7, 9, 148, 150
second ending, 13
second inversion, 82–85, 116–117, 123, 150
   four-three chord ($_3^4$ position), 117–118, 126–127, 130
   six-four chord ($_4^6$ position), 82–85, 123–124
second principle of intervals (re-sizing principle), 51–52, 57–58
secundal harmony, 77, 151

semitone, 25, 147, 148, 151
seventh, 54, 77, 109–122, 124–133, 135–140
sextuplet, 20
sharp, 26–28, 35, 37–39
simple intervals, 49, 59–60, 62, 151
simple meters, 5–8, 17–18, 22, 151
six-five chord ($_5^6$ position), 117–118, 121–122, 126–127
six-four chord ($_4^6$ position), 82–85, 123–124
sixteenth note, 1–3, 5–10, 12–15, 19–20, 22, 24
sixteenth rest, 1–2
six-three chord ($_3^6$ position), 82–85, 91, 123–125
sixty-fourth note, 1–3
sixty-fourth rest, 1–2
small triplet, 18–21
staff, 1, 12, 16–17, 29–31, 33, 44, 46, 49, 54, 62, 77–79, 123, 139, 151
stems, 1, 3, 18–20, 22, 54, 62
subdominant, 36, 65–66, 78–79, 81, 86–92, 113–115, 118, 151
submediant, 36, 65–66, 71, 78–79, 81, 86–92, 113–115, 151
subtonic, 36, 66, 71, 86–87, 89–91, 113–115, 120, 151
supertonic, 36, 65–66, 78–79, 81, 86–92, 113–115, 151
suspension, 63, 119, 130
symmetrical meters, 4, 23, 151
syncopation, 9–10, 63, 151

T

tempo, 14, 16, 151
tertian harmony, 77–78, 109, 128, 136–139, 146, 150, 151
tetrachords, 36–41, 66, 72, 151
third, 78–86, 88, 90–91, 109–110, 116–119, 121, 127–130, 133–135, 137, 140
third inversion, 116–118, 126–127, 130, 139
   four-two chord ($_2^4$ position), 117–118, 126–127, 130, 139
thirty-second note, 1–3, 6–9, 14–15
thirty-second rest, 1–2
ties, 3, 9–11, 152
timbre, 92, 149, 152
time signature, 5–8, 23–24, 148, 152

tonal center, 36, 65, 90, 102, 147, 152
tonality, 47–48, 90–93, 119, 152
tonic, 36, 48, 65–68, 71, 78–79, 81, 86–91, 95–102, 113–115, 119–120, 147, 152
transposed modes, 99–108
treble clef, 29, 44, 123, 146, 152
triad, 54, 76, 77–93, 123–133, 135–140
triple meter, 4–6, 10, 11, 22–23
triplet, 17–21, 152
tritone, 61–62, 90, 91, 102, 152
two-measure repeat, 13
    See also repeat signs

U

upbeat, 15
upper leading tone, 114
upper tetrachord, 37–40, 66, 72, 152

V

variable scale degrees, 73–74, 85–86, 88–89, 120

W

whole notes, 1–3
whole rests, 1, 3